Central Banking Systems Compared

The introduction of the euro as a new currency was a huge step for European banking and finance. Although the new European Central Bank's organisation, monetary instruments and objectives are very similar to those of the pre-euro Bundesbank, there are still notable differences.

This new study provides a comprehensive comparison of the recently established European central bank system with the previous German central bank system and the US Federal Reserve. This book covers such themes as:

- historical information on the basic features of each system
- comparison and analysis of each system's statutory objectives
- the recent policy actions of different banking systems
- economic policy in the eurozone

This well-written contribution to financial economics should be of interest to academics and students as well as being an excellent resource for professionals concerned with central banking systems around the world.

Emmanuel Apel is Associate Professor of Economics at the University of Ottawa, Canada.

Routledge International Studies in Money and Banking

1 Private Banking in Europe
Lynn Bicker

2 Bank Deregulation and Monetary Order
George Selgin

3 Money in Islam. A Study in Islamic Political Economy
Masudul Alam Choudhury

4 The Future of European Financial Centres
Kirsten Bindemann

5 Payment Systems in a Global Perspective
Maxwell J. Fry, Isaak Kilato, Sandra Roger, Krzysztof Senderowicz, David Sheppard, Francisco Solis and John Trundle

6 What is Money?
John Smithin

7 Finance
A characteristics approach
Edited by David Blake

8 Organisational Change and Retail Finance. An Ethnographic Perspective
Richard Harper, Dave Randall and Mark Rouncefield

9 The History of the Bundesbank. Lessons for the European Central Bank
Jakob de Haan

10 The Euro. A Challenge and Opportunity for Financial Markets
Published on behalf of *Société Universitaire Européenne de Recherches Financières (SUERF)*
Edited by Michael Artis, Axel Weber and Elizabeth Hennessy

11 Central Banking in Eastern Europe
Nigel Healey

12 Money, Credit and Prices Stability
Paul Dalziel

13 Monetary Policy, Capital Flows and Exchange Rates
Essays in memory of Maxwell Fry
Edited by William Allen and David Dickinson

14 Adapting to Financial Globalisation
Published on behalf of *Société Universitaire Européenne de Recherches Financières (SUERF)*
Edited by Morten Balling, Eduard H. Hochreiter and Elizabeth Hennessy

15 Monetary Macroeconomics. A New Approach
Alvaro Cencini

16 Monetary Stability in Europe
Stefan Collignon

17 Technology and Finance. Challenges for Financial Markets, Business Strategies and Policy Makers
Published on behalf of *Société Universitaire Européenne de Recherches Financières (SUERF)*
Edited by Morten Balling, Frank Lierman and Andrew Mullineux

18 Monetary Unions. Theory, History, Public Choice
Edited by Forrest H. Capie and Geoffrey E. Wood

19 HRM and Occupational Health and Safety
Carol Boyd

20 Central Banking System Compared. The ECB, The Pre-Euro Bundesbank and the Federal Reserve System
Emmanuel Apel

Central Banking Systems Compared
The ECB, the pre-euro Bundesbank, and the Federal Reserve System

Emmanuel Apel

LONDON AND NEW YORK

First published 2003
by Routledge
2 Park Square, Milton Park, Abingdon, Oxon, OX14 4RN

Simultaneously published in the USA and Canada
by Routledge
270 Madison Ave, New York NY 10016

Routledge is an imprint of the Taylor & Francis Group

Transferred to Digital Printing 2007

© 2003 Emmanuel Apel

Typeset in Times by Wearset Ltd, Boldon, Tyne and Wear

All rights reserved. No part of this book may be reprinted or reproduced or utilised in any form or by any electronic, mechanical, or other means, now known or hereafter invented, including photocopying and recording, or in any information storage or retrieval system, without permission in writing from the publishers.

British Library Cataloguing in Publication Data
A catalogue record for this book is available from the British Library

Library of Congress Cataloging in Publication Data
Apel, Emmanuel, 1944–
  Central banking systems compared : the ECB, the pre-euro Bundesbank, and the Federal Reserve System / Emmanuel Apel.
    p. cm. – (Routledge international studies in money and banking; 20)
  Includes bibliographical references and index.
  1. European Central Bank. 2. Deutsche Bundesbank. 3. Board of Governors of the Federal Reserve System (U.S.) 4. Banks and banking, Central–European Union countries. 5. Banks and banking, Central–United States. 6. Monetary policy–European Union countries. 7. Monetary policy–United States. I. Title. II. Series.
HG2976 .A64 2003
332.1'1'094–dc21

2002031944

ISBN10: 0–415–30042–8 (hbk)
ISBN10: 0–415–45922–2 (pbk)

ISBN13: 978–0–415–30042–1 (hbk)
ISBN13: 978–0–415–45922–8 (pbk)

Dedicated to the memory of my late parents

Contents

List of illustrations	ix
List of abbreviations and acronyms	xii
Preface	xiv

1 Historical background and basic institutional features   **1**

The European Central Bank 1
The pre-euro Bundesbank 14
The Federal Reserve System 17

2 Objectives, independence, transparency and accountability   **28**

Principal statutory objective(s) of, and interpretation by, the three central banks 28
Central bank independence 33
Transparency and accountability 57

3 Monetary policy: strategy, instruments and actions   **64**

Monetary policy strategy of the Eurosystem 65
Operational instruments of the Eurosystem 81
Monetary policy decisions of the Eurosystem 90
Monetary policy strategy and instruments of the pre-euro Bundesbank 117
The Fed's monetary policy strategy 133
The Fed's principal operational instruments 139

4 Economic policy coordination in the eurozone   **143**

The economic policy framework 144
Banking prudential supervision and financial stability 175
Concluding remarks 190

Appendix	193
Notes	195
References	205
Index	213

Illustrations

Tables

1.1	Capital and foreign reserve assets transferred by the National Central Banks to the European Central Bank	11
2.1	Summary of institutional characteristics of the ECB/Eurosystem, the pre-euro Deutsche Bundesbank, and the US Federal Reserve System	34–38
3.1	The major macroeconomic indicators, with release frequency, used in the framework of the ECB's broadly based assessment of future price developments in the eurozone	74–77
3.2	Monetary policy instruments of the Eurosystem, the pre-euro Bundesbank and the Federal Reserve System	82–83
3.3	Convergence of key official short-term interest rates, in per cent, of eurozone National Central Banks, from mid-1997 to end of 1998	92
3.4	Key ECB interest rate, the main refinancing rate: 1999–2001	107
3.5	Bundesbank monetary targets, inflation objective and the outcomes (with eurozone and US memorandum data)	110–15
3.6	FOMC's target ('intended') federal funds rate, future policy bias and disclosure policy: 1990–2002	126–27
4.1	General government balance (as a percentage of GDP, 1998–2004)	152
4.2	GDP growth rates and HICP inflation rates, 1998–2002 for the eurozone and its Member States (EUR-11 prior to 2001 and EUR-12 from 2001 onwards)	155
4.3	Representation of the Eurosystem/ESCB in external and EU bodies	167–69
4.4	Bank supervisory structure in EU countries and the US	178–79
4.5	Market share of branches and subsidiaries of foreign credit institutions as a percentage of the total assets of domestic credit institutions, end-1997	184

x *Illustrations*

4.6	Concentration at the national level: assets of the five largest credit institutions as a percentage of the total assets of domestic credit institutions	185

Boxes

1.1	Composition of the 18-member ECB Governing Council	6–7
1.2	Enlargement of the European Union and the ECB	9
1.3	Changes to the organisational structure of the Deutsche Bundesbank as of 30 April 2002	15–16
1.4	Composition of the Federal Open Market Committee (FOMC), January 2002	25–27
2.1	Macroeconomic benefits of 'price stability'	29–30
2.2	ECB's coordinated and unilateral foreign exchange interventions of September and November 2000	45–48
3.1	Timeliness of four major economic indicators released by the three largest eurozone Member States (Germany, D; France, F; and Italy, I), the eurozone (EUR-12), and the US	78
3.2	The declining euro from 1999–2000: a possible explanation	99–103
3.3	Some recent large takeovers resulting in Foreign Direct Investment (FDI) outflows from the eurozone, 1999–2001	105–06
3.4	Statements of eurozone officials and key events, January 1999–November 2001	118–24
4.1	Examples of recent domestic and cross-border mergers or acquisitions (or proposals) in the eurozone banking sector	186–90

Figures

1.1	The Eurosystem and the European System of Central Banks	5
1.2	Organisation of the pre-euro Bundesbank with respect to monetary policy decisions	18
2.1(a)	€/$ trading history: 1975–2000	43
2.1(b)	Euro against the dollar: September–November 2000	44
3.1	Schematic presentation of ECB's monetary policy strategy	65
3.2	M3 growth and the reference value: 1999–2001	72
3.3	ECB interest rates and money market rates: 1999–2001	88
3.4	Breakdown of HICP inflation in the euro area by component	94
3.5	Pre-euro Bundesbank targets of M3: 1995–98	129

3.6(a)	Pre-euro Bundesbank's Lombard, Discount and Repo rates: 1985–95	131
3.6(b)	Pre-euro Bundesbank's Lombard, Discount and Repo rates: 1995–98	132
3.7	US discount rate and targeted Federal funds rate: 1998–2002	137

Abbreviations and acronyms

BAFin	Federal Agency for Financial Services Supervision (Germany)
BEPG	Broad Economic Policy Guidelines (EU)
BIS	Bank for International Settlements (Basel)
CECEI	Comité des Etablissements de Crédit et des Entreprises d'Investissement (France)
ECB	European Central Bank
Ecofin	The EU Council meeting composed of the Ministers of Finance and Economy representing the Member States of the European Union
ECU	European Currency Unit, replaced by the euro
EEA	European Economic Area (the EU plus Norway, Iceland and Liechtenstein)
EFC	Economic and Financial Committee (EU)
EMU	Economic and Monetary Union (EU)
EONIA	Euro OverNight Index Average (of interest rates)
ERM II	Exchange Rate Mechanism II (EU)
ESCB	European System of Central Banks
EUR	Official three-letter abbreviation of euro
Eurogroup	The informal group composed of the members of the Ecofin Council (see above) who represent the Member States of the eurozone
FDIC	Federal Deposit Insurance Corporation (US)
FOMC	Federal Open Market Committee (US)
FRS	Federal Reserve System (US)
FSF	Financial Stability Forum
GAB	General Arrangements to Borrow (IMF)
G-7	Group of Seven (United States, Japan, Germany, Britain, France, Italy and Canada)
G-10	Group of Ten (G-7 plus the Netherlands, Belgium, Sweden and Switzerland)

G-20	Group of Twenty (G-7 plus Argentina, Australia, Brazil, China, India, Indonesia, Mexico, Russia, Saudi Arabia, South Africa, South Korea and Turkey, as well as representatives from the IMF-World Bank)
HICP	Harmonised Index of Consumer Prices (EU)
IAIS	International Association of Insurance Supervisors
IMF	International Monetary Fund
IMFC	International Monetary and Financial Committee (of the IMF)
IOSCO	International Organization of Securities Commissions
MRO	Main Refinancing Operation (ECB)
M1, M2, M3	Various definitions of monetary aggregates with different degrees of liquidity
NCB	National Central Bank
NOW	Negotiable Order of Withdrawal account (US)
OCC	Office of the Comptroller of the Currency (US)
OECD	Organization for Economic Cooperation and Development
OMIC	Open Market Investment Committee (US, historical)
OMPC	Open Market Policy Conference (US, historical)
OTS	Office of Thrift Supervision (US)
Repo rate	Repurchasing rate
RP	Repurchase Agreements
SOMA	System Open Market Account (of the US Federal Reserve System)
SP	Sale–Purchase transactions
'Statute'	Statute of the European System of Central Banks and of the European Central Bank, which is a Protocol attached to the Maastricht Treaty (Protocol no. 18 to the Treaty establishing the European Community)
'Treaty'	Maastricht Treaty or Treaty on European Union, signed on 7 February 1992 and entered into force on 1 November 1993

Preface

This book is a comparative study of the newly established European Central Bank (the Eurosystem) with the pre-euro Bundesbank and with the US Federal Reserve System. The institutional framework, the monetary policy strategies and the operational mechanisms of the three central banks are presented and compared, with an assessment of the monetary policy strategy and results of the new European Central Bank (ECB) during its first three years of operation. Although the Eurosystem's organisation, monetary instruments and primary objective of price stability are very similar to the Bundesbank model, the 'two-pillar' monetary policy strategy of the ECB is a departure from the 'monetary targeting' strategy adopted by the pre-euro Bundesbank. In fact, the eclectic nature of the ECB's monetary policy strategy borrows from both the pre-euro Bundesbank's and the Federal Reserve System's strategies. The statutory independence of the ECB is very similar to the regime that existed for the pre-euro Bundesbank. However, unlike the Bundesbank and more like the Federal Reserve System, the ECB has numerous legal requirements to communicate, without compromising its independence, with the European Parliament and to engage in a dialogue with other EU bodies. Like the pre-euro Bundesbank but unlike the US central bank, the ECB refuses to publish the minutes of its Governing Council or to publish the vote of the Governing Council – or even the results of the vote whilst keeping the voting patterns of the members secret. Following the tradition of the pre-euro Bundesbank, the ECB, initially in early 1999, took the financial markets by surprise in terms of the timing of the monetary policy changes. More recently, after having been much criticised for its confusing, and at times contradictory, public statements, the ECB seems to be preparing the market for monetary policy changes, in line with the strategy of the Federal Reserve System. The Eurosystem is a central bank whose organisation and monetary policy strategy will evolve over time, just as the Federal Reserve System has evolved over the past 90 years. Already, the first pillar of the ECB monetary policy strategy (the reference value of the broad monetary aggregate) is becoming less important and will probably be formally abandoned in the near future, just as some current members of the Governing Council are willing to support the publication of the votes of that policy-making body, while maintaining secret the votes of each member. Moreover, once the ECB's independence and credibility have been well-established, the ECB Governing Council will not be so reluctant to engage in an ongoing dialogue with the Eurogroup Ministers of Finance to discuss the interaction between monetary, fiscal and structural policies – and may even be willing to discuss the operational definition of price stability, without giving the impression that it is compromising its 'operational independence'.

Text organisation

Since the historical background to the creation of each of the three central banks is not well known to most readers, Chapter 1 provides the required minimum historical information, as well as basic institutional features of each central bank. Relatively more space is devoted to the US central bank for two reasons: (i) the Federal Reserve System was not the first US central bank to be established and (ii) the organisational structure of the Federal Reserve System has evolved over its 90-year history. Chapter 2 examines and compares the statutory objectives of the three central banks and the issues of central bank independence, transparency and accountability. Chapter 3 compares the monetary policy strategies, instruments and recent policy actions of the three central banks. An evaluation of the performance of the ECB is also presented. Finally, Chapter 4 deals with economic policy coordination in the eurozone. Since monetary policy is only one aspect of the overall economic policy of a 'nation', it is important to understand how the eurozone's European Central Bank, a supranational institution, fits into the general economic policy framework and institutions of the European Union. Since this European policy framework is *sui generis* and has evolved as a result of the creation of the single currency area, we believe that it is important to outline its main features, which involve 12 national governments, the European Commission, the Council of Ministers of Economics and Finance of the European Union, and the European Parliament. We also describe the external representation of the new European Central Bank at the level of international organisations and forums.

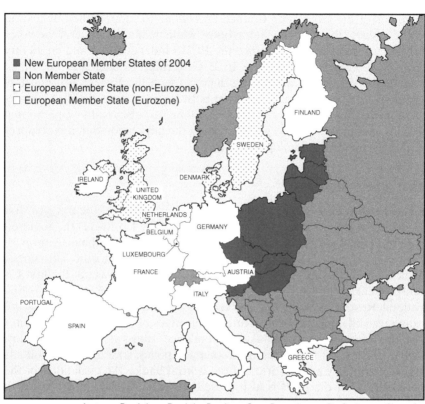

	Area (1000 km²)	Population (million)	Population Density (inhabitants per km²)	Gross Domestic Product (1000 million PPS)*	Per Capita Gross Domestic Product (PPS)	Share of Eurozone GDP (%)**
Austria	84	8.1	96	202	24900	3.1
Belgium	31	10.2	330	255	25000	3.8
Denmark	43	5.3	124	140	26400	—
Finland	337	5.2	15	120	23000	2.0
France	544	59.1	109	1312	22200	21.3
Germany	357	82.2	230	1973	24000	31.1
Greece	132	10.5	80	159	15100	1.9
Ireland	70	3.7	54	97	26300	1.6
Italy	301	57.6	192	1284	22300	17.8
Luxembourg	3	0.4	145	17	41600	0.3
Netherlands	41	15.8	373	409	25900	6.1
Portugal	92	10.0	109	171	17100	1.7
Spain	505	39.4	78	733	18600	9.3
Sweden	411	8.9	22	206	23200	—
United Kingdom	244	59.6	244	1377	23100	—
EU 15	3191	376.1	118	8462	22500	—
USA	9373	275.1	29	9573	34800	—
JAPAN	378	126.5	335	3011	23800	—

*Figures for 2000. Gross domestic product is the total value of all goods and services produced within a country in a year – it is often used to express wealth. PPS, purchasing power standard, is a unit representing an identical volume of goods and services in each country, irrespective of price levels. The value of 1 PPS unit corresponds roughly to 1 euro (source: European Commission services).
**Figures are calculated on basis of 2000 GDP at market prices

Key characteristics of the euro area including and excluding Greece

	Reporting period	Unit	Euro area incl. Greece	Euro area excl. Greece	United States	Japan
Population[1]	2000	m	302	292	272	127
GDP (share of world GDP)[2]	1999	%	16.2	15.8	21.9	7.6
GDP	1999	€bn	6,245	6,127	8,666	4,081
GDP per capita	1999	€	20,667.5	21,013	31,916	32,205
Sectors of production[3]						
Agriculture, fishing, forestry	1999	% of GDP	2.8	2.6	1.6	1.8
Industry (including construction)	1999	% of GDP	28.5	28.6	27.3	36.4
Services	1999	% of GDP	68.7	68.7	71.1	61.9
Unemployment rate (share of labour force)	1999	%	10.0	9.9	4.2	4.7
Labour force participation rate[4]	1999	%	67.3	67.4	77.2	72.4
Employment rate[4,5]	1999	%	60.5	60.6	73.9	68.9
Exports of goods[6]	1999	% of GDP	12.9	13.3	7.4	9.3
Exports of goods and services[6]	1999	% of GDP	16.9	17.2	10.3	10.7
Import of goods[6]	1999	% of GDP	11.8	11.9	11.1	6.4
Import of goods and services[6]	1999	% of GDP	15.9	16.1	13.2	9.1
Exports (share of world exports)[7]	1999	%	18.9	19.0	15.2	9.1
Current account balance[6]	1999	% of GDP	−0.2	−0.1	−3.6	2.5
General government						
Surplus (+) or deficit (−)	1999	% of GDP	−1.3	−1.3	1.0	−8.9
Gross debt	1999	% of GDP	72.7	72.2	63.2	125.6
Revenue	1999	% of GDP	47.7	47.8	32.9	31.0
Expenditure	1999	% of GDP	49.0	49.1	31.9	39.9
Bank deposits[8]	1999	% of GDP	79.4	80.0	41.0	134.5
Stock of loans to the private sector[9]	1999	% of GDP	90.1	91.1	76.1	136.3
Outstanding domestic debt securities[10]	1999	% of GDP	89.8	90.1	178.0	157.9
Stock market capitalisation	1999	% of GDP	66.1	64.7	128.7	73.9

Sources: Eurostat, IMF, European Commission, OECD, Reuter's, ECB and ECB calculations.

Notes
1. As of January 2000.
2. GDP shares are based on a purchasing power parity (PPP) valuation of country GDPs.
3. Based on real value added. Data for the United States and Japan refer to 1997.
4. Data for Greece refer to 1998.
5. As a ratio of the number of persons in employment to the working age population (those aged between 15 and 64).
6. Balance of payments data, only extra-euro area trade flows for the euro area. For euro area imports and exports including Greece. ECB estimate based on Eurostat and ECB balance of payments data.
7. External trade statistics, world exports exclude intra-euro area trade flows.
8. Euro area: total deposits with MFIs; United States: demand, time and savings deposits with banking institutions; Japan: demand and time deposits with deposit money banks.
9. Euro area: MFI loans to other euro area residents; United States and Japan; domestic credit.
10. Data for domestic debt securities refer to December 1999.

1 Historical background and basic institutional features

This chapter presents a short historical background of each central bank, starting with the European Central Bank (ECB), followed by the pre-euro Bundesbank and the Federal Reserve System. The basic institutional structure of each central bank is presented as a prerequisite to an understanding of the issues of independence, transparency and accountability, which are discussed in Chapter 2.

THE EUROPEAN CENTRAL BANK

Historical background

The idea of creating a single European currency with a single European central bank pre-dates the Maastricht Treaty (1992), which outlined the organisation, powers and functions of the European Central Bank. In the post-war period, at The Hague Summit of December 1969, the Heads of State or Government of the six original Member States of the Community (France, Germany, Italy and the Benelux countries – Belgium, the Netherlands and Luxembourg), declared in a communiqué that the Community should work, in stages, towards the goal of achieving an Economic and Monetary Union:

> They have reaffirmed their wish to carry on more rapidly with the further development necessary to reinforce the Community and its development into an economic union. They are of the opinion that the process of integration should end in a Community of stability and growth. With this object [sic] in view they have agreed that on the basis of the memorandum presented by the Commission on 12 February 1969 and in close collaboration with the Commission a plan by stages should be drawn up by the Council during 1970 with a view to the creation of an economic and monetary union ... They have agreed that the possibility should be examined of setting up a European reserve fund, to which a common economic and monetary policy would lead.
> (Point no. 8 of the final Communiqué of the Conference of the Heads of State or Government on 1 and 2 December 1969 at The Hague, Appendix 1 of the Werner Report 1970)

2 *Historical background*

The Werner Committee, established in 1970 with a view to proposing a road map to achieve such a goal, recommended that the Treaty of Rome establishing the European Economic Community (1957) be amended to set fixed and irreversible exchange rates between the currencies of the Member States, followed by the creation of a European System of Central Banks, which would be responsible for setting a single monetary policy for the Community:

> The constitution of the Community system for the central banks could be based on organisms of the type of the Federal Reserve System operating in the United States. This Community institution will be empowered to take decisions, according to the requirements of the economic situation, in the matter of internal monetary policy as regards liquidity, rates of interest, and the granting of loans to public and private sectors.
>
> (Werner Committee 1970: 7)

Although the Community adopted various resolutions in the early 1970s to implement gradually the recommendations of the Werner Report (e.g. 22 March 1971, 19–21 October 1972),[1] and in fact had launched the first stage of the step-by-step process, the demise of the Bretton Woods international monetary system, coupled with the German view that European economic and political union was a prerequisite to the formation of a monetary union, forced the Community Council of Finance Ministers (Ecofin Council) to postpone *sine die* the creation of a legal framework to launch a single currency with the establishment of a European central bank. It was not until the late 1980s, after measures to create a single market were adopted in line with the provisions of the Single European Act (1986) and after it was agreed, in the wake of German reunification, to introduce a 'political union' pillar in the Common Foreign and Security Policy in the Maastricht Treaty, that the general outline of the Delors Report on Economic and Monetary Union (Delors Committee 1989) was adopted as the basis for the negotiations that eventually led to the provisions of the Maastricht Treaty to establish a European Central Bank with a single currency.

The text of the Treaty and its Protocols dealing with 'Economic and Monetary Policy' was the result of negotiations undertaken at the Intergovernmental Conference on Economic and Monetary Union (EMU). This conference, composed of representatives of the then 12 Member States of the Community, opened in Rome on 15 December 1990 and closed with an agreement one year later in Maastricht. The speedy outcome of these negotiations, held in parallel with the Intergovernmental Conference dealing with Political Union, was the direct result of the impetus provided by the French President, François Mitterrand, and the German Chancellor, Helmut Kohl, to deepen European integration in view of the fall of the Berlin Wall in November 1989, leading to the economic and political reunification of Germany in 1990. The major draft treaties on EMU – including draft statutes on the European Central Bank – were submitted by the Commission (European Commission 1991), by the governments of France (France 1991) and Germany (Deutschland 1991), by the Committee of Governors of the Central Banks of the European Communities (1990), and by the Monetary Committee of the European Communities (1990). The Deutsche Bundesbank (1990) also submitted a position paper on EMU. At the very start of the negotiations, the British Conservative government, under John Major, who could not accept the idea of creating a single European currency that would replace, inter alia, the British pound, submitted a proposal for the creation of a 'hard ECU', which would become the common currency of Europe, managed by a new institution, the European Monetary Fund (HM Treasury 1991). The 'hard ECU' would coexist with the other national currencies and was not intended to replace them. Since the British proposal was never seriously considered by the other Member States, the UK government had to request an 'opt-out' clause from the final stage of EMU so as to be able to sign the Maastricht Treaty.

The Delors Committee which, in the late 1980s, had the mandate to study and propose concrete recommendations on how an economic and monetary union should be established, recommended the adoption of a single currency with a European System of Central Banks responsible for formulating and implementing monetary policy in the single currency area (Delors Committee 1989). This new central bank was to be organised with a federalist structure, 'in what might be called the European System of Central Banks (ESCB)' (Delors Committee 1989: 25). Although the proposed central bank appeared to be based on the model of the US Federal Reserve System (Delors, the President of the European Commission from 1985–94, often used the term 'EuroFed' to refer to the ESCB), the structural organisation, the assigned functions, the monetary policy instruments and the primary objective of the ECB/ESCB – as laid out in the Maastricht Treaty, in its Protocol dealing with the central bank, and in secondary legislation – are rooted in the model of the pre-euro Deutsche Bundesbank. However, the ECB modus operandi dealing with monetary policy strategy and communication policy is a combination taken from the Bundesbank and Federal Reserve models.

The organisation, powers and functions of the European Central Bank are outlined in Articles 105 to 115 of the Treaty on European Union (1992, also known as the 'Maastricht Treaty' and hereafter referred to as the 'Treaty') and in Protocol number 18 on the 'Statute of the European System of Central Banks and of the European Central Bank', hereafter referred to as the 'Statute'.[2] This Protocol, which contains 53 articles, in combination with the 'Treaty' articles, defines the role of the European Central Bank in formulating and executing monetary policy for the single currency area, a power that this supranational body does not share with any Community or national institution. The Council of Ministers of Economics and Finance of the European Union (composed of the Finance Ministers from each of the 15 EU Member States and hereafter indicated as the 'Ecofin Council') retains its powers in formulating broad guidelines on macroeconomic policies for EU Member States (Article 99), in conducting multilateral surveillance in policy areas such as the ceilings on public deficit and debt ratios (Article 104 and European Commission 1999b: Part F), in harmonising the tax laws of the 15 Member States of the European Union, and in formulating the euro exchange rate policy, which is a shared responsibility with the European Central Bank.

Basic institutional features: ECB, Eurosystem and ESCB

The European Central Bank (ECB) with the 15 national central banks of the EU Member States is known, according to the 'Treaty', as the *European System of Central Banks* (ESCB). The ECB, with the national central banks of the EU Member States that have introduced the single currency (originally 11, now 12, Member States), is known as the *Eurosystem*. The Governing Council of the ECB, analogous to the pre-euro Bundesbank's Central Bank Council or to the Federal Open Market Committee of the Federal Reserve System (see below), is the highest decision-making body of the Eurosystem and is responsible for monetary policy decisions in the eurozone (see Figure 1.1 and Box 1.1). The ECB Governing Council is composed of a six-member Executive Board, which is analogous to the pre-euro Bundesbank's Directorate or to the Board of Governors of the Federal Reserve System (see below), and the current 12 Governors of the National Central Banks of the Member States participating in the eurozone, which is analogous to the Presidents of the pre-euro Land Central Banks in Germany or to the Presidents of the district Federal Reserve Banks in the US (see below). The members of the Executive Board are appointed for a non-renewable term of eight years by a common accord of the Heads of State or Government of the Member States constituting the eurozone, on a recommendation from the Eurogroup Finance Ministers after consulting the European Parliament and the ECB Governing Council.[3] One member of the Executive Board is designated President of the ECB and another is designated Vice-President of the ECB. The members of the Executive Board must have professional qualifications. The Governors of the National Central Banks of the 12 Member States participating in the eurozone, are appointed for a minimum term of five years by their respective national governments or parliaments.

Monetary policy decisions are taken by a simple majority of the members of the Governing Council, with the President having a casting vote in case of a tie.[4] This rule reinforces the view that each member has an equal weight, independent of national origin. The vote of a member of the Governing Council from Luxembourg has the same weight as the vote

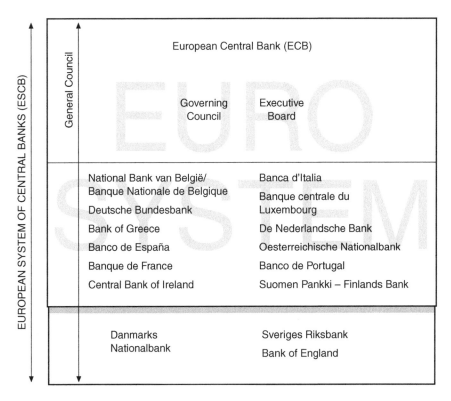

Figure 1.1 The eurosystem and the European System of Central Banks.

Source: European Central Bank, *Annual Report 2001*.

Note: As of 1 January 2001, Bank of Greece is part of the Eurosystem. Hence, with a six-member Executive Board and 12 Governors of the eurozone National Central Banks, the Governing Council of the ECB, the monetary policy decision-making body, is composed of 18 members. The Eurosystem is composed of the ECB and the 12 National Central Banks of the Member States composing the eurozone. The European System of Central Banks (ESCB) is composed of the ECB and all 15 EU National Central Banks, with a General Council composed of two Executive Board members (President and Vice-President of the ECB) and the Governors of all 15 EU National Central Banks.

of a member from Germany, meaning that the Governing Council does not practice 'qualified majority' voting on monetary policy decisions, in contrast to the rules used by the Council of Ministers of the European Union.

The Governing Council of the ECB is responsible for the eurozone's monetary policy and the Executive Board of the ECB is responsible for implementing monetary policy in accordance with decisions taken by the Governing Council. The Eurosystem adheres to the principle of decentralisation. This principle stipulates that, to the extent deemed possible and appropriate, the ECB shall have recourse to the eurozone National

Box 1.1 Composition of the 18-member ECB Governing Council

The European Central Bank was established on 1 June 1998, therefore allowing some seven months during which the operational decisions and the testing of the communication and payment systems could be undertaken before the launching of the single currency[a] and the single monetary policy on 1 January 1999. The Governing Council holds a monetary policy meeting once a month[b], with all but two of the meetings per year held at its headquarters in Frankfurt am Main, Germany. Since 2000, the eurozone National Central Banks (with the exception of the Bundesbank) host each year, on a rotating basis, the two meetings held outside Germany.

The members of the Executive Board appointed in June 1998 and their respective responsibilities are as follows:

W. Duisenberg (The Netherlands), President, who was pressured by France to promise to resign before his eight-year term expires so as to make room for a French candidate. He is responsible for External Relations, Secretariat, Protocol and Conferences, and Internal Audit. In early 2002, he announced his resignation effective July 2003.
C. Noyer (France), Vice-President with a four-year term. He is responsible for Administration and Personnel, Legal Services and is one of the ECB's two members who sit on the Economic and Financial Committee, a consultative Community body; **L. D. Papademos** (Greece) was appointed Vice-President for a regular eight-year term to replace Noyer whose term expired on 31 May 2002.
E. Domingo-Solans (Spain), with a six-year term. He is responsible for Information Systems, Statistics and Banknotes.
S. Hämäläinen (Finland), with a five-year term. She is responsible for Operations and Controlling.
O. Issing (Germany), with an eight-year term. He is responsible for Economics and Research, a very important position since he presents the economic analysis to argue the case for or against any change in monetary policy at the monthly monetary policy meetings of the Governing Council. He is also one of the ECB's two members who sit on the Economic and Financial Committee.
T. Padoa-Schioppa (Italy), with a seven-year term, is responsible for International and European Relations, Payment Systems and Prudential Supervision.

The other members of the Governing Council, the 12 National Central Bank Governors, in alphabetical order according to the names of the Member States in their own language, are as follows.

G. Quaden, as from 1 March 1999 [preceded by A. Verplaetse, until 28 February 1999]; *Nationale Bank van België/Banque nationale de Belgique*.
E. Welteke as from 1 September 1999 [preceded by H. Tietmeyer, until 31 August 1999]; *Deutsche Bundesbank*.
N. Garganas as from 14 June 2002 – [preceded by L. D. Papademos, as from 1 January 2001 when Greece joined the single currency area[c] until 31 May 2002 when he was appointed ECB Vice-President], *Bank of Greece*.
J. Caruana as from 12 July 2000 [preceded by L. Rojo, until 11 July 2000]; *Banco de España*.
J.-C. Trichet, *Banque de France*.
J. Hurley as from 11 March 2002 [preceded by M. O'Connell, until 10 March 2002]; *Central Bank of Ireland*.
A. Fazio, *Banca d'Italia*.
Y. Mersch, *Banque centrale du Luxembourg*.
N. Wellink, *De Nederlandsche Bank*.
K. Liebscher, *Oesterreichische Nationalbank*.
V. Constâncio as from 23 February 2000 [preceded by A. de Sousa, until 22 February 2000]; *Banco de Portugal*.
M. Vanhala, *Suomen Pankki*.

Notes
a It is important to underline that the single currency was introduced in 1999, not in 2002. From January 1999 to January 2002, the legacy bills and coins used at the retail level, and the cheques written in the legacy units of account were all, legally speaking, only non-decimal subdivisions of the euro.
b Prior to November 2001, the ECB Governing Council, like the pre-euro Bundesbank's Central Bank Council, held a monetary policy meeting every fortnight. To reduce the frequency of interest rate volatility, which usually occurs around the time of a monetary policy meeting, the ECB Governing Council decided in November 2001 to meet only once a month to consider monetary policy changes. It still holds two meetings per month, but one of the meetings per month deals with issues other than monetary policy decisions.
c Since Greece had not qualified for membership in the eurozone with the first wave of countries in 1999, the Greek government applied for membership in early 2000. Following the positive recommendation by the Heads of State or Government, the Ecofin Council in June 2000 approved the Greek request to join the eurozone as of 1 January 2001.

Central Banks (NCBs) to carry out operations that form part of the tasks of the Eurosystem. Whereas the principle of decentralisation applies to operations only (e.g. the basic open-market operations, called the 'main refinancing operations', are executed by each euro NCB with the credit institutions located on its national territory), the monetary policy decisions remain centralised (e.g. the interest rate of the main refinancing operations is decided by the ECB Governing Council and the overall amount of short-term liquidity provided each week to the credit institutions in the Eurosystem is decided by the ECB Executive Board). This principle is very similar to the one that was applied to the allocation of responsibilities and functions between the Central Bank Council/Directorate of the pre-euro Bundesbank and the Land Central Banks (see below).

A General Council, composed of the President and Vice-President of the ECB and the Governors of the 15 EU National Central Banks, has been established for the transition period when some national central banks of the ESCB do not participate in the Eurosystem. The General Council coordinates monetary policies between the Eurosystem and the 'out' NCBs (which retain their powers in the field of monetary policy, which has to be consistent with the goal of price stability), cooperates on issues dealing with prudential supervision of credit institutions in the European Union, and contributes in the preparations for irrevocably fixing the exchange rates of the euro against the currencies of the 'out' Member States that have made a formal request to join the eurozone.

When the other three current EU Member States (Denmark, Sweden and the United Kingdom[5]) eventually join the eurozone, the Governing Council will be composed of 21 members, with the NCB governors effectively holding 71 per cent of the votes in that decision-making body of the Eurosystem. This is in contrast to the case of the pre-euro Deutsche Bundesbank, where the Presidents of the Land Central Banks held only 53 per cent of the votes in the Central Bank Council, and to the case of the US Federal Reserve System where the five voting Presidents of the district Federal Reserve Banks hold only 42 per cent of the votes of the Federal Open Market Committee, the decision-making body of the US central bank (see below). In a Eurosytem composed of the 15 National Central Banks – and many more in the future, with the enlargement of the EU (see Box 1.2) – the Executive Board (the centre) will clearly be in the minority with six votes out of a total of 21. The 'executive' of the Eurosystem is relatively less important than the 'executive' of either the Directorate of the pre-euro Bundesbank or the Board of Governors of the Federal Reserve System.

Income of the ECB

The eurozone National Central Banks, not the governments of the Member States constituting the eurozone, are the shareholders of the

Box 1.2 Enlargement of the European Union and the ECB

With the enlargement of the European Union from the current 15 Member States to 27 Member States, the Governing Council would be composed of ultimately 33 members, as the new Member States were eventually accepted to join the eurozone. Such a large Governing Council would both change the balance of power strongly towards the national central bank governors and away from the six Executive Board members, and render it unwieldy. The Treaty of Nice (2001) opens the way to change the ECB's decision-making procedures without requiring another intergovernmental conference to modify the voting rules in the Governing Council of the ECB. The Treaty of Nice, which was ratified by all 15 EU Member States by the end of 2002, allows the Council of the European Union, meeting in the composition of the Heads of State or Government and acting unanimously, to recommend to Member States an amendment to the provision of Article 10.2 of the ECB 'Statute' concerning the general voting rules of the ECB Governing Council. The amendment would enter into force after having been ratified by all the Member States. The current principle of the voting procedure in the ECB Governing Council on monetary policy is 'one member, one vote'. An amendment could envisage a voting system similar to the one existing in the Federal Open Market Committee of the Federal Reserve System (see below). In line with the provisions of this system, all NCB governors would participate in the discussions of the ECB Governing Council, but in any given year only a limited number of governors would have the right to vote, the voting rights rotating among the governors from year to year. A further condition could be envisaged whereby the Governors of National Central Banks from large Member States, such as from Germany and France, would have a permanent voting seat on the ECB Governing Council, as is the case, for example, for the President of the Federal Reserve Bank of New York, who has a permanent voting seat on the FOMC.

ECB; the eurozone NCBs, not the ECB, receive the so-called 'seigniorage income' of the Eurosystem. The ECB receives investment income derived from its capital base and holdings of foreign reserve assets, both of which were provided by the eurozone NCBs. The 12 NCBs participating in the eurozone paid up in full their respective subscriptions to the ECB's capital according to their calculated share, as provided in the Maastricht Treaty. The shares and amounts of the capital subscription to the European

10 *Historical background*

Central Bank are calculated on the basis of the relative size of each Member State's population and gross domestic product (see Table 1.1). As a result, the ECB is endowed with a capital of €4 billion, out of an authorised initial capital base of €5 billion.[6] This capital, as well as its holdings of foreign reserve assets (see Table 1.1), generates its regular income to cover its administrative expenses on salaries, services and rental of premises. As 'shareholders' of the ECB, the eurozone NCBs are entitled to receive any profit (the difference between the income and expenses) earned by the ECB, in proportion to their paid-up capital.[7]

Seigniorage income of the NCBs

The income accruing to a national central bank in the performance of its monetary policy operations is known as *seigniorage income*, since it arises from the seigniorage rights granted to a central bank. Seigniorage income is derived from the assets held by the central bank against notes in circulation and deposit liabilities to credit institutions (or, more generally, to counterparties). When a central bank engages in an open market operation to provide liquidity, it purchases – albeit temporarily – an interest-bearing security from a counterparty, who in turn receives a deposit (or banknotes, if requested) from the central bank. The security provides seigniorage income to the central bank. Although all open-market policy decisions are taken by the ECB Governing Council, it is important to note that the ECB does not directly engage in these open-market operations, which are carried out directly by the National Central Banks of the Eurosystem, in keeping with the principle of decentralisation. Consequently, the NCBs receive seigniorage income, not the ECB.

The 'Treaty' (see Article 32.5 of the 'Statute') provides that each eurozone National Central Bank's seigniorage income derived from its assets held against notes in circulation and deposit liabilities to credit institutions (less any interest paid on reserves held by credit institutions) is pooled and then redistributed to each eurozone NCB in proportion to its paid-up shares in the capital of the ECB. However, the Governing Council of the ECB decided that, for the first three years (1999–2001), seigniorage income derived from the banknotes in circulation would *not* be pooled and redistributed to the eurozone NCBs prior to the introduction of the euro banknotes (European Central Bank 1998b). In accordance with this interim decision, based on Article 32.3 of the 'Statute', only the seigniorage income derived from the *deposit* liabilities of the euro NCBs to credit institutions is to be pooled and redistributed to the eurozone NCBs, in proportion to the paid-up shares of the NCBs in the capital of the ECB.[8]

This interim decision was taken to avoid the contentious issue of the full application of Article 32.5, which would have meant a reallocation of seigniorage income from the Deutsche Bundesbank to the Banque de France (see *Central Banking* 1997). On the basis of data from the

Table 1.1 Capital and foreign reserve assets transferred by the National Central Banks to the European Central Bank

National Central Bank	Key (%)	Subscribed Capital (in euro)	% of capital paid up	Total amount of capital paid (in euro)	Foreign Reserve Assets transferred to ECB (in euro)*
Deutsche Bundesbank	24.4935	1,224,675,000	100.0	1,224,675,000	12,246,750,000
Banque de France	16.8337	841,685,000	100.0	841,685,000	8,416,850,000
Banca d'Italia	14.8950	744,750,000	100.0	744,750,000	7,447,500,000
Banco de España	8.8935	444,675,000	100.0	444,675,000	4,446,750,000
De Nederlandsche Bank	4.2780	213,900,000	100.0	213,900,000	2,139,000,000
Banque nationale Belgique	2.8658	143,290,000	100.0	143,290,000	1,432,900,000
Oesterreichische Nationalbank	2.3594	117,970,000	100.0	117,970,000	1,179,700,000
Bank of Greece	2.0564	102,820,000	100.0	102,820,000	1,028,200,000*
Banco de Portugal	1.9232	96,160,000	100.0	96,160,000	961,600,000
Suomen Pankki	1.3970	69,850,000	100.0	69,850,000	698,500,000
Central Bank of Ireland	0.8496	42,480,000	100.0	42,480,000	424,800,000
Banque centrale Luxembourg	0.1492	7,460,000	100.0	7,460,000	74,600,000
Subtotal-Euro NCBs	80.9943	4,049,715,000		4,049,715,000	40,497,150,000
Bank of England	14.6811	734,055,000	5.0	36,702,750	Nil
Sveriges Riksbank	2.6537	132,685,000	5.0	6,634,250	Nil
Danmarks Nationalbank	1.6709	83,545,000	5.0	4,177,250	Nil
Subtotal-non Euro NCBs	19.0057	950,285,000		47,514,250	Nil
TOTAL	100.000	5,000,000,000		4,097,229,250	40,497,150,000

Source: European Central Bank, *Annual Report 2001*.

Note
*Euro value calculated by using the euro exchange rates of the US dollar and the Japanese yen and the gold price denominated in euro that prevailed at the time of the transfer of these assets in early January 1999. Since the Bank of Greece transferred its foreign reserve assets in early January 2001 when Greece joined the eurozone, the figure shown here for the Bank of Greece incorporates the adjustment made for the depreciation of the euro against the US dollar and Japanese yen between 1999 and 2001 (for details, see European Central Bank, *Annual Report 2001*: 189).

12 Historical background

eurozone comprising the original 11 NCBs, the Bundesbank would have received each year only 31 per cent of the pooled seigniorage income derived from the eurozone's banknotes in circulation whereas the value of the Deutsche mark banknotes in circulation accounts for an estimated 38 per cent of the eurozone's total value of banknotes in circulation. On the other hand, the Banque de France would have been allocated 21 per cent of that pooled income whereas the value of the French franc banknotes represents only 12 per cent of the eurozone's total value of banknotes in circulation.[9] The question of the calculation of the pooled seigniorage income derived from the banknotes was revisited by the Governing Council just prior to the introduction of the euro banknotes in 2002. Following the decision of the Governing Council, as from calendar year 2002, the seigniorage income derived from euro banknotes is pooled and allocated to the eurozone NCBs in proportion to their paid-up shares in the capital of the ECB. However, there is a transitional period up to the end of 2007, during which the seigniorage income (monetary income) derived from banknotes and allocated to the NCBs, is adjusted by taking into account the differences between the average value of banknotes in circulation of each eurozone NCB in the period from July 1999 to June 2001 and the average value of banknotes that would have been allocated to each eurozone NCB during that period under the ECB's paid-up capital formula. This adjustment is to be reduced in annual stages until the end of 2007 (see European Central Bank 2001b). Again, this procedure of calculating the allocation of monetary income prevents a sudden change of seignoriage income as a result of the pooling of income derived from banknotes after the end of calendar year 2001.

Foreign reserve assets of the ECB

The Eurosystem may conduct foreign exchange intervention either on its own or within the framework of coordinated intervention involving other central banks. The intervention may be carried out by the ECB, or by the NCBs acting on behalf of the ECB, or by a combination of the two (see Chapter 2). To carry out the task of foreign exchange intervention, the ECB is authorised to hold and manage some of the official foreign reserves of the Member States participating in the eurozone. To that end, the ECB was initially provided by the participating national central banks with foreign reserve assets – other than the national currencies of the Community Member States, IMF reserve positions, and Special Drawing Rights – up to an amount equivalent to €50 billion. The foreign reserve assets initially transferred to the ECB were essentially composed of US dollars and gold, the latter composing 15 per cent of the total value transferred. The original 11 NCBs of the eurozone transferred to the ECB in early January 1999, a total of almost €40 billion in foreign reserve assets (precisely €39.5 billion, composed of €30.2 billion in US dollars in the form of securities and cash, €3.4 billion in Japanese yen in the form of securities and cash, and €5.9 billion in gold, equal to 750 tonnes) which represents the maximum allowable amount of €50 billion authorised by the 'Treaty' and adjusted downwards for the 'out' NCBs by deducting their share, approximately 20 per cent. Each National Central Bank's contribution is fixed in proportion to its share in the subscribed capital of the ECB (see Table 1.1). For instance, the Bundesbank transferred to the ECB reserves amounting to €12.2 billion (=24.4935 per cent of €50 billion). When Greece joined the eurozone on 1 January 2001, the Bank of Greece, which became the 12th participating NCB, transferred to the ECB foreign reserve assets, also composed of gold, US dollars and Japanese yen, with a total value equivalent to €1,278,260,161. The ECB remunerates the participating NCBs for the transfer of these foreign reserve assets at an interest rate equal to the Eurosystem's main refinancing rate (see Chapter 3), adjusted to reflect a zero return on the gold component of these reserve assets. In calendar years 1999, 2000 and 2001, the ECB earned respectively €1.5 billion, €2.5 billion and €1.7 billion on the foreign reserve assets (primarily interest income from US government securities), but paid only €913 million, €1.4 billion and €1.5 billion respectively to the participating NCBs on their claims on the foreign reserve assets transferred at the beginning of 1999 (European Central Bank, *Annual Report 1999*: 156; *Annual Report 2000*: 174; *Annual Report 2001*: 186).

On the recommendations of the ECB (ECB/1999/1) and the Commission, the Ecofin Council adopted on 8 May 2000 a Regulation (2000/1010/EC) that allows the Governing Council to request further calls of foreign reserve assets from participating NCBs. When implemented, and provided that all 15 EU Member States participate in the eurozone, this measure will bring the total amount of foreign reserve assets held by the ECB to €100 billion. The new higher ceiling would strengthen the ECB's credibility on the international markets, in the event of a decision to execute foreign exchange interventions.

While foreign reserve assets in excess of those transferred to the ECB are held and managed by the participating NCBs,[10] market transactions conducted with those assets are monitored by the ECB to ensure the singleness of the Eurosystem's exchange rate policy and monetary policy. The ECB issued guidelines to eurozone NCBs, whereby each NCB's operation in foreign reserve assets, including gold, which exceed a certain amount is subject to prior approval by the ECB. A similar monitoring framework has been put in place for transactions performed by eurozone Member States and the European Commission involving the use of their foreign exchange working balances.

THE PRE-EURO BUNDESBANK

Historical background

The Deutsche Bundesbank was established in 1957 to replace the two-tier central bank system of West Germany set up by the Allied Control Commission in March 1948. The two-tier system of 1948, in part based on the model of the US Federal Reserve System, was designed to maintain the central bank's independence of the future West German federal government. It was composed of the legally independent Land Central Banks, which operated in the individual Länder (States) of the western occupied zones, and the Bank deutscher Länder, established in Frankfurt am Main and responsible for issuing banknotes, the Deutsche mark, created in June 1948. In each West German State, the Land Central Bank acted as a central bank, just as each of the 12 district Federal Reserve Banks had done in the US until the 1930s. The difference was that, whereas the shareholders of the Land Central Banks were each Land Government, the shareholders of each district Federal Reserve Bank were, and still are, the member commercial banks in each district (see below). In 1957, the two-tier central bank system was abolished and a unified central bank was set up, but which retained the feature of being independent of all governments (state and federal) in the key area of interest rate decisions. The Land Central Banks, along with the Berlin Central Bank, were amalgamated with the Bank deutscher Länder, which then became the Deutsche Bundesbank, with the German Federal government as its sole shareholder. The Land Central Banks became part of the Bundesbank as Main Offices. However, they retained the name of 'Land Central Bank'. Since 1 November 1992, following German reunification, the administrative areas of the Land Central Banks do not necessarily coincide with the territory of a Land. Of the nine Land Central Banks of the reunified Germany, five are responsible for two or three Länder each. Thus, only the Land Central Banks of North Rhine-Westphalia, Hesse, Baden-Wüttemberg, and Bavaria coincide with the territory of the Land.

Basic institutional features

The governing bodies of the Deutsche Bundesbank were – until the reorganisation of the Deutsche Bundesbank that became effective at the end of April 2002 (see Box 1.3 for details) – the Directorate and the Central Bank Council. The Directorate was composed of eight members, including the President and Vice-President. The members of the Directorate were nominated by the Federal Cabinet, after consulting the Central Bank Council, and were appointed by the President of the Federal Republic for a term of eight years, or in exceptional cases for a shorter term of office, but not for less than two years.[11] Members of the Directorate had to possess professional qualifications.

Box 1.3 Changes to the organisational structure of the Deutsche Bundesbank as of 30 April 2002

The launch of the single currency area and the transfer of monetary policy decisions to a supranational institution in January 1999 changed the principal role of the Bundesbank. The Bundesbank, like all the other eurozone NCBs, became part of the Eurosystem and, since that time, contributed to the monetary policy decisions of the eurozone through its President's direct participation in the policy council meetings of the European Central Bank and through its 'involvement in the preparation, implementation and public explanation of monetary policy decisions' (Deutsche Bundesbank 1999: 7).

In the monetary policy field, the Bundesbank's policy-making council is required to provide its expertise to brief and recommend arguments to its President and to all Bundesbank members who participate in the ESCB committees. The Bundesbank must also maintain operational functions – all with due regard to the instructions given by the ECB – such as the execution of refinancing operations for credit institutions in Germany, payment and clearing transactions in Germany, management of foreign reserve assets of the Bundesbank, and supply of currency to the German financial institutions.

Although the role and powers of the Bundesbank changed significantly when it was integrated into the Eurosystem, the organisational structure of the Bundesbank remained essentially unchanged. In January 2001, the German government proposed (see Bundesministerium der Finanzen 2001), after consulting the Bundesbank (see the Bundesbank proposal, 'option 1', in Deutsche Bundesbank 1999), that the organisational structure of the Bundesbank be streamlined through the creation of a single governing body composed of six members, plus a President and Vice-President. Under this proposal, which was later adopted by both houses of the German Parliament, the Central Bank Council, was replaced as of 30 April 2002 by one governing body, called the 'Executive Board', headquartered in Frankfurt am Main. Nominally, the regional structure of the Bundesbank is maintained through the preservation of the present nine Main Offices, each headed by a regional *director*. In keeping with the federative structure of Germany, the President, Vice-President and two other members of the new Executive Board are nominated by the Federal Government and the four other members are nominated by the Bundesrat (the upper legislative chamber representing the Länder), but conditional on the approval of the Federal Government.

Under the rules of the Eurosystem, the governing body of the Bundesbank has the right to brief, and to make recommendations to the Bundesbank President, who sits on the governing body of the European Central Bank.[a] By excluding the representatives of the nine Land Central Banks, now called Main Offices, from the Bundesbank's Executive Board, the new organisational structure eliminates the current indirect role of the Land Central Banks in the eurozone monetary policy and strengthens the position of the Bundesbank President within the Bundesbank's Executive Board. It also deals with the problems created by the tendency of the Bundesbank officials from the Land Central Banks to comment, not only publicly but also critically, on ECB monetary and exchange rate policies, which added to the impression that eurozone monetary authorities did not speak with one voice. Moreover, these critical public comments irritated the current President of the Bundesbank, Mr. Welteke, who feared that the market could at times interpret them as a reflection of his views as a member of the ECB Governing Council.

Note

a This must be done without prejudice to the President's independence of instructions in his capacity as a Member of the Governing Council of the European Central Bank, as is stipulated in the revised Article 6.1 of the Bundesbank Act, adopted in 1997, to be in line with the provisions of the Maastricht Treaty dealing with the institutional independence of the decision-making bodies of the ECB. Thus, the Bundesbank President may be briefed and given advice by the Bundesbank's governing body, but he may not receive instructions on how to vote when he sits on the Governing Council of the European Central Bank.

This restriction on a NCB's governing body also appears in the new Statute of the Banque de France (Loi 98-357 of 12 May 1998), which legally integrates the Banque de France in the ESCB and which strengthens its independence granted in the law of 4 August 1993:

Le Conseil de la politique monétaire [the Banque de France's still-existing Monetary Policy Council established in 1993 and composed of nine members, including its Governor] examine les évolutions monétaires et analyse les implications de la politique monétaire élaborée dans le cadre du Système européen de banques centrales (Art. 7, par. 1).

Le Conseil de la politique monétaire délibère dans le respect de l'indépendance de son président [the Governor of the Banque de France], membre du conseil des gouverneurs de la banque centrale européenne, et des règles de confidentialité de celle-ci (Art. 9, par. 4).

These two paragraphs entered into force as of 1 January 1999.

The Central Bank Council was composed of 17 members: the eight members of the Directorate and nine Presidents of the Land Central Banks (see Figure 1.2). Presidents of Land Central Banks were nominated by the Bundesrat (the upper chamber of the Federal Parliament representing the Länder) and were appointed by the President of the Federal Republic for a normal term of eight years, but not for less than two years.[11] The members of the Central Bank Council, responsible for monetary policy decisions, could not be removed from office before the end of their term except for a limited number of reasons related to personal behaviour, such as the inability to perform duties.

While the Central Bank Council was responsible for monetary policy decisions (e.g. setting the key official short-term interest rates), the Directorate was responsible for the implementation of the decisions taken by the Central Bank Council (e.g. determining the aggregate amount of liquidity that should be provided to the entire banking sector). Execution of open-market operations was decentralised. Bids for funds were submitted by the credit institutions to their respective Land Central Bank, but the aggregate amount of liquidity provided to the entire banking system was set by the Directorate of the Bundesbank in Frankfurt, consistent with the interest rate decisions taken by the Central Bank Council.

The Central Bank Council generally met on alternate Thursdays; monetary policy decisions were taken by a consensus or, if necessary, by simple majority. Whenever the Central Bank Council decided to change monetary policy, a Bundesbank press officer would hold, immediately following the meeting, a short press conference to announce the results of the meeting. This announcement would include the change of the key official short-term interest rates controlled by Bundesbank and the reason or reasons behind the change in monetary policy. No further details would be released and, in particular, the minutes of the Central Bank Council meetings and the votes of each individual member were never released to the public.

THE FEDERAL RESERVE SYSTEM

Historical background

In US history, there is a long-standing distrust of centralised power and of central banks in particular. These views were first represented by Thomas Jefferson (President, 1801–09) who argued against the principles of the centralisation of power. The plan to establish a centralised national issuing bank was the subject of enduring dispute. The US Constitution did not include explicit power to establish a central bank. Between the end of the eighteenth century and the first part of the nineteenth century, the US had twice established a central bank to stabilise the private banking system. However, the charter of the First Bank of the United States (1791–1811),

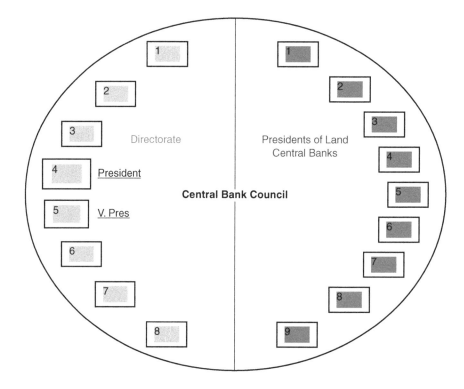

The *Central Bank Council* was composed of the President and Vice-President of the Bundesbank, the other six members of the Directorate and the Presidents of the nine Land Central Banks. The Central Bank Council determined the Bundesbank's monetary policy. The Directorate was the central executive of the Bundesbank. The eight members of the Directorate were nominated by the Federal Cabinet and appointed by the President of the German Federal Republic. The Presidents of the nine Land Central Banks were nominated by the Bundesrat (upper legislative chamber) and appointed by the President of the Federal Republic.

The nine Land Central Banks, which are the Main Offices of the Deutsche Bundesbank, each responsible for one or more of the German Länder (States), are as follows:

> **Baden-Württemberg;**
> **Free State of Bavaria;**
> **Berlin and Brandenburg;**
> **Free Hanseatic City of Bremen, Lower Saxony and Saxony-Anhalt;**
> **Free and Hanseatic City of Hamburg, Mecklenburg-West Pomerania and Schleswig-Holstein;**
> **Hesse;**
> **North Rhine-Westphalia;**
> **Rhineland-Palatinate and Saarland;**
> **Free States of Saxony and Thuringia**

Figure 1.2 Organisation of the pre-euro Bundesbank with respect to monetary policy decisions.

which had been opposed by Thomas Jefferson and James Madison, but proposed by Alexander Hamilton (Secretary of the Treasury, 1789–95) who argued in favour of the principles of the centralisation of power, was not renewed in 1811 when James Madison was President. The charter of the Second Bank of the United States (1816–36), granted as a result of the war with Britain and the revival of Hamilton's ideas, was not renewed upon expiration primarily because of political distrust of the eastern financial establishment and a desire by western farmers for inexpensive credit. The struggle over the attempt to re-charter the Second Bank of the United States, brought to the fore by the bitter controversy between Nicholas Biddle, President of the Bank, and President Andrew Jackson (1829–37), left a legacy such that, for some 75 years, the United States was a sovereign nation without a central bank.[12] In his veto message of a Congressional bill to renew the charter of the Second Bank, President Jackson stated:

> It is regretted that the rich and powerful too often bend the acts of government to their selfish purposes ... In the full enjoyment of the gifts of Heaven and the fruits of superior industry, economy, and virtue, every man is equally entitled to protection by law; but when the laws undertake to add to these natural and just advantages artificial distinctions, to grant titles, gratuities, and exclusive privileges, to make the rich richer and the potent more powerful, the humble members of society – the farmers, mechanics, and laborers – who have neither the time nor the means of securing like favors to themselves, have a right to complain of the injustice of their Government ... In the act before me there seems to be a wide and unnecessary departure from ... just principles.
> (Reprinted in US House of Representatives 1894)

The veto message declared the Bank unconstitutional and condemned it as a device for giving financial advantage and power to a small and irresponsible group of wealthy persons living in eastern cities and even in foreign countries.

The original charter of the Second Bank of the United States provided that the capital should be $35,000,000, of which one fifth was to be subscribed by the federal government. The shareholders were to elect 20 directors of the Bank and the President of the United States was to appoint five. The new institution could issue notes in denominations of not less than $5, which would be accepted by the government in payment for taxes; the total value of notes issued could not exceed $35,000,000. Notes had to be redeemed in specie or the Bank was to forfeit 12 per cent per annum of the notes in circulation. The federal government was to receive $1,500,000 from the Bank in return for the charter privilege. On the expiration of its United States charter in 1836, the Bank secured a new one from the state of Pennsylvania (since its offices were in Philadelphia) and continued in business as a state bank until it was forced into liquidation in 1841.

From the 1840s to the beginning of the twentieth century, the United States did not have any central bank. The Independent Treasury System of the federal government, established in 1846, was little more than a receiving and disbursing instrument for the Federal treasury. The need for funds during the Civil War (1861–65) led to the establishment of the National Banking System in 1864. Under this system, 'country banks' were required to hold reserves at larger banks, called 'reserve city banks' which in turn were required to hold deposits in 'central reserve city banks'. The US Treasury Department attempted to have some control of the money supply by adding or draining funds that it kept on deposit at central reserve city banks. Under the National Banking Act, the Treasury also granted concessions to national banks. By 1880, over 2,000 national banks issued notes; by 1905, they were over 56,000.

The series of serious financial panics, culminating with the banking panic of 1907, which forced 243 banks, including 31 national banks, to suspend payments, was the driving force behind the proposals to establish some form of central bank. Although that banking panic was bought under control by the actions of a group of commercial banks, led by J. Pierpont Morgan, it led to the establishment by Congress of a National Monetary Commission, whose mandate was to propose changes to the then existing banking system. The original legislative framework of the Federal Reserve System was based on two old American principles: the distrust of centralised power and the ambivalent attitude towards the establishment of new government institutions to deal with the shortcomings of the private market system. After several years of studying the proposals submitted by the Commission and by other authorities, Congress adopted the Federal Reserve Act of 23 December 1913, establishing a Federal Reserve System that embodied these two principles, namely setting up a decentralised regional system of central banks that were controlled by both the private business sector and the federal government. The establishment of one central bank that had been proposed in the Aldrich plan of 1912, named after the Republican Senator from Rhode Island, had been firmly repudiated in the presidential election of 1912 between the Democratic candidate Wilson, who was elected, and the Republican candidate Taft. Under the adopted proposal, the regional central banks were to be owned by the private commercial banks, and Washington and the regional central banks would jointly manage the monetary system so as to avoid financial crises that could lead to the collapse of the private commercial banks. In contrast to the post-war Bundesbank and the European Central Bank, which were both established to manage monetary policy with the primary objective of maintaining price stability, the Federal Reserve System was created out of a desire to avoid banking panics. Thus, it is not surprising that the Federal Reserve System did not originally have 'price stability' as one of its objectives and that it retains today a role of 'lender of last resort'.

Organisational structure of the Federal Reserve System: an evolving process

The Federal Reserve System was composed of 12 regional Federal Reserve Banks, coordinated by a Federal Reserve Board in Washington, DC. Under the 1913 Act, the Board consisted of *seven* members, five of whom were appointed by the President, with the consent of the Senate, for terms of *ten* years, each term staggered in such a way that one term expired every two years. The Secretary of the Treasury and the Comptroller of the Currency[13] were *ex officio* members of the Board. In 1922, the number of appointed members was increased to six, and in 1933 the term of office was raised to 12 years.

Under the 1913 Act, the Board was thus a wholly public body, but *not* independent of the Executive branch of government. In fact, the Secretary of the Treasury was designated *ex-officio* Chairman of the Board, whereas one of the five appointed members was designated simply 'Governor of the Board'. Conversely, the district Federal Reserve Banks were not public bodies; the member banks (private commercial banks) in each district owned them. The Act provided that the affairs of each Reserve Bank would be administered by a board of nine directors, six elected by member banks and three appointed by the Federal Reserve Board in Washington, DC. Each of the 12 district Reserve Banks had the authority to engage in open-market operations, to rediscount commercial paper from member banks and, subject to review and approval by the Federal Reserve Board, to set the discount rate.

Almost immediately after the creation of the Federal Reserve System, the district Federal Reserve Banks began to maintain a considerable degree of independence from the Federal Reserve Board in Washington, insisting on the division of powers, as provided in the Act. The district Federal Reserve Banks began to create an administrative structure that was not prescribed by the Federal Reserve Act of 1913. First, each district Federal Reserve Bank appointed a chief executive officer, with the title of 'Governor of the Federal Reserve Bank'. Then, these 12 Governors set up an important administrative entity, which they called the *Conference of Governors of the Federal Reserve Banks*. This committee rivalled the Federal Reserve Board in its power to control the operation of the System and quickly assumed an importance that has been significant in defining the structure and function of the Federal Reserve System to the present day (see Mealendyke 1998).

From the outset, each Federal Reserve Bank purchased, for its own account, both Treasury securities and bankers acceptances (BAs). These decentralised open-market purchases were executed more as a source of revenue rather than as a tool for regulating reserves to control the money supply in each Federal Reserve district. Discount rate changes, which had to be approved by the Board in Washington, were the main instrument to vary credit availability, with the typical result that discount rates varied from one Federal Reserve district to another. Starting in the early 1920s, Benjamin Strong, the influential Governor of the New York Federal Reserve Bank, argued that open-market operations could be used to stabilise the economy, but that they had to be coordinated among the regional Reserve Banks and executed by the New York Federal Reserve Bank. This led to the creation in 1923 of the *Open Market Investment Committee* (OMIC), consisting of the Governors of the Federal Reserve Banks of New York, Boston, Philadelphia, Cleveland, and Chicago, thus excluding the Governors of the other seven Federal Reserve Banks[14] and the members of the Federal Reserve Board in Washington. However, this Committee, chaired by Strong himself, did not have the exclusive power to approve the open market operations of the regional Federal Reserve Banks. The Trading Desk at the New York Fed simply carried out operations for all the Federal Reserve Banks, including the New York Federal Reserve Bank.

In 1930, power shifted from the five large Federal Reserve Banks to Washington. The OMIC was replaced by the *Open Market Policy Conference* (OMPC), composed of all 12 Federal Reserve Bank governors and the members of the Federal Reserve Board. In the early 1930s, the Federal Reserve Board, with the Treasury Secretary as one of its members, argued in favour of counter-cyclical open-market operations in the face of the deteriorating economic situation. However, it was not until the Roosevelt administration and a Democratic Congress took power in March 1933 during the Great Depression, that major changes in the organisation and in the operating mechanisms of the Federal Reserve System were introduced. The major modifications were as follows.

(i) Under the Banking Act of 1933:
- The Federal Deposit Insurance Corporation (FDIC) is created to insure bank deposits, beginning 1 July 1934. All the banks that are part of the Federal Reserve System must have their deposits insured by the FDIC.

(ii) Under the Banking Act of 1935:
- The 'Federal Reserve Board' is renamed the 'Board of Governors of the Federal Reserve System' composed of seven appointed members, who are now designated 'Governors', with a non-renewable full term set at 14 years.[15] Once appointed, a Board Governor cannot be dismissed by the President. One Board Governor is appointed and designated as Chairman, for a term of four years, renewable as long as his term as a regular Board member has not expired. The Secretary of the Treasury and the Comptrol-

ler of the Currency can no longer be members of, or sit on, the Board.
- The chief executive officer of each district Federal Reserve Bank, previously designated 'Governor', is re-designated as 'President'. His appointment by the board of directors of his Bank, for a five-year, renewable term, is now subject to the approval of the Board of Governors. The name change reflects a change in the power relationship between the Federal Reserve Banks and the Board in Washington. Heretofore, the 'Governors' of the System were the 12 chief executives of the Federal Reserve Banks, whereas the Board in Washington was simply composed of 'Members', except for its appointed chairman who was designated '*Governor* of the Federal Reserve Board'. Under the new law, the members of the Board are designated 'Governors', with one member designated 'Chairman'.
- The Open Market Policy Conference, which had been renamed the *Federal Open Market Committee* (FOMC) under the Banking Act of 1933, has its voting membership limited to five, instead of all 12, Presidents of Federal Reserve Banks at any one time. This measure, which has not been modified since its implementation, gives the Board of Governors relatively more power. Furthermore, the Federal Open Market Committee by-laws, under the Banking Act of 1935, stipulate that the President of a Federal Reserve Bank, in his role as a member of that Committee, may not act as a representative of the Federal Reserve Bank that appointed him and may not receive instructions by his Bank.
- The district Federal Reserve Banks no longer have the power to buy or sell government securities, except with the explicit permission of the FOMC. Since then, only the Federal Reserve Bank of New York has been designated by the FOMC to execute open market operations on its behalf.
- The Board of Governors is given the power to double the minimum reserve requirements of banks under the jurisdiction of the Federal Reserve System ('member banks') from the percentages specified in the amended Act of June 1917.
- The Board of Governors is granted the power to regulate credit advanced by bankers and brokers to their customers for purchasing securities (the authority to set the so-called 'margin requirements').

Seigniorage income in the Federal Reserve System

Since 1935, all open-market operations of the Federal Reserve System have been carried out by the Federal Reserve Bank of New York under the explicit authority of the Federal Open Market Committee. The assets acquired from these open-market operations are held in an account called the *System Open Market Account* (SOMA). These assets, including the interest income, are allocated to each of the 12 Federal Reserve Banks in proportion to the relative value of the banknotes issued by each of them, unlike the Eurosystem's allocation formula for interest income, which is based on the proportion of paid-up capital to the ECB by each NCB. On the basis of the allocation formula used by the Federal Reserve System, the Federal Reserve Bank of New York has an estimated 39 per cent claim on the total amount of SOMA balances, composed of primarily US government and Federal agency securities.[16] This arrangement ensures that all open market operations are centralised, while at the same time allowing each district Federal Reserve Bank to share in the interest earned on the assets derived from these operations ('seigniorage income').

In the US Federal Reserve System, the question of the distribution of the seigniorage income among the 12 Federal Reserve Banks does not pose a problem since the seigniorage income of each Federal Reserve Bank is transferred to a single government, namely the United States Treasury. In the eurozone, the issue of the allocation of seigniorage income among the NCBs is contentious because the seigniorage income of each NCB ultimately goes to its respective government, not to a single government. In the US, the 'excess earnings' of each Federal Reserve Bank are transferred to the US Treasury. 'Excess earnings' are defined as interest income derived from the interest earned on the US government and Federal agency securities allocated to each Federal Reserve Bank stemming from the centralised open market operations, less the following items: operating costs, which include the shared costs of operating the Board of Governors (the Board has no income of its own); payment of annual dividends to its member banks, equal to 6 per cent of the paid-in capital from its member banks; and the amount necessary to equate the Federal Reserve Bank's surplus with its paid-in capital (see Federal Reserve System 1998: 301).

Current institutional features of the FOMC

The most important governing body of the Federal Reserve System in setting monetary policy is the Federal Open Market Committee (FOMC), which is composed of the seven-member Board of Governors (including the Chairman of the Board, who is also the Chairman of the Committee), the President of the Federal Reserve Bank of New York (who is also the Vice-Chairman of the Committee), and the Presidents of four other Federal Reserve Banks, who serve on a one-year rotating term (see Box 1.4). Since 1982, the FOMC normally meets eight times a year in Washington, DC, although the Committee may have also teleconferences in addition to the regularly scheduled meetings. Prior to 1982, the Committee met approximately once a month; in fact in the 1950s and 1960s, the Committee met every two or three weeks; by law, at least four meetings per year are required. All the Presidents of the Federal Reserve Banks participate in FOMC discussions, but only the five Presidents who are members of the Committee have the right to vote. Decisions in the FOMC are taken by simple majority voting, with each member having one vote. In case of a tie, the Chairman has also a casting vote. Alan Greenspan, the current Chairman who was appointed in 1987 and whose term as Chairman expires in 2004, tries to maintain a consensus on the FOMC. Although no member of the Executive branch of the US government sits or participates at the meetings of the FOMC, regular informal contacts take place between the Chairman and other members of the Board of Governors of the Federal Reserve System, on the one hand, and the Secretary of the Treasury and the President's Council of Economic Advisers, on the other hand, to exchange views on the macroeconomy and to discuss monetary and fiscal policies.

Box 1.4 Composition of the Federal Open Market Committee (FOMC), January 2002

The Federal Open Market Committee of the Federal Reserve System is composed of 12 voting members: the seven members of the Board of Governors of the Federal Reserve System and five Presidents of Federal Reserve Banks. The current members are:

Alan Greenspan, Board of Governors, Chairman
William J. McDonough, President, Federal Reserve Bank of New York, Vice Chairman
Susan Schmidt Bies, Board of Governors
Roger W. Ferguson, Board of Governors
Edward M. Gramlich, Board of Governors
Jerry L. Jordan, President, Federal Reserve Bank of Cleveland
Robert D. McTeer, President, Federal Reserve Bank of Dallas
Mark W. Olson, Board of Governors
Anthony M. Santomero, President, Federal Reserve Bank of Philadelphia
Gary H. Stern, President, Federal Reserve Bank of Minneapolis
Donald Kohn (nomination submitted to Senate in May 2002), Board of Governors
Ben Bernanke (nomination submitted to Senate in May 2002), Board of Governors

Board of Governors

Each of the seven appointed members of the Board of Governors must come from a different Federal Reserve District. Each member on the Board of Governors fills a position that has a term of 14 years. The expiration dates of each position are staggered so that a position expires every two even-dated years on 31 January. A member can serve more than a complete term of 14 years only if he/she was reappointed after a first appointment that completed the unexpired term of a member who resigned or died.

Alan Greenspan of New York was first appointed in 1987 to complete an unexpired term ending in 1992; he was reappointed in 1992 with the term of office expiring in 2006. The designation of Chairman, which Greenspan has held since 1987, expires every four years, with the current term as Chairman ending in June 2004.

Roger Ferguson of Massachusetts was first appointed in 1997 to complete an unexpired term ending in 2000; he was reappointed in 2000 with the term of office expiring in 2014. Ferguson is the Vice Chairman of the Board of Governors; the designation as Vice Chairman expires every four years, with the current term ending in October 2003.

Edward Gramlich of Virginia was appointed in 1997 to complete an unexpired term ending in 2008.

Susan Bies of Missouri took office in 2001 to fill the position of a full term ending in 2012 (this position was left vacant for a long period as a result of delays in the nomination and in the Senate confirmation).

Mark Olson of Minnesota took office in 2001 to complete an unexpired term ending in 2010.

The two vacant positions, for which nominations were confirmed by Senate in July 2002, have terms ending in 2004 (Ben Bernanke) and 2016 (Donald Kohn).

Presidents of the 12 Federal Reserve Banks

The President of the New York Federal Reserve Bank has a permanent voting seat on the FOMC.

The other four voting seats on the FOMC are held on a yearly rotating basis by the Presidents of the other 11 Federal Reserve Banks. The rotation cycle is as follows: one seat rotates among the Presidents of the Federal Reserve Banks of Boston, Philadelphia and

Richmond; another seat rotates between the Presidents of the Federal Reserve Banks of Cleveland and Chicago; another seat rotates among the Presidents of the Federal Reserve Banks of Atlanta, St Louis and Dallas; the final seat rotates among the Presidents of the Federal Reserve Banks of Minneapolis, Kansas City, and San Francisco.

Whenever the President of a Federal Reserve Bank does not have a voting seat on the FOMC, he or she still attends the monetary policy meetings, with only the right of participation.

2 Objectives, independence, transparency and accountability

PRINCIPAL STATUTORY OBJECTIVE(S) OF, AND INTERPRETATION BY, THE THREE CENTRAL BANKS

When established, the pre-euro Bundesbank and the European Central Bank were assigned a single primary statutory objective of 'safeguarding the currency' and 'price stability', respectively. Both central banks interpreted their primary objective in very similar terms, which are now outlined. A detailed presentation of the quantitative definition of price stability by these two institutions is presented in Chapter 3. The evolution of the statutory objectives of the Federal Reserve System is also presented here. The standard macroeconomic benefits of maintaining 'price stability' are explained in Box 2.1.

The pre-euro Bundesbank and the ECB/Eurosystem

The pre-euro Bundesbank was assigned a statutory primary objective of 'safeguarding the currency' (Bundesbank Act of 1957, Article 3[1]), which the Bundesbank interpreted as maintaining a 'low inflation' regime. The pre-euro Bundesbank often referred in a vague sense to the goals of 'monetary stability' and 'price stability': 'Monetary stability can in general be equated with stability of the price level, from which a constant purchasing power of money follows' (Deutsche Bundesbank 1995: 24). Although there is a difference between an objective of 'low inflation' and of 'price stability' (see Kenny and McGettigan 1997; Issing *et al.* 2001: 71–75),[2] the Bundesbank preferred to refer to its mandate as 'price stability', with 'normative price increases' to account for the statistical upward bias in the measurement of the general price index. The medium-term maximum inflation of 2 per cent per annum that the Bundesbank incorporated as of 1985 in its basic formula for the derivation of the monetary target was to be interpreted as that 'normative price increase' or

> the maximum inflation rate to be tolerated in the medium term ... in light of the possibility of statistical recording errors and of a slight

Box 2.1 Macroeconomic benefits of 'price stability'

Since most central banks are given 'price stability' as an objective, or the only objective, to achieve and maintain, it is natural to ask, 'what are the macroeconomic benefits of price stability?', or conversely, 'what are the macroeconomic costs of inflation?'. The standard answers to this question are presented in this box. Everyone seems to know the answer to the question, 'what are the macroeconomic costs of an economy operating at a level of aggregate demand less than its potential output (a negative output gap)? So, if there is a macroeconomic cost to an economy operating with inflation and there also is a macroeconomic cost to an economy operating with a negative output gap, the natural question to ask is, 'why are all central bankers not given two objectives to achieve and maintain: price stability and a level of aggregate demand equal to potential output?' The answer to this latter question is presented below in this chapter under the section dealing with central bank independence.

The main reason that a central bank is given 'price stability' as an objective is to reap the long-run macroeconomic benefits of 'price stability' (see Bakhshi *et al.* 1998). Some of these macroeconomic benefits are as follows.

A macroeconomic benefit of pursuing a monetary policy leading to 'price stability', which is usually operationally defined as a low rate of inflation, is that it allows households and firms to base their economic decisions on more reliable information, as they find it easier to distinguish movements in relative prices from movements in the general price index. Since production, investment and consumption/saving decisions are based on the movement of relative prices, high rates of inflation – which are also associated with more variable rates of inflation – may lead economic agents to confuse absolute price changes with relative price changes. This results in an inefficient allocation of resources, which in the long run decreases macroeconomic welfare (O'Reilly 1998).

A macroeconomic cost of the existence of inflation is the result of the positive relationship between the *real* interest rate and the rate of inflation. Since economies with high rates of inflation also have more variable rates of inflation, the *real* interest rate, which incorporates a risk premium to cover the greater *variability* of the inflation rates, is higher the greater the rate of inflation. The long-run consequence of an inflationary environment is a higher real rate of interest leading to a lower stock of capital and, consequently, lower per capita income.

Other macroeconomic welfare benefits associated with a low rate of inflation are the elimination of so-called 'menu costs' and 'shoe-leather costs'. In an inflationary environment, even if predictable, sellers must continually update price lists, leading to 'menu costs'. Mankiw (1985) has shown that in an inflationary environment, the small 'menu costs' prevent each firm from continually adjusting prices, as would occur in a world without these transaction costs. Thus, in the context of imperfect competition, small 'menu costs' may lead to large welfare losses for the whole economy.

'Shoe-leather costs' occur whenever households and firms spend needless time and energy in economising on liquid balance and/or cash, which pay very little or no interest at all. As the nominal interest rates on other financial assets are positively related to the (expected) rate of inflation, the opportunity cost of holding liquid balances and/or cash increases with the diminishing purchasing power of these money balances. Thus, as household and firms try to reduce their money balances in the face of higher rates of inflation by holding, on average, more of the alternative financial assets, they are forced to spend more time switching between money balances and other financial assets. These implicit costs are called 'shoe-leather costs', which are incurred as a result of the more numerous trips to the bank in an inflationary environment.

> overstating of price rises in the price statistics (because of substitution effects and quality changes are not taken into consideration, and because of the inevitable incompleteness of the range of prices covered).
>
> (Deutsche Bundesbank 1995: 81)

The European Central Bank has been assigned a statutory primary objective of maintaining 'price stability' in the eurozone (Article 105.1 of the 'Treaty'). The ECB has the authority to define the operational meaning of its primary objective (Article 105.2 of the 'Treaty'[3]). Like the pre-euro Deutsche Bundesbank, the ECB defines 'price stability' as the year-on-year price increase of a maximum of 2 per cent over the medium term. The ECB, like the Bundesbank, only explicitly stipulates the upper bound of a price increase range that implicitly has a lower bound of 0 per cent.

The Federal Reserve System

The Federal Reserve System never had, and still does not have, 'price stability' as its *single* assigned statutory objective. In fact, its original mandate did not even mention 'price stability'. Instead, the Federal Reserve System was established in 1913

> [to] provide for the establishment of Federal reserve banks, to furnish an elastic currency, to afford means of rediscounting commercial paper, to establish a more effective supervision of banking in the United States, and for other purposes.
> (Preamble to the Federal Reserve Act of 1913 [Federal Reserve System 1994: 2])

In those early days, 'to furnish an elastic currency' meant that the Federal Reserve Banks had a mandate to provide reserves to accommodate routine variations in the need for credit to finance trade so as to avoid financial panics. In other words, the regional Federal Reserve Banks had to have a pro-cyclical monetary policy. During an expansionary period when the demand for money was higher, the Federal Reserve System had to provide more credit to commercial banks and thus increase the money supply. Inversely, during a contractionary period when the demand for money was lower, the System had to provide less credit to commercial banks and thus decrease the money supply. It is clear that the Federal Reserve System did not originally have a mandate to keep prices stable. The architects of the System were not concerned about the inflationary (or deflationary) potential of an accommodative credit provision since the international monetary system, based on the gold standard with its international gold flows, would limit inflationary (or deflationary) tendencies.

The Employment Act of 1946

All Congressional attempts in the 1920s and early 1930s to introduce a 'price stability' objective in the official mandate of the Federal Reserve System were defeated. Opposition to those proposals came from various officials of the Federal Reserve System – both from the Federal Reserve Banks and from the Board members.[4] Instead, under the provisions contained in the post-war Employment Act of 1946, the primary objectives of national economic policy were addressed to the entire Federal Government, which includes the Federal Reserve System. These policy goals were put in terms of promoting 'maximum employment, production, and purchasing power.'[5] The Act was a product of the experiences of the Great Depression, which had destroyed the faith in the automatic tendency of the economy to find an equilibrium at or near full employment. Congress feared not so much the inflationary pressures of excess demand but a relapse into depressed levels of economic activity with the end of military spending after the end of the Second World War. The Employment Act of 1946 did not *explicitly* provide for price stability as a statutory objective, although it did *implicitly* by using the expression 'maximum purchasing power'. In any event, monetary policy at the time was tied to a policy of supporting Government bond prices and thus could not be used to combat inflation since the US Treasury was reluctant to give up the ability acquired during the Second World War to finance the debt cheaply. Automatic fiscal stabilisers were expected to contain inflation whenever 'maximum employment' placed too much pressure on available resources. By March 1951, an 'Accord' was reached that allowed the Federal Reserve System to resume an active and independent monetary policy.

The Federal Reserve Reform Act of 1977 and the Full Employment and Balanced Growth Act of 1978 (Humphrey–Hawkins Act)

During the post-war era, up until the beginning of the 1970s, the American economy had remained free from the two major macroeconomic problems of the first half of the twentieth century: periods of economic depression and periods of high rates of inflation. The immediate post-war period (1946–48) and the early months of the Korean War were the two episodes of inflationary problems caused by excessive demand. Apart from these two intervals, the Employment Act of 1946 had not led to budgetary and monetary policies that created inflation. With the appearance in the 1970s of inflation and aggregate demand below potential output, Congress passed two new laws, one in 1977 to clarify the multiple-policy objectives of the Federal Reserve System, the other in 1978 to strengthen the Employment Act of 1946. The Federal Reserve Reform Act of 1977 for the first time specifies that the Fed is to 'promote effectively the goals of maximum employment, stable prices, and moderate long-term interest rates.' (Federal Reserve Reform Act, Section 2A, November 16, 1977).[6] The Full Employment and Balanced Growth Act of 1978 sets national economic policy objectives of 'full employment and production, increased real income, balanced growth, a balanced Federal budget ... and reasonable price stability' (Federal Reserve System 1978: 338–39). Since the Federal Reserve System must work within the framework of the overall objectives of national economic policies established by Congress, this Act, also known as the Humphrey–Hawkins Act, confirms the multiple statutory objectives of the Federal Reserve System. It identifies national economic priorities and objectives; it directs the President to establish, and the Congress to consider, policies to eliminate the negative output gap and inflation within a five-year time frame; and it sets new procedures and requirements for the President, the Congress, and the Federal Reserve to improve the coordination and development of economic policies, consistent with these objectives.

CENTRAL BANK INDEPENDENCE

The various aspects of central bank independence – institutional, operational and personal – are now examined for each of the three central banks. A comparative overview is presented in Table 2.1.

Institutional independence

Institutional independence is measured by the degree to which a central bank may act to achieve its defined objectives without government bodies trying to influence those monetary policy decisions. The degree of institutional independence is related both to the statutory relationship between the central bank and the other government bodies and to the mandate given to the central bank. In principle, a central bank that has multiple policy goals is subject to more political pressures than a central bank that has only a single primary objective. This is particularly the case whenever the multiple policy goals cannot be achieved simultaneously. For instance, if an economy receives a negative supply shock that creates both a negative output gap and inflation, a central bank that has the statutory goals of maintaining price stability and an output gap close to zero may be put under political pressure to emphasise one goal over the other in the short run.

The European Central Bank

The statutory relationship between the ECB/Eurosystem and all other governmental bodies is clearly and unambiguously specified in the 'Treaty':

> When exercising the powers and carrying out the tasks and duties conferred upon them by this Treaty and the Statute of the ESCB, neither the ECB, nor a national central bank, nor any member of their decision-making bodies shall seek or take instructions from Community institutions or bodies, from any government of a Member State or from any other body....
> (Article 108 of the 'Treaty' and Article 7 of the 'Statute')

In the case of the ECB, 'institutional independence' does not mean that the monetary authority does not communicate with the other EU bodies responsible for eurozone economic policies, such as the EU Council composed of the Ministers of Finance or the European Parliament, but that, whenever formal contacts take place between the ECB and other EU bodies to exchange information and views, the institutional independence of the central bank must be respected.

Moreover, since the ECB is given a single primary statutory objective

Table 2.1 Summary of institutional characteristics of the ECB/Eurosystem, the pre-euro Deutsche Bundesbank, and the US Federal Reserve System

	ECB/Eurosystem	Pre-euro Bundesbank	Federal Reserve System
Principal statutory objective(s)	Price stability	Safeguarding the currency	Maximum employment, stable prices, and moderate long-term interest rates
Interpretation of statutory objective(s)	Annual rate of inflation of not more than 2% in medium term	Annual rate of inflation of not more than 2% in the medium term	An undefined low rate of inflation and sustainable growth in output
Monetary policy strategy used to achieve and maintain objective(s)	Two pillar strategy based on (i) a monetary reference value, and (ii) an analysis of a large number of economic and financial variables	Monetary targeting	Evolved over time; in the 1970s and 1980s, a strategy based on some form of monetary targeting; now uses an analysis of a large number of economic and financial variables to assess whether the federal funds target rate should be modified to achieve twin objectives
Principal governing bodies	Governing Council; Executive Board	Central Bank Council; Directorate	FOMC; Board of Governors
Institutional independence			
(1) Is central bank given an unambiguous statutory primary mandate?	Yes	Yes	No
(2) Can central bank receive instructions from government authorities?	No	No, except a 2-week suspension of decision possible at request of Government, but government privilege never exercised	Yes, in the form of legislative Acts from Congress, such as the Humphrey–Hawkins Act of 1978

Operational independence			
(1) Does central bank have the sole legal authority to define operationally the meaning of its statutory objective(s)?	Yes, and defined it as indicated above	Yes, and defined it as indicated above	No, since Congress has the authority to legislate operational meaning of statutory objectives
(2) Does central bank have legal authority to set its monetary policy strategy and to use, and set targets for, monetary policy instruments, e.g. short-term interest rate, open-market operations, required reserves?	Yes	Yes	In general yes, but Congress has at times set, by legislation, framework of Fed's monetary policy strategy, i.e. the Full Employment and Balanced Growth Act of 1978
(3) Can there be a conflict of interest between monetary policy decisions and the central bank's responsibility to safeguard the banking system?	No	No	Yes, since the Fed has the responsibility to safeguard the stability of the financial system
(4) What is the central bank's authority with respect to			
• the establishment of a formal exchange rate regime?	Eurogroup Finance Ministers, after consulting the ECB and without prejudice to the ECB's statutory objective of price stability	Government, after consulting the Bundesbank and without prejudice to the Bundesbank's objective of price stability	US Treasury
• foreign exchange intervention?	Governing Council, unless given directives by Eurogroup Finance Ministers, but must not be in conflict with ECB's statutory objective	Central Bank Council, unless given directives by Minister of Finance, but must not be in conflict with price stability objective	US Treasury and FOMC, in close and continual consultation and cooperation with each other; division of responsibilities is not clear

continued

Table 2.1 Continued

	ECB/Eurosystem	Pre-euro Bundesbank	Federal Reserve System
Personal independence			
(1) Appointment of President/Chairman and other members of executive governing body of central bank	Eurozone Heads of State or Government, on proposal of Eurogroup Finance Ministers and after consulting the Governing Council and the European Parliament, for a term of 8 years, non-renewable; President and other members of Executive Board may only be dismissed by European Court of Justice	President of Federal Republic, on proposal of government after consulting Central Bank Council, for a normal term of 8 years, with a minimum term of 2 years, renewable; Bundesbank President and other members of Directorate may not be dismissed arbitrarily and only on the initiative of Central Bank Council	US President with the consent of the US Senate; Chairman is appointed for a 4-year term, renewable as long as the Chairman's full 14-year, non-renewable term as a regular Board member has not expired; Chairman and other Board members may not be dismissed by President, only by Congress
(2) Appointment of other members of Governing body	Eurozone NCB Governors are appointed according to national laws with a minimum term of five years, renewable; once appointed, cannot be arbitrarily dismissed	Presidents of the Land Central Banks are nominated by the Bundesrat and appointed by the President of the Federal Republic for a normal term of 8 years, but not for less than 2 years, renewable; grounds for dismissal must be well-founded	Presidents of Federal Reserve Banks are appointed for a 5-year, renewable term by their directors, subject to the approval of the Board of Governors of FRS; may be dismissed by those directors, but reasons for dismissal must not be related to positions taken as a member of FOMC

(3) Publication of minutes with votes attributed to members of governing body?	No	No	Yes
Geographical representation	No specific requirements for the six Executive Board members, but political agreement to have four members selected from the 'large' States and two members selected from the 'small' States	No specific requirements for the eight members of the Directorate	Not more than one member of the seven-member Board of Governors may be selected from any one of the 12 Federal Reserve Districts and due regard must be given for a fair representation of financial, agricultural, industrial and commercial interests of the country
Professional qualifications of members	Executive Board members must have professional qualifications	Members of the Directorate must have professional qualifications	No requirements
Centralisation or decentralisation of execution of monetary policy decisions?	Refinancing operations (open market operations) with credit institutions are executed by NCBs	Refinancing operations (open market operations) with credit institutions are executed by Land Central Banks	All open market operations are centralised at the Federal Reserve Bank of New York; discount window operations executed by each district Federal Reserve Bank
Transparency and accountability			
(1) Objectives:			
• Price stability overriding?	Yes	Yes	No
• Quantified inflation objective?	Yes	Yes	No
(2) Is the monetary policy strategy simple and easy to follow, which includes, for instance, a monetary *target* value?	No, complicated strategy, with only a monetary *reference* value	Yes, with a monetary target range	No, complicated strategy with a monetary reference range,[a] which was officially abandoned as of 2001
(3) Immediate announcement of monetary policy decisions?	Yes, which includes a detailed statement and press conference following the monetary policy meeting	Yes, with no details	Yes since 1994, with a short statement explaining reasons for policy change

continued

Table 2.1 Continued

	ECB/Eurosystem	Pre-euro Bundesbank	Federal Reserve System
(4) Announcement of expected future path of policy?	Yes, informally and immediate[b]	No	Yes, and since 1999 immediately[c]
(5) Publication of minutes?	No	No	Yes, with six week lag and with votes attributed to members
(6) Publication of internal forecasts/projections?	Yes, projections[d]	No	Yes[e]
(7) Regular congressional/parliamentary hearings?	Yes; accountable to public via European Parliament but EP cannot change status of ECB	No; accountable to public	Yes; accountable to Congress via the twice-yearly monetary policy report and Congressional oversight of Board of Governors

Notes:

a Only a reference range is set for the growth rates of M2, M3 and domestic non-financial debt. As of mid-2001, FOMC no longer sets reference ranges.

b During their press conference that immediately follows the monthly monetary policy meeting, the President and Vice-President of the ECB may provide, by way of answers to questions from reporters, some indication of the probable future move of official short-term interest rates. These views are repeated in the 'Editorial' section of the ECB *Monthly Bulletin*.

c In 1994, the FOMC began releasing an immediate public statement whenever a decision was taken to change the monetary policy stance, which was phrased for the public in terms of raising or lowering the target federal funds rate. However, the FOMC waited the usual six-week period to release its decision on the so-called inter-meeting 'policy bias', but in December 1998, the FOMC decided to release immediately its decision on major shifts in its inter-meeting policy bias, regardless of the current decision taken on the target federal funds rate. This was first implemented in May 1999, when no change in the target federal funds rate was decided, but the inter-meeting policy bias was announced as 'tilted toward tightening'. The so-called inter-meeting monetary 'policy bias' was designed to communicate to the public the FOMC's views, based on the information available at that time, about the likely direction of future policy during the inter-meeting period. Furthermore, in order to avoid some of the confusion on the part of the public regarding the meaning of future policy bias, the FOMC decided, as of February 2000, to release immediately after each meeting a statement that includes its views on the foreseeable future of the risks for the attainment of its two policy goals: price stability and sustainable economic growth. These risks are couched in the following language: balanced with respect to prospects for both goals, or weighted mainly toward conditions that may generate heightened inflation pressures, or weighted mainly toward conditions that may generate economic weakness. In a further move to be more transparent, the FOMC decided as of March 2002 to include in its immediate announcement following each meeting the roll call of the vote on the federal funds rate target.

d The ECB published for the first time in December 2000 its twice-yearly projections. Projections are calculated assuming constant short-term interest rates and a constant euro exchange rate.

e Forecasts of GDP growth rate, unemployment rate and inflation rate are released in the twice-yearly 'Monetary Policy Report to Congress'. The July Report revises the February forecasts and provides the forecasts for the following year. Prior to July 2000, these reports were submitted to Congress in accordance with the requirements of the Full Employment and Balanced Growth Act (1978). Since July 2000, the reports are submitted to Congress in accordance with the requirements stipulated under Section 2B of the Federal Reserve Act.

of price stability, the institution's performance can only be formally judged on whether it has maintained price stability over the medium term, as defined by the ECB. The ECB has an obligation to focus on other objectives as long as they do not compromise its primary statutory mandate. Thus, the ECB/Eurosystem is granted a high degree of 'institutional independence'.

The pre-euro Bundesbank

The pre-euro Bundesbank was the European national central bank that had enjoyed *de jure* and *de facto* the greatest degree of institutional independence from its national government and legislature. The Bundesbank Act of 1957 had given Germany's central bank a high degree of 'institutional independence' from the government and the legislature. In exercising its monetary policy functions to achieve and maintain its primary statutory objective of 'safeguarding the currency', the Bundesbank could not receive instructions from either the German Federal Cabinet[7] or the legislature (Bundestag or Bundesrat). While there was a formal channel for the exchange of information between the Bundesbank and the Federal Cabinet, there was no statutory relationship between the Bundesbank and the German federal parliament, which meant that Bundesbank officials did not have to appear before the German parliament to explain, or engage in a dialogue about, the conduct of monetary policy. Members of the Federal Cabinet, generally the Finance Minister, were entitled to attend, without having the right to vote, the meetings of the highest decision-making body of the Bundesbank, the Central Bank Council, and could even propose motions. Similarly, the Federal Cabinet could invite the President of the Bundesbank to attend its deliberations to comment on issues that may have had indirect effects on monetary policy. As is the case for the ECB vis-à-vis the eurozone economic policy, the pre-euro Bundesbank had to support the German national economic policy, as long as such support was not in conflict with the Bundesbank's single primary objective of 'safeguarding the currency':

> Without prejudice to the performance of its duties [such as safeguarding the currency], the Deutsche Bundesbank is required to support the general economic policy of the Federal Cabinet.
> (Article 12 of the Bundesbank Act of 1957)

In addition to the statutory provisions that guaranteed the 'institutional independence' of the pre-euro Bundesbank, there existed in post-war Germany a broad consensus that the Bundesbank's independence should be respected to ensure a non-inflationary economic system. Thus, the Bundesbank could rely on broad public support to guarantee its 'institutional independence'.

The Federal Reserve System

The Federal Reserve System was formally granted institutional independence from the Executive branch of the US government when the Secretary of the Treasury and the Comptroller of the Currency were removed from the FOMC in 1935. However, the US central bank is not granted 'institutional independence' from the Legislative branch of the US government. Under the US Constitution (Article I, Section 8), Congress has the legal authority to regulate the quantity and the value of money. By passing the Federal Reserve Act of 1913, Congress delegated that power to the Federal Reserve System. Without an explicit clause to the contrary, the delegation of power implied that Congress retained responsibility for overseeing the conduct of the Federal Reserve System, with the implicit authority to request the testimony of the Chairman of the Board of Governors at Congressional committee hearings. The Congressional oversight of the Fed was formalised with the application of the original terms of the Humphrey–Hawkins Act of 1978. Under those provisions, the Federal Reserve Board has to present to Congress, twice a year, a report setting forth a review and analysis of recent developments, and prospects for the future, of the major macroeconomic variables, combined with a discussion of the conduct of monetary policy. The conduct of monetary policy includes the activities, objectives and plans of the Board and the Federal Open Market Committee, but since the changes made to the Federal Reserve Act in December 2000 as a result of the application of the Federal Reports Elimination and Sunset Act of 1995, it no longer includes annual target ranges of the monetary aggregate growth rates.[8] The semi-annual written and oral reports, submitted to House and Senate Congressional committees by the Chairman of the Board of Governors, must include the Board's two-year economic projections, which are compared with those submitted by the President in his Annual Report to Congress. The Congress then considers jointly the policies of the President and those of the Federal Reserve Board.

Although Congress considers the Fed to be an independent agency of the US government, and therefore does not address specific instructions to it, Congress sets the Fed's autonomy. Congress retains the ultimate power under the Constitution to instruct the Federal Reserve by law. This creates, under certain conditions, a subtle form of political influence on the Fed. Since the Fed does not have a single primary statutory objective, Congressional committee members can at times challenge the Fed's emphasis of one objective over the other – in particular whenever the policy of maintaining price stability appears in the short run to be in conflict with the policy of maintaining a high level of employment. This form of political influence is, of course, not possible between the ECB and the European Parliament, which has the right to question, and often does question, the appropriateness of monetary policy decisions at Parliamentary committee hearings, with the understanding that the hearings serve only as a means to 'inform' Parliament. Moreover, whenever challenged about the appropriateness of its monetary policy decisions, the ECB can always argue that its primary single objective of maintaining price stability cannot be compromised to achieve other economic objectives or that maintaining price stability is the best way to achieve the other economic objectives, such as a high level of employment.

Operational independence

The second aspect of central bank independence has to do with its operational independence. The degree of the central bank's operational independence depends on whether:

- the central bank has the sole legal authority to *operationally* define the meaning of its mandate;
- the central bank has the legal authority to decide on a monetary policy strategy and to use, and set targets for, monetary policy instruments, such as short-term interest rates and open-market operations;
- the central bank must share with a governmental authority its decision-making powers in the area of foreign exchange policy, which may be in conflict with the central bank's monetary policy;
- the central bank has a statutory responsibility to safeguard the stability of the financial system, which may be in conflict with its monetary policy.

The European Central Bank

The ECB and the pre-euro Bundesbank are identical in terms of their operational independence as defined by the above-cited points (see Table 2.1). Soon after the establishment of the ECB in mid-1998, the ECB Governing Council defined, in accordance with the powers granted to it under Article 105.2 of the 'Treaty',

- the operational meaning of price stability, as a year-over-year rate of inflation in the eurozone not greater than 2 per cent over the medium term;
- a monetary policy strategy based on 'two pillars' by using a broad monetary aggregate reference value and a broad range of economic and financial variables to assess future price developments;
- the instruments to implement its monetary policy strategy, such as the main refinancing operations with credit institutions, the lending and deposit facilities, and the required reserves to be held by the credit institutions.

The ECB's operational independence in the area of monetary policy decisions is not restricted by the possible conflict of interest that may exist whenever a central bank has a responsibility to safeguard the stability of the financial system. Under the provisions of the Maastricht Treaty, the ECB/Eurosystem does not have a statutory responsibility to act as the 'lender of last resort' whenever the stability of the financial system is placed at risk from the failure, or potential failure, of one or more credit institutions. To that extent, the ECB's monetary policy decisions, which may adversely affect financial institutions, are not compromised by an explicit responsibility to rescue weak financial institutions. The responsibility of safeguarding the stability of the financial system remains a national responsibility in the eurozone, as described in Chapter 4.

In the area of foreign exchange policy, which may have spillover effects on monetary policy, the ECB/Eurosystem is not fully operationally independent. The Maastricht Treaty assigns to the Ecofin Council the responsibility to define the exchange rate regime of the euro against non-Community currencies and assigns to the central bank the responsibility to decide how and when to carry out foreign exchange intervention in the context of a given exchange rate regime. However, in all cases, whether the exchange rate regime is fixed or flexible, the intervention on the foreign exchange market must not prejudice the central bank's statutory objective of maintaining price stability. This means, for instance, that if the Ecofin Council were to establish a fixed exchange rate regime requiring foreign exchange intervention that would increase the money supply in a way contrary to the monetary policy objective of the ECB, the central bank could either request a change in the parity rate of the euro or abandon the intervention. The legal framework of the shared responsibilities between the Ecofin Council and the ECB in this area is outlined in the Maastricht Treaty. Article 111 of the 'Treaty' stipulates that the Ecofin Council, with the eurozone Ministers acting unanimously[9] on a recommendation from the ECB or from the Commission, may conclude 'formal agreements on an exchange rate system for the Euro in relation to non-Community currencies'. In the absence of formal agreements, the Ecofin Council, acting by a qualified majority of the eurozone Ministers and on a recommendation from the ECB or from the Commission, may also issue 'general orientations' to the Eurosystem regarding exchange rate policy. This may consist of instructions to intervene, either to raise or lower the value of the euro, or to slow the speed of an appreciation or depreciation of the euro on the foreign exchange market. However, in a report to the European Council in December 1997, the EU Finance Ministers declared that the Ecofin Council would issue exchange rate policy orientations only in exceptional circumstances, such as in the case of a clear misalignment of the euro with non-Community currencies. In the present circumstances, where there is neither a formal exchange rate regime nor a general orientation policy for the euro against non-Community currencies, the ECB

Objectives, independence and accountability 43

Governing Council is free to decide whether to intervene on the foreign exchange market. Until September 2000, neither the ECB nor the eurozone NCBs had intervened in the foreign exchange market to support the falling euro, which had declined from a value of $1.1789 on the first trading day of 4 January 1999 to $0.8450 on 20 September 2000. That policy changed on 22 September 2000 when, at the initiative of the ECB, the monetary authorities of the US and Japan joined the ECB in a concerted intervention to support the falling euro. The ECB also engaged in unilateral intervention during the month of November 2000 to support the euro against the US dollar (see Figures 2.1(a, b), and Box 2.2 for details).

Exchange Rate Mechanism II (ERM II)

Foreign exchange intervention with respect to the currencies of EU Member States outside the eurozone is governed by the rules and regulations of the Exchange Rate Mechanism (ERM II) agreement, signed between the ECB and the 'out' NCBs (European Central Bank 1999a: 96–102). For the non-eurozone Member States, participation in ERM II is voluntary, but officially required for a period of two years without any 'own-initiative devaluation' prior to entry into the eurozone. Only Denmark and Greece agreed to participate as of 1999 in this system of a fixed but adjustable exchange rate, defined as a band against the euro. Britain, with its calamitous experience with the Community Exchange Rate Mechanism of the early 1990s, declined to participate in the ERM II.

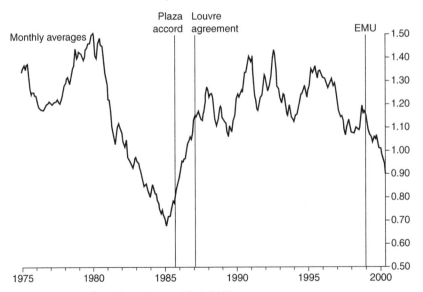

Figure 2.1(a) €/$ trading history: 1975–2000.
Source: Bank of England.
Note: €/$ defined until EMU as dollars per synthetic euro, using a weighted average of the 11 component currencies (IMF weights).

44 Objectives, independence and accountability

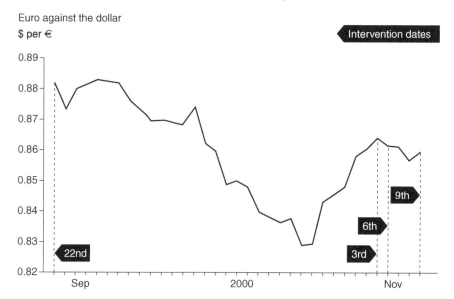

Figure 2.1(b) Euro against the dollar.
Source: *Financial Times* (London)

Sweden, whose economy is relatively more dependent on natural resources, also declined to participate in ERM II, arguing on the necessity of maintaining a flexible exchange rate to absorb asymmetric shocks.

The operational provisions of ERM II are similar, but not identical, to the ones of the Community Exchange Rate Mechanism established in 1979, which replaced the Basel Accord of 1972, known as the 'snake', and which attempted to maintain a bilateral exchange rate between any two Community currencies fluctuating in a band defined around a fixed, but adjustable, bilateral parity. Under ERM II, the standard fluctuation band of a participating 'out' currency is defined at ±15 per cent around its euro central rate. Intervention at the margins of the defined band is, in principle, automatic, the central bank with the weak currency being allowed to borrow unlimited amounts from a very short-term financing facility. The very short-term financing facility, managed by the ECB, is an account that allows the ECB to lend euros to the 'out' NCBs and, conversely, the 'out' NCBs to lend their currency to the ECB for purposes of intervention. The initial maturity for repayment in the creditor's currency, with interest, of a very short-term financing operation is three months. At the request of the debtor central bank, the initial maturity for a financing operation not exceeding a specified ceiling may be extended automatically for a period of three months, renewable – subject to the agreement of the creditor central bank – for another three months. Any debt exceeding the specified ceiling may be renewed once for three months subject to the agreement of the creditor central bank. Unlike the official rules adopted in the original

Box 2.2 ECB's coordinated and unilateral foreign exchange interventions of September and November 2000

The euro's relentless decline against the US dollar from its high of $1.1789 on 4 January 1999 to $0.8450 on 20 September 2000 (see Figures 2.1(a) and 2.1(b)), a decline of some 28 per cent over a period of 21 months, set the stage for the ECB to engage in intervention to arrest a further decline that most EU and national authorities from the eurozone Member States believed to be inconsistent with the underlying economic and financial fundamentals of the eurozone. Moreover, and notwithstanding the relatively closed economy of the eurozone,[a] the magnitude of the euro's decline, if sustained over a period of time, was expected to have a significant impact on the ECB's primary objective of maintaining the eurozone's medium term inflation rate below 2 per cent. The rise in imported prices would eventually filter through the general price index. All other euro exchange rate indices measuring the decline of the euro provided essentially the same picture: the nominal, or the real, effective exchange rate of the euro[b] for the narrow group of the then 13 major trading partners of the eurozone had declined by 20 per cent for that same period of time.

After a number of contradictory statements from eurozone finance ministers, heads of government, and ECB/NCB officials (see Box 3.4) regarding their views on the decline of the euro, the Eurogroup Finance Ministers and the ECB, prior to the Versailles Informal Ecofin Council meeting, declared on 8 September 2000:

> The Eurogroup and the ECB reiterate their common concern that the current level of the euro does not reflect the strong economic fundamentals of the Euro area. They agree to follow closely the situation. A strong euro [rather than a stable euro] is in the interest of the Euro area.
> (Statement of the Eurogroup, Versailles, 8 September 2000, http://www.presidence-europe.fr)

At its press conference, the then-President of the Eurogroup Finance Ministers, Laurent Fabius, of France, added that intervention on the foreign exchange markets was always a tool available to the ECB (*Financial Times* [European Edition], 9/10 September 2000: 1). It was later reported by the *Financial Times* (Beattie and Fidler 2000: 3) that Fabius had telephoned Lawrence Summers, the US Treasury

Secretary, during and after the Versailles meeting to obtain an agreement in principle that the US Federal Reserve System would be willing, if requested, to join the ECB in a coordinated intervention to support the euro. The ECB was reluctant to engage in intervention to support the euro without the participation of the US central bank, which usually requires the agreement of the US Secretary of Treasury, for fear that intervention on its own would fail, with the resulting loss of credibility and prestige of this newly established central bank.

As a way of testing the impact of ECB intervention, the ECB President, W. Duisenberg, announced at his regular monthly press conference on 14 September 2000 that the ECB Governing Council had decided to convert the interest earnings on its foreign currency reserves into euro. This income, primarily composed of US dollars and amounting to €2.5 billion, would be sold against the euro over a period of a few days. The ECB bought on the foreign exchange market the equivalent of €1.9 billion the day after the announcement and €0.7 billion soon thereafter (see the ECB's weekly 'Consolidated Financial Statement of the Eurosystem as at 22 September 2000 and 29 September 2000'). The measure, which was the equivalent of foreign exchange intervention in all but name, was not successful in arresting the decline of the euro against the US dollar. When the euro breached the lower end of $0.85 line, the US Treasury, in consultation with the Chairman of the Federal Reserve Board, reluctantly agreed (the US Treasury Secretary added in his post-intervention announcement that the US still favoured a strong dollar, see 'Statement of Treasury Secretary Lawrence H. Summers at the Pre-G7 Press Conference, US Treasury Department, LS-902, September 22, 2000') to a coordinated intervention request by the ECB to support the euro with the participation of the other G7 Group of central banks: the Bank of Japan, the Bank of England and the Bank of Canada.

Coordinated Intervention of 22 September 2000

On 22 September 2000, one day prior to a meeting of the G7 Group of Finance Ministers and Governors, approximately €6.5 billion were bought, primarily against the US dollar. The Federal Reserve System bought €1.4 billion; the Bank of Japan, €1.5 billion; the Bank of England, €85 million; the Bank of Canada, €110 million; and the ECB, €3.41 billion. The immediate impact of this coordinated intervention, which was undertaken as the euro was already rising off its low, was successful in taking the euro from about $0.87 to $0.90. Later in the day, the euro retreated to $0.8790. The G7 Group of Ministers and Governors warned the foreign exchange markets that they were prepared to repeat this type of intervention: 'We will continue to monitor developments closely and to cooperate in exchange markets as appropriate' (G7 Press Release, 23 September 2000, Prague). However, when Duisenberg openly discussed in an interview (*The Times*, 16 October 2000) the unlikely prospect of ECB intervention in the event of a war in the Middle East, as well as the unlikely prospects of the US, in the run-up to its presidential election, of repeating coordinated intervention, the euro promptly fell to the low range of $0.83. When the G7 Ministers of Finance and Central Bank Governors failed to mention the euro at the Group of 20 meeting in Montreal in late October 2000, and when just prior to that meeting, the US Treasury Secretary reaffirmed his commitment to a 'strong dollar', the euro fell to a low of $0.8226.

Unilateral intervention of 3 November 2000

On Friday, 3 November 2000, just prior to the US presidential election, the European Central Bank surprised the markets by launching its first unilateral intervention to support the euro's recovery, which had begun the previous week with the announcement by the US Department of Commerce of a significant deceleration of the quarter-to-quarter growth rate of real GDP from an annual rate of 5.6 per cent during the second quarter to an annual rate of 2.7 per cent during the third quarter. The first bout of intervention on that day, estimated at €1 billion, pushed the euro from about $0.865 to $0.88. After a second bout of intervention in late afternoon, the euro settled at $0.8671 in late North American trading. Thus, this unilateral intervention by the ECB to the amount of €1 to 2 billion was barely able to maintain the euro at a level higher than the one immediately prior to the ECB intervention.

Unilateral intervention of 6 November 2000

Fearing that a Bush victory in the US would result in speculative sale of the euro, the ECB unilaterally intervened again on Monday, 6 November. It entered the foreign exchange market when the euro was trading at about $0.8640 (see Fig. 2.1(b)). The euro immediately moved to a high of $0.8732 to settle in late New York trading at $0.8619. The amount of intervention was reported to be between €500 million and €1 billion. It appeared that the ECB's unilateral intervention was more of an attempt to impose a floor of $0.86 on the euro than trying to raise its value. In view of eurozone data indicating a slowing economy, the ECB apparently concluded that the economy was not strong enough to use the interest rate instrument to put a floor on the euro; it would have to use foreign exchange intervention.

Unilateral intervention of 9 November 2000

As the euro started to decline below $0.86 when markets began to assume that the Republican contender Bush[c] would emerge victorious in the contested US presidential election returns, the ECB again intervened unilaterally, pushing the euro from $0.8580 to about $0.8630. It intervened twice: the first time in the afternoon on the European market, and the second time after 20: 00 GMT when the markets had assumed that the ECB had finished its operation. The ECB also intervened for the first time on the yen–euro cross to suggest that the Bank of Japan might participate in euro intervention. In late New York trading, the euro settled at about $0.8574. Data released later indicated that about €1 billion had been bought on the foreign exchange market by the Eurosystem on that day ('Consolidated Financial Statement of the Eurosystem as at 10 November 2000', ECB Press Release of 21 November 2000).

Notes:
a In 1999, the value of imported goods and services for the eurozone (EUR-11) represented 16.1 per cent of its GDP; for the US, the value of imported goods and services represented 13.2 per cent of its GDP. The comparable percentages of GDP for the value of exported goods and services are 17.2 per cent and 10.3 per cent, respectively.
b The nominal effective exchange rate of the euro is calculated by the European Central Bank on a daily basis, back to 1990. It is based on weighted averages of bilateral euro exchange rates against 13 major trading partners of the euro area (12 major trading partners since January 2001, with the entry of Greece in the eurozone). Weights are based on the 1995–97 manufacturing goods trade and capture third market effects. For data prior to 1999, a proxy for the exchange rate of the euro is constructed by the ECB based on a basket of the currencies of those countries that now constitute the euro area (see European Central Bank, *Monthly Bulletin*, April 2000: 39-48).
c At the time, the foreign exchange market assumed that the Republican presidential candidate Bush would carry out his promise to cut income taxes, leading to a tighter monetary policy and a 'policy mix' similar to the Reagan era when the dollar climbed to historical levels.

ERM, the ECB and the non-euro area NCBs participating in ERM II may suspend marginal intervention whenever such actions have an impact on the domestic money supply that is inconsistent with their primary objective of price stability.

For intra-marginal intervention, which also was undertaken under the framework of the first Community ERM, the cumulative amount of euros available to the debtor central bank is subject to a ceiling. The Danmarks Nationalbank, which has established a narrow fluctuation band of ±2.25 per cent around its euro central rate and which is the only 'out' NCB currently participating in ERM II, has a ceiling of €520 million available from the ECB for eventually engaging in intra-marginal intervention to support a weakening krone against the euro. Under the terms of ERM II, the decision to change the parity of the 'out' currency against the euro is to be taken on the basis of economic grounds, not political ones that were too often used to delay the devaluation of a weak currency under the first ERM regime.

The pre-euro Bundesbank

The pre-euro Bundesbank, like the current ECB, was given a large degree of operational independence. Under Article 6.1 of the Bundesbank Act of 1957, the pre-euro Bundesbank was given the authority both to define operationally the meaning of its statutory objective and to set a monetary policy strategy to achieve it.[10] The Bundesbank had operationally interpreted its assigned objective of 'safeguarding the currency' as a maximum annual rate of inflation equal to 2 per cent in the medium term, with a monetary policy strategy formulated in terms of controlling the money supply growth rate within some defined target rate band. Under Articles 15 and 16 of that same Bundesbank Act,[11] the German central bank was also authorised to define the monetary policy instruments to carry out that strategy. Its three principal monetary policy instruments were:

- the open market operations that took the form of securities repurchase agreements ('repos') with credit institutions to guide short-term interest rates;
- the discount and Lombard rates at which credit institutions could borrow upon request from the Bundesbank and which established a floor and a ceiling, respectively, around the repo rate; and
- the setting of required reserve ratios for credit institutions.

As in the case of the ECB/Eurosystem, the pre-euro Bundesbank did not have full operational independence in the area of foreign exchange policy. The role of the German government and the role of the Bundesbank in that area were completely analogous to the ones described above for the Ecofin Council and the Eurosystem in the case of the eurozone. The

German government, after consulting the Bundesbank, was responsible for the establishment of a formal exchange rate regime of the Deutsche mark, such as the one that existed under the Bretton Woods Agreement until 1973 or the one that existed under the European Monetary System during the 1980s and 1990s. The Bundesbank's Central Bank Council was responsible for carrying out the necessary foreign exchange intervention under the terms of those fixed but adjustable exchange rate regimes, but the intervention could be terminated whenever its impact was deemed to be in conflict with the Bundesbank's price stability objective. Even under the so-called unlimited marginal intervention provision of the European Exchange Rate Mechanism, the Bundesbank had a 'side agreement' with the German government that whenever such unlimited marginal intervention (i.e. usually selling the Deutsche mark against the weaker currencies participating in the ERM) threatened the loss of control of the German domestic money supply, the Bundesbank had the right to abandon the intervention, as it did during the ERM crisis of September 1992 (see Pringle 1992: 12–21). This was also the case under the fixed exchange rate regime of Bretton Woods in the late 1960s/early 1970s, when the Deutsche mark was allowed temporarily to float against the dollar in September 1969 and again in May 1971, when the Bundesbank was unwilling to support the US dollar in the face of heavy market speculation against the US dollar and in favour of the Deutsche mark. The Bundesbank would have lost control of the German money supply if it had tried to maintain the fixed parity by selling such large quantities of Deutsche marks against the US dollar.

The pre-euro Bundesbank had neither the explicit responsibility to maintain the stability of the German financial system, nor the power to act as the 'lender of last resort'. Thus, the Bundesbank's operational independence was not restricted by the Central Bank Council facing a potential conflict between taking the appropriate monetary policy decisions to maintain price stability and taking the appropriate monetary policy decisions to maintain the stability of the German banking system. In the event of a financial crisis, the statutory responsibility to act rested with government and private institutions. Deposit insurance and government funds were used to address the problems of insolvent banks, and short-term liquidity problems of solvent banks were settled with the Liquidity Consortium Bank. The Liquidity Consortium Bank, which is a specialised institution established in 1974 with 30 per cent of its capital held by the Bundesbank and with the remainder held by all categories of German banks, deals with short-term liquidity problems of solvent banks created as a result of one insolvent bank unable to honour its inter-bank settlement commitments. It ensures the timely settlement of domestic and external inter-bank payments and thus reduces the systemic risk created by one insolvent bank. The Liquidity Consortium Bank is sometimes referred to as the 'lender of next-to-last resort'.

The Federal Reserve System

Compared with the high degree of operational independence that was enjoyed by the pre-euro Bundesbank and that is currently enjoyed by the ECB today, the statutory operational independence of the Federal Reserve System is clearly restricted, stemming from the combination of the multiple statutory policy objectives assigned to the Fed and the oversight role of Congress on the Fed. The Federal Open Market Committee has been reluctant to adopt a numerical definition of price stability for fear that it may be challenged by Congress whenever the policy of maintaining the 'price stability' goal may appear, in the short run, to be in conflict with the policy goal of maintaining a 'maximum level of employment'. Instead, the Federal Reserve has chosen to operationally define price stability in more qualitative terms. The Chairman of the Board of Governors of the Federal Reserve System, Mr Greenspan, has stated that price stability can be broadly defined to mean, 'that the expected changes in the average price level are small enough and gradual enough that they do not materially enter business and household financial decisions' (Greenspan 1989). The FOMC also has interpreted the objective of promoting 'maximum employment' as the equivalency of promoting long-run 'sustainable economic growth', which presumably refers to the condition that, in the long-run, aggregate demand should be close to the potential level of aggregate output. Unlike the ECB, which defines the long-run sustainable economic growth of the eurozone as approximately equal to 2 to 2.5 per cent per annum, the Federal Reserve does not officially announce a figure, although Greenspan has informally indicated that the figure may be around 4 per cent per annum, owing to the technological changes that have occurred since the mid-1990s. Paradoxically, the Federal Reserve's limited operational independence to define its statutory objectives has given the FOMC more flexibility in its strategy to achieve its vaguely defined objectives – as long as Congress does not use its power to define them for the Fed.

The Federal Reserve has been granted the operational independence to choose, and set targets for, the instruments of monetary policy (Sections 13 and 14 of the Federal Reserve Act). For instance, the Fed may engage in open-market operations, may set the discount rate, and may target the federal funds rate (the overnight interbank rate) as its principal instruments to guide short-term market-determined interest rates. With the Monetary Control Act of 1980, the Board of Governors was given the right to decide whether to impose reserve requirements on all depository institutions and to set and modify the required reserve ratios. On the other hand, Congress required the Fed, from the period 1978 to mid-2000, to set yearly target growth rates of monetary aggregates as part of its monetary policy strategy and to explain any deviations of the monetary aggregates from the announced targets.

The statutory treatment of the prerogatives and responsibilities of the Treasury and the Federal Reserve in exchange rate management provides a wide latitude in interpreting the practical responsibilities of these two agencies (Destler and Henning 1989: 83–90). Both agencies have the authority to intervene in the foreign exchange market, but there is an implicit agreement that the ultimate authority in foreign exchange intervention policy rests with the Treasury. In practice, the Federal Reserve has played a subordinate role in foreign exchange intervention activity, taking its cue from the Treasury and acting as its agent. Even if the Federal Reserve were to consider an intervention directive from the Treasury to be inconsistent with its current monetary policy stance, the Federal Reserve would not have the privilege, like the ECB or the pre-euro Bundesbank, to decide to suspend foreign exchange intervention. The operational independence of the Fed is significantly restricted in this area. In practice, while the Treasury has the authority to decide when to intervene in the foreign exchange market, with the Fed acting as an agent of the Treasury, these decisions are in fact taken in close consultation with the Fed. The Treasury understands that foreign exchange intervention has implications for monetary policy. For instance, a US Treasury intervention policy to lower the external value of the US dollar increases the US domestic money supply, which may be inconsistent with the monetary policy stance pursued by the FOMC. The Fed may then wish to sterilise the impact of foreign exchange intervention on the domestic money supply, in which case the intervention would have little lasting effect on the foreign exchange rate.

Under the flexible exchange rate regime that exists since the demise in the early 1970s of the Bretton Woods system of fixed exchange rates, the Federal Reserve has not been granted much operational independence in the area of foreign exchange intervention policy. The FOMC has only been given the *explicit* authority to request the New York Fed to engage in foreign exchange intervention in order to prevent 'disorderly market conditions' in the foreign exchange market, where the US dollar floats vis-à-vis the major currencies. However, the FOMC directive to the New York Fed stipulates that all foreign exchange intervention operations must be conducted 'in close and continuous consultation and cooperation with the United States Treasury', which suggests that the Treasury could even override the Fed's interpretation of the existence of 'disorderly market conditions'.

Personal independence

The institutional independence of a central bank would be meaningless if the governmental authorities, who appointed or nominated the members of the central bank's governing body, were then able to place indirect political pressures on these members. The right of those governmental authorities arbitrarily to dismiss a member from, or not renew a member's term of office to, the central bank's governing body is one way indirect political influence could be exercised on individual members.

The European Central Bank

The personal independence of the members of a central bank's decision-making body may be affected by the terms of tenure of their position. The Maastricht Treaty and the ECB's internal rules of procedure guarantee a high degree of personal independence for the members of the ECB Governing Council as they take positions on monetary policy. In order to ensure a reasonable security of tenure, a member of the ECB's Governing Council may not be arbitrarily dismissed at the discretion of the authorities who appointed that member. This means that the Heads of State or Government of the eurozone do not have any authority to dismiss an Executive Board member (Article 11.4 of the 'Statute'), and that a eurozone national government or parliament may not dismiss its NCB Governor for reasons other than being guilty of serious misconduct or being unable to fulfil the conditions required for the performance of his/her duties (Article 14.2 of the 'Statute'). An Executive Board member may only be dismissed by the European Court of Justice, upon the request of the ECB Governing Council or Executive Board, based solely on grounds of serious misconduct or inability to fulfil the conditions required for the performance of duties. The eight-year term[12] of the members of the Executive Board is non-renewable in order to preclude the possibility of members taking monetary policy positions with a view to being reappointed to the Board. Although the term of each NCB Governor is renewable, each term must be for a minimum period of five years so as to reduce the possibility of a Governor taking monetary policy positions to accommodate the government in power, with a view to being reappointed by that same government.

The internal rules of procedure of the ECB also guarantee the personal independence of each Governing Council member as he/she takes monetary policy positions at the monthly meetings. Decisions taken by the ECB Governing Council are depersonalised, which means that the Governing Council's proceedings, in particular the vote or the position taken by each member, remain confidential (Article 23.4 of the Rules of Procedure of the European Central Bank, European Central Bank 1999a). Publishing the argument and vote of each member of the Governing Council may ultimately erode the personal independence of the members of that Council from national governments since the members may be subject to indirect political pressures from their national governments. According to Otmar Issing, a current member of the Executive Board:

[such a] practice would seriously undermine the functioning of the Governing Council. In the context of the Eurosystem, it would subject NCB Governors to national and other pressures and would be detrimental to a frank and constructive exchange.

(Issing 1999)

The pre-euro Bundesbank

The members of the pre-euro Bundesbank's Central Bank Council had a similar degree of personal independence from the German governmental authorities who appointed them. Once appointed, a member of the Central Bank Council could not be arbitrarily dismissed. The grounds for dismissal had to be well founded and unrelated to the positions taken by the member on monetary policy. A member of the Bundesbank's Directorate, the governing body analogous to the ECB's Executive Board, could not be removed from office at the initiative of the German government, but only at the initiative of the Central Bank Council. The Presidents of the Land Central Banks were appointed for a normal term of eight years, renewable. The members of the Directorate were also appointed for a normal term of eight years, renewable, which is in contrast to the non-renewable term of the members of the ECB's Executive Board.

The monetary policy positions taken by the members of the Central Bank Council of the pre-euro Bundesbank also remained confidential in order to guarantee the personal independence of its members. The Central Bank Council published neither the minutes of its meetings nor the votes or arguments of its members.

The Federal Reserve System

Once appointed, the members of the Board of Governors of the Federal Reserve System may not be removed from office by the US President, who appoints them with the consent of the US Senate. Only Congress has the power to initiate and complete the process to dismiss a Board member. These powers have never been exercised by Congress. The President of a Federal Reserve Bank, who is appointed by the Bank's nine-member board of directors and with the approval of the Board of Governors of the Federal Reserve System, may be dismissed 'at [the] pleasure' of its board of directors, with the reasons communicated in writing to the Board of Governors of the Federal Reserve System (see Section 4, par. 4 and Section 11, par. 7 of Federal Reserve Act). However, since 1935, the reasons for dismissal may not be related to the positions taken by the Federal Reserve Bank President on monetary policy in his/her role as a member of the FOMC. With the adoption of the Banking Act of 1935, the FOMC by-laws stipulated that the President of a Federal Reserve Bank, in his/her role as a member of that Committee, may not act as a representative of the Federal Reserve Bank that appointed him/her and may not receive instructions from his/her Bank. With the publication of the FOMC minutes, which include the vote of each member of the Committee and the argument of each dissenting member of the Committee, the FOMC members do not enjoy the same degree of statutory personal independence as the members of the governing body of the ECB or of the pre-euro Bundesbank.

Does central bank independence lead to lower inflation?

The usual argument advanced for giving the central bank a single primary objective of 'price stability' is that a central bank that has multiple objectives may attempt – even with *benevolent* central bankers – to exploit the short-run trade-off between the inflation rate and output (employment), either by trying to guide output (employment) above its 'natural' rate in the face of structural market imperfections (see an example of a 'time-inconsistent' monetary policy strategy model in Blanchard and Fischer 1989: 596–600) or by trying to accommodate a negative supply shock in the face of rising prices, in order to avoid the negative output gap and thus stabilise output (Eijffinger *et al.* 1998). Given the fact that economic agents adjust their price expectations in light of current and past rates of inflation, using monetary policy to achieve these employment/output goals *in the longer term* does not provide sustainable gains in employment and output, but only leads to higher, and more variable, rates of inflation, which – following the arguments given in Box 2.1 above – is a clear macroeconomic cost. Thus, the conclusion derived from this analysis is to give the central banker one objective, namely price stability, and to guarantee his/her independence from the politicians, who would always be tempted to force the central bank to exploit the short-run trade-off between the inflation rate and output.

The above models do not prove that the independent central banker who is given the single objective of price stability necessarily provides a lower variation of output than the 'benevolent' central banker who looks at both inflation and output. The above models only show that, with a 'benevolent' central banker, there is, in the long-run, no gain in output and a loss in terms of inflation.

In the Rogoff (1985) model, a central banker who is given a primary objective of price stability and who is independent of the politicians can achieve a low and stable rate of inflation but at the cost of more variation in the output variable. In Rogoff's model, output is subjected to a random aggregate supply shock. A central bank that is not independent of the politicians will achieve a higher and more variable rate of inflation. This is because politicians who have the power to influence the central bank will place, in addition to the price stability objective,

56 *Objectives, independence and accountability*

some importance on stabilising output variations. For instance, suppose that the economy receives a transitory negative supply shock that reduces output. The politician who wishes to stabilise output, forces the central bank to change its monetary policy towards a more expansionary stance, which is effective in increasing output to offset the negative supply shock as long as price expectations remain constant. When price expectations catch up with the change in the monetary policy stance and the central bank loses its credibility regarding the price stability objective, the economy will be operating at a higher rate of inflation, with no gains in the long-run level of output – given the random nature of the supply shocks.

By examining the institutional characteristics of a large number of central banks over the 1970s and 1980s, some studies, such as those by Grilli *et al.* (1991), Alesina and Summers (1993) and Eijffinger *et al.* (1998), confirm empirically the notion that there exists an inverse relationship between the degree of central bank independence and the inflation rate (and its variation).[13] Moreover, contrary to the implications derived from the Rogoff model, the empirical results obtained by the Alesina–Summers and Eijffinger *et al.* studies show that the inverse relationship between the degree of central bank independence and the inflation rate does not come at the expense of a higher variation of economic growth. They show that there is *no* (statistically) significant relationship between the degree of central bank independence and the variation of economic growth. In fact, Eijffinger *et al.* (1998) find that the relationship between the degree of central bank independence and the variation of economic growth is (weakly) negative, which would suggest that a country with an independent central bank committed to price stability is receiving a 'free lunch'. Given the long and variable 'outside lags' of monetary policy on output and the uncertainty in assessing the state of the world, with or without forecasting models (see Bryant *et al.* 1988), using monetary policy as a counter-cyclical instrument to fine tune output can destabilise – create more amplitude to – the output path of an economy that, in the absence of counter-cyclical monetary policy, would automatically return to its natural rate of output. Under these conditions, a non-independent central bank that is forced by the politicians to react to random supply shocks could result in more, not less, variability of output growth compared with an independent central bank that focuses on price stability – an argument often used by the pre-euro Bundesbank and the current ECB.

The conclusions obtained from the empirical studies that examine the relationship between the degree of central bank independence and the inflation rate are controversial because of the difficulty of obtaining a reliable index to measure the degree of central bank independence. This important issue is raised and studied by Forder (1998). He examines in detail the measures of central bank independence that appear in the Parkin and Bade (1980), Alesina (1989), Alesina and Summers (1993) and

Emerson *et al.* (1992) studies. He shows that there are clear errors in the construction of these indexes of central bank independence and, after a proper recalculation of the indexes, concludes that there is no 'evident relationship between central bank independence and inflation ... [that] is, more independent central banks, as measured by these influential studies, do not systematically yield lower inflation' (Forder 1998: 67). A similar study by Mangano (1998), who examines the measures of central bank independence calculated by Cukierman (1992) and Grilli *et al.* (1991), raises important questions about the accuracy of these indexes.

TRANSPARENCY AND ACCOUNTABILITY

Transparency

The degree of central bank transparency pertains to the number of objective(s) assigned to the central bank, the precision of the operational definition of the assigned objective(s), the clarity of the monetary policy strategy used by the central bank to achieve those defined objectives, the simplicity of the instruments used to implement the bank's monetary policy strategy, and the quantity, timeliness and quality of information released to the public on how the monetary policy committee reached its decision. By all these criteria, with the exception of its monetary policy strategy, the ECB is as – or more – transparent than the pre-euro Bundesbank. The pre-euro Bundesbank's monetary policy strategy of targeting a monetary aggregate was more transparent than the ECB's current strategy based on 'two pillars', one of which uses the broad monetary aggregate only as a reference value. With the exception of its refusal to publish the minutes of its policy meetings with the votes of the Governing Council members, the European Central Bank is as – or more – transparent than the Federal Reserve System on all the other criteria.

In line with the pre-euro Bundesbank model, but in contrast to the Federal Reserve System, price stability is assigned as the ECB's overriding objective, with no other objective – such as maintaining a maximum level of employment – allowed to compromise its primary objective. Furthermore, the ECB Governing Council provided a quantitative definition of price stability, as the pre-euro Bundesbank had done. It also defined, in some detail, the monetary policy strategy – based on two pillars – to achieve its price stability objective. This strategy, based on a monetary reference value and a broad assessment of economic and financial variables, was considered to be less transparent than the pre-euro Bundesbank's monetary policy strategy based on setting target growth rates for a broad monetary aggregate (see Chapter 3). The ECB Governing Council thoroughly explained to the public the Eurosystem's interest rate instrument, which is simply described as the main refinancing interest rate bounded by a ceiling and a floor equal to the ECB's interest rates on the lending facility and on the deposit facility, respectively, set to implement and signal changes in monetary policy (see Chapter 3). Immediately following the monthly monetary policy meeting, the ECB and the eurozone NCBs release, in the nine official languages of the eurozone, a short statement indicating the monetary policy decision. This is followed by a press conference with the ECB President and Vice-President, at which the President, in an introductory statement, explains in some detail the reasons underlying the monetary policy decision. The explanation uses the framework of the ECB's defined monetary policy strategy. The President's introductory statement is amplified a few days later on the 'Editorial' page of the ECB's *Monthly Bulletin*, which may also include the Governing Council's assessment of the probable impact of future economic and financial developments on its price stability objective, as a way of indicating the future bias of monetary policy. The ECB considers the President's introductory statement to be the equivalent of the 'minutes' of the Governing Council meeting, since the drafted statement is approved by the Governing Council prior to its delivery at the press conference. A question-and-answer period with reporters follows the introductory remarks by the President of the ECB. This part of the press conference has been criticised for not being very informative owing to the terse, 'cute', and less than forthcoming answers from the President.

Like the pre-euro Bundesbank, but unlike the post-1967 Federal Reserve System, the official minutes of the ECB Governing Council meetings, accompanied by the votes and arguments of its members, remain confidential. However, according to the first President of the ECB, Mr Duisenberg, they could be released to the public after 16 years, although the internal ECB Rules of Procedures stipulate a 30-year time period before the release of confidential information. The ECB argues that disclosing how each member voted to arrive at the decisions taken by the Governing Council may place undue 'nationalistic' overtones in an institution that is to be supranational and that has no long-term track record in that regard. This would not be in line with the responsibility of the members of the Governing Council who must think and act in terms of a euro-wide monetary policy, without bringing nationalistic considerations into play, just as the Presidents of the regional Federal Reserve Banks sitting on the post-war Federal Open Market Committee bring very few regional arguments around the table when setting a US-wide monetary policy. The ECB Governing Council, in the near future, may consider a compromise solution of releasing, with the monetary policy decision, the overall result of the vote without revealing how each individual member of the Governing Council voted.

Following the tradition of the pre-euro Bundesbank, which never released its internal macroeconomic forecasts, the ECB Governing Council decided in the beginning not to publish any internally generated forecasts or projections of inflation and other various macroeconomic indicators for the eurozone, initially arguing that the release of the forecasts may lead the public to conclude that the ECB follows an 'inflation-targeting' strategy, but later arguing that it first had to solve technical issues related to its macroeconometric model and acquire some experience with the projections (Duisenberg 1999d; Jones 2000a). In late 2000, following numerous requests from the European Parliament's Monetary and Economic Affairs Committee, the ECB decided to publish these internal projections, which are calculated by the ECB staff in conjunction with the eurozone NCBs. The December 2000 issue of the *Monthly Bulletin* provided the first of the twice-yearly publication of the two-year horizon of the inflation rate projection and of the growth rate of the real GDP projection for the eurozone, based on constant short-term interest rates and on a constant euro exchange rate. The ECB emphasises that these projections are the responsibility of the ECB staff and the Monetary Policy Committee of the Eurosystem and not of the Governing Council (Duisenberg 2000b). The Eurosystem is now in line with the Board of Governors of the Federal Reserve System, which publishes its twice-yearly forecasts of the major macroeconomic indicators.

Evolution of the Fed's disclosure policy

Until 1967, the FOMC did not have a policy of releasing its monetary policy actions to the public. The only disclosure requirement imposed on the Federal Reserve, pursuant to the Banking Act of 23 August 1935, was the publication, in the Board's *Annual Report* to Congress, of the FOMC policy actions taken over the previous 12 months.[14] In mid-1967, against the background of the newly adopted Congressional Freedom of Information Act, the FOMC decided to change the rules regarding the availability of information. From mid-1967 to 1975, the FOMC decided to release to the public the policy actions of each meeting, with a delay of approximately 90 days. Then, in a quest to provide information on a more timely basis, the FOMC decided in 1976 to release the policy actions of each meeting shortly after the next regularly scheduled meeting. In those days, and until 1982, the FOMC met approximately once a month. Thus, the publication delay was approximately 30 days from the date of the meeting. Since 1982, the publication delay of the minutes of each meeting is approximately 45 days, since the regularly scheduled meetings are approximately every six weeks.

The FOMC's disclosure policy of not releasing any statement immediately following the monetary policy meeting, but of only releasing the minutes with a delay, meant that the markets were never fully informed immediately of the decisions taken at the FOMC meeting.[15] The public had to wait until the conclusion of the next FOMC meeting to know, with certainty, the decision taken at the previous meeting. The reasons advanced to explain the FOMC's disclosure policy were twofold. First, an immediate disclosure of a change in monetary policy, if unexpected, may destabilise financial markets. The argument was that it is better to let financial market participants gradually infer the changes of the monetary policy stance by observing the impact of the daily actions taken by the New York Fed Trading Desk on the short-term market-determined interest rates. The money market, in conjunction with the 'Fed watchers', would gradually filter the information contained in the FOMC directive addressed to the New York Fed Trading Desk. Second, by not immediately disclosing to the public its monetary policy directive, the New York Fed Trading Desk was given more flexibility in implementing it in the event that new, unexpected macroeconomic data should be released during the inter-meeting period. The Committee expressed this idea when it considered, in 1993, the possibility of releasing an immediate statement after each meeting:

> ...the Committee wanted to give further consideration to the risk that the adoption of a different schedule for releasing information about policy decisions might have the effect, in difficult circumstances, of reducing its willingness to make needed policy adjustments promptly.
> (Federal Reserve System 1993: 124)

In 1994, after much deliberation and in the interest of communicating monetary policy changes without leading to misunderstandings or delays in recognising the changes, the FOMC decided to release an immediate public statement[16] whenever a decision was taken to alter the monetary policy. However, the FOMC waited the usual six-week period to release its decision concerning the inter-meeting policy bias or tilt, which was only included in the publication of the minutes.

The terminology used in the FOMC's directive was not very transparent to the general public. Expressions such as, 'the Committee seeks to increase slightly the existing degree of pressure on reserve positions' meant an immediate increase in the federal funds target rate. Additionally, the FOMC's policy inclination (the policy bias or tilt) over the inter-meeting period was couched in code-like expressions such as 'slightly greater reserve restraint *would*, or slightly lesser reserve restraint *might*, be acceptable', which meant that the policy decision over the inter-meeting period had a greater chance of targeting a small increase in the federal funds rate rather than a small decrease. The expression 'would be acceptable' suggested a higher probability than 'might be acceptable'. The magnitude of the target federal funds rate variation over the inter-meeting period was indicated by the use of the word 'slightly' or 'somewhat', with the latter suggesting a larger change than the former. It was only as of the August 1997 meeting that the FOMC directive addressed to the New York Fed Trading Desk and publicly released as part of the Committee minutes

Objectives, independence and accountability 61

was clearly phrased in terms of a target federal funds rate, both for the immediate policy change and the inter-meeting policy bias.

The FOMC took additional measures to provide the public with more timely and clearer information on policy decisions. As of the meeting of May 1999, the FOMC decided to include the statement on the inter-meeting policy bias in the immediate press release, which was now issued after each meeting, regardless of whether the Committee had decided to change the monetary policy or not. In addition, effective with the meeting of February 2000, the FOMC clarified the meaning of its inter-meeting policy bias. The private sector considered the future policy bias statement of referring to the relative chances of an increase, decrease or no change in the intended federal funds rate during the inter-meeting period, to be opaque both in terms of determining whether it simply referred to the direction of monetary policy during the inter-meeting period or at the next meeting, and in terms of the commitment of the FOMC to implement the policy 'bias'. To resolve this problem, the FOMC decided to phrase the future policy bias in terms of an assessment of the relative risks posed by future economic and financial developments for the attainment of the twin objectives of the Fed: price stability and sustainable economic growth. The risks are couched in the following language:

> Against the background of its long-run goals of price stability and sustainable economic growth and of the information currently available, the Committee believes that the risks are [balanced with respect to prospects for both goals] [weighted mainly toward conditions that may generate heightened inflation pressure] [weighted mainly toward conditions that may generate economic weakness] in the foreseeable future.
>
> (Federal Reserve System 2000a)

Thus, a statement, for instance, to the effect 'that the risks are weighted mainly toward conditions that may generate heightened inflation pressure' should be interpreted as a tightening bias of future monetary policy, i.e. a bias towards an increase in the intended federal funds rate. The 'foreseeable future' is a time frame intended to cover an interval beyond the next FOMC meeting. Since the 'foreseeable future' no longer refers to the inter-meeting period, the future risk-assessment statement is removed from the directive addressed to the New York Fed Trading Desk, which is responsible for implementing the FOMC's monetary policy decisions, but is included both in the minutes and in the immediate press release addressed to the public.

The FOMC minutes of the monetary policy meetings include a detailed assessment of the US and international economic and financial conditions, based on all the information available at the time of the meeting. This includes information obtained from the so-called 'Beige Book', which is a timely survey of economic conditions in each of the 12 Federal Reserve districts, undertaken by each Federal Reserve Bank in its respective district, and released to the public some two weeks prior to the regularly scheduled FOMC meetings. The minutes of the meetings contain the votes on the policy decisions made at those meetings, as well as a summary of the discussions that led to the decisions. Committee members who dissent from a decision are identified in the minutes with the reasons for their dissent and, since March 2002, the dissenters are also identified, along with their preferred target federal funds rate, in the immediate press release issued after each meeting. Decisions of the Committee are usually adopted by unanimity, with only occasional dissent. A dissenting vote may signal to the public a possible change in the future policy, to the extent that the views of the dissenter may be accommodated in the future to maintain a consensus. Neither the release of the minutes of the FOMC nor the release of the immediate press statement issued after each meeting is accompanied by any comments at a press conference.

The members of the FOMC occasionally give public speeches to indicate their views on the current and future macroeconomic environment. These speeches are sometimes given with a view to guide market expectations with regard to the direction of the monetary policy stance to be taken at the next meeting of the FOMC. The current Chairman of the FOMC rarely gives speeches on the topic of current US monetary policy, unless he wishes to 'telegraph' to the market his current macroeconomic preoccupations, which may be translated into policy at the next meeting of the FOMC. He never grants press interviews.

Accountability

In a democracy, a central bank, like all government institutions, must be accountable to the people, either directly or indirectly, by way of their representatives. Moreover, the accountability of a central bank can only be assessed with reference to the objectives assigned to the central bank. For the ECB, this is stated in terms of a achieving and maintaining price stability, which has been numerically defined over the medium term by the ECB.

Given its high degree of institutional independence, without any statutory relationship with the German parliament, the pre-euro Bundesbank could only be directly accountable to the German people. In contrast, the Board of Governors of the Federal Reserve System, being subject to Congressional oversight, and whose institutional independence is therefore limited, is indirectly accountable to the people through the US Congress. The ECB's accountability requirements are very similar to the pre-euro Bundesbank model. Given its high degree of institutional independence, the ECB is accountable to the people of the eurozone. Although the ECB reports to the European Parliament, the European Parliament does not,

Objectives, independence and accountability 63

by itself, have the legal powers to alter the fundamental terms of reference of the Eurosystem since these terms are enshrined in a European treaty. An EU treaty can only be changed by negotiations between the governments of EU Member States, the results of which must be unanimously ratified by all national parliaments and the European Parliament (EP). The European Parliament can only pressure the ECB Governing Council to change its 'rules of procedures', such as the release of minutes or the publication of ECB internal forecasts. The ECB reports submitted to the EP are not analogous to the Fed reports submitted to Congress (see above section on 'institutional independence') since Congress has oversight responsibilities combined with the legislative power over the Fed, while the EP has oversight responsibilities with no substantive legislative powers over the ECB. It is also clear that the ECB is accountable neither to *national* governments nor to *national* parliaments. Neither the President of the ECB nor any other member of the Executive Board appears before any national parliament or its committees. However, nothing prevents the governor of a eurozone NCB appearing before his/her own parliamentary committees to explain the monetary policy decisions of the ECB, provided that he/she does not reveal any confidential information about the Governing Council, such as voting patterns, and does not receive any instructions from those committees. In fact, according to Article 19 of the new 'Statut de la Banque de France' (Loi [Law] 98–357 of 12 May 1998, applicable as of 1 January 1999), the Finance Committee of the French 'Assemblée nationale' and of the French 'Sénat' may request the Governor of the Banque de France to testify while respecting the ECB rules of confidentiality. Moreover, the Governor of the Banque de France may request to be heard by those two parliamentary committees.

The 'Treaty'[17] requires the ECB to submit an annual report to the European Parliament, the Council of Ministers, the European Commission, and the European Council. After the ECB Vice-President's and President's presentations of the Annual Report to the European Parliamentary Committee on Economic and Monetary Affairs and to the European Parliament's plenary session, respectively, the European Parliament holds a plenary debate. The ECB President also appears four times a year before the European Parliamentary Committee on Economic and Monetary Affairs to exchange views on the current and recent performance of the ECB. The 'Statute'[18] also requires the ECB to publish quarterly reports. In fact, the ECB decided to publish monthly reports in the form of the *Monthly Bulletin*, in which the ECB extensively explains to the public the monetary policy decisions taken by the Governing Council. In addition to the 'Treaty' requirements, the members of the Executive Board communicate with the public through regular speeches and interviews.

3 Monetary policy
Strategy, instruments and actions

A central bank is assigned an objective, or objectives, to achieve and maintain. To achieve the objective, or objectives, the central bank's decision-making body usually defines a set of procedures to guide its actions. This set of procedures is called the *monetary policy strategy*. The pre-euro Bundesbank used a monetary policy strategy that is called 'monetary targeting'. Under such a strategy, the central bank chooses a monetary aggregate and determines its monetary policy actions on the basis of comparisons between the target value of the monetary aggregate and the actual value of the monetary aggregate. The target value of the monetary aggregate must be defined so as to be consistent with the central bank's definition of the 'price stability' objective. Another well-known and widely used (Bank of Canada, Bank of England) monetary policy strategy is the 'inflation targeting' strategy. Under such a strategy, the central bank's decision-making body takes monetary policy actions on the basis of a comparison between the target for inflation and the forecast inflation rate. The monetary authority steers the final target variable (the policy objective of 'price stability') directly without the use of a separate intermediate target variable, such as the 'monetary target'. The inflation targeting strategy requires an inflation forecast since monetary policy actions (i.e. changing short-term interest rates) affect the final objective with a lag. The inflation forecast is usually based on a wide range of economic and financial variables to estimate, for example, the future 'output gap', which has an impact on price developments. The current value of a monetary aggregate may even be considered as one of the many informational variables used to forecast inflation.

As described below, the ECB Governing Council decided to use neither a pure 'monetary targeting' nor a pure 'inflation-targeting' strategy to achieve and maintain its primary objective of price stability. It decided to use a combination of both strategies, which it called a monetary policy strategy based on 'two pillars'. In that sense, the ECB is more like the Fed. The FOMC's monetary policy strategy, which has evolved over time, uses a combination of both of these strategies to achieve not one, but two objectives, namely price stability, which has never been numerically defined, and a sustainable growth rate of output, which presumably means a growth rate of aggregate demand equal to the potential growth rate of output.

MONETARY POLICY STRATEGY OF THE EUROSYSTEM

In May 1998, after the 15 EU Heads of State or Government had designated the first group of 11 EU Member States that would constitute the eurozone, the Heads of State or Government from those Member States appointed the members of the Executive Board of the European Central Bank, which was established in June 1998. At that point, the Governing Council of the ECB had the authority to define and outline the monetary policy strategy to be implemented by the Eurosystem as of 1 January 1999 to achieve its primary goal of maintaining price stability in the eurozone. First, the ECB Governing Council defined the price stability objective, which is entrenched in the 'Treaty', in quantitative terms. Second, it set out the strategy to achieve its quantitative definition of price stability. This strategy is based on 'two pillars' used to assess future price developments (European Central Bank, *Monthly Bulletin*, January 1999; see Figure 3.1):

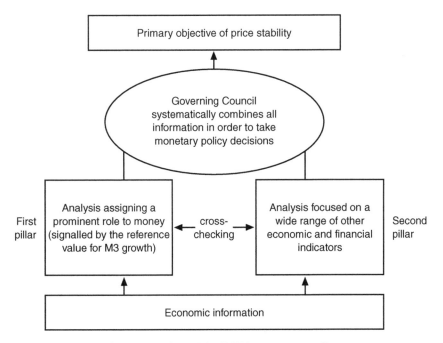

Figure 3.1 Schematic presentation of the ECB's monetary policy strategy.
Source: ECB *Monthly Bulletin*, November 2000.

Quantitative definition of price stability

The ECB Governing Council defined price stability over the medium term as a year-on-year[1] increase of less than 2 per cent, as measured by the Harmonised Index of Consumer Prices (HICP) for the eurozone. Although such a definition seems to indicate an inflation range with a lower bound of 0 per cent and an upper bound of 2 per cent, the ECB only sets explicitly the upper bound because of possible measurement errors in the consumer price index, as shown in most studies (e.g. Hoffmann 1998). These errors arise from changing spending patterns and quality improvements in goods and services included in the basket used to define a specific price index. The measurement bias causes consumer price indexes to overstate slightly the 'true' rate of inflation. Hoffmann estimates the bias to be in the order of 0.75 percentage points per year for Germany. For instance, an observed zero rate of price increase on the basis of the measured price index would actually mean a decline in prices (i.e. deflation), which is what the ECB wishes to avoid by using the word 'increase' in its definition of price stability. The ECB's refusal to specify explicitly the lower bound of the inflation rate range in its definition 'price stability' allows both for the existence of measurement bias in the HICP and for uncertainty regarding its magnitude.

By focusing on the HICP for the entire eurozone, the ECB bases its decisions on data relating to the entire zone and does not react to regional or national developments that have no impact on the overall eurozone inflation rate. The HICP adjusts national consumer price indexes – which vary because of conceptual measurement differences across Member States – so as to make them comparable and to obtain a meaningful weighted average of the national indexes for the 12 Member States. Each country weight, equal to the country's share of the total eurozone private final domestic consumption expenditure, for 2002, in percentages, is as follows (Eurostat 2002):

Belgium	3.40	Italy	19.34
Germany	30.56	Luxembourg	0.26
Greece	2.47	The Netherlands	5.20
Spain	10.34	Austria	3.18
France	20.41	Portugal	2.04
Ireland	1.21	Finland	1.59

The harmonised consumer price indexes of the three major economies of the eurozone (Germany, France and Italy) constitute 70 per cent of the total weight of the eurozone HICP. The HICP of an economy like Ireland with a weight of approximately 1 per cent cannot have any significant impact on the eurozone HICP.

The HICP is produced under an EU legal umbrella adopted in 1995. Since 1995, a number of technical implementing regulations covering a wide range of aspects of index methodology have been adopted. The index is more comprehensive in terms of product coverage than most national consumer price indexes. For example, expenditures of people living in institutions, such as retirement homes, and of foreign visitors, as well as prices of health and educational services are also included. The HICP is calculated and released every month by Eurostat, the statistical agency of the European Commission. The definitive figure is usually released 18 days following the end of the reference month. Since the end of 2001, Eurostat calculates each month a 'flash estimate' of HICP, released at the end of the reference month. The 'flash estimate' is based on preliminary consumer price data from Italy and Germany, as well as energy prices.

The ECB statement stipulating that 'price stability is to be maintained over the medium term' acknowledges the existence of short-term volatility in prices caused, for example, by variations in indirect taxes, food or energy prices, which cannot be controlled by monetary policy. Presumably, the ECB will not react to those variations, provided that they do not spillover into other prices or wages. This means that whenever the ECB perceives a temporary shock that either increases or decreases the rate of price change outside of its defined range of price stability, the monetary policy will not react, provided that the temporary shock does not have secondary effects on other prices and wages. Thus, the central bank will allow the temporary shock to have a one-off effect on the HICP, even if the HICP's rate of increase or decrease is temporarily outside the defined range for a period extending from one to two years.[2] The ECB's strategy seems to consider the narrow index (all items listed in the HICP excluding energy, food, alcohol and tobacco, which account for 30 per cent of the total weight of the HICP) in assessing the underlying inflation rate, provided that the rate of change of the overall price index eventually converges to the rate of change of the narrow index, also referred to as the *core rate of inflation*. This would suggest that, as long as the volatile components of the price index do not risk having spillover effects on the general price index, their temporary impact on the HICP could be ignored in assessing the underlying rate of inflation, as was the case for the period June 2000 to April 2002. During this period, the year-on-year rate of inflation released each month was above the 2 per cent ceiling, due in part to the temporary price shock emanating from the energy sector, the 'mad-cow'/foot-and-mouth diseases, and the 1999–2000 depreciation of the euro, but the core rate of inflation was well within the defined range of price stability. The Governing Council was vigilant in assessing the medium term risk of inflation, yet it did not tighten monetary policy after

November 2000, arguing that by 2002 the eurozone year-on-year inflation rate, measured by the HICP, would be back under the 2 per cent ceiling (for a discussion of the core rate of inflation, see Wynne 1999). When the May 2002 inflation figures were released, showing a 2 per cent headline year-on-year inflation rate, the ECB focused on the core inflation rate of 2.6 per cent to argue that the risks remained high that inflation would remain above the 2 per cent ceiling for the rest of the year. The core inflation rate was driven higher by service price increases, in part explained by the many service sector businesses that took advantage of the euro cash changeover in early 2002 to push up prices.

First pillar: monetary reference value

A broad monetary aggregate is assigned an important role as an intermediate indicator in the central bank's pursuit of price stability, for two reasons. First, the ECB believes that, in the medium to long term, inflation is always a monetary phenomenon. Second, since monetary policy has an impact on inflation with a long and variable lag, once inflation shows up in the numbers it is already too late to react. Consequently, the ECB believes that current deviations of the growth rate of a broad monetary aggregate from a set reference growth rate, signals to the monetary authorities future risks to price stability. However, any deviation of the broad monetary aggregate from its reference value would not automatically lead to a change in monetary policy. It would first lead to a further analysis to identify and interpret the cause of the deviation. Only if that analysis concluded that such a deviation is a threat to maintaining price stability, would the ECB change its monetary policy to bring the monetary aggregate back in line with the reference value. Thus, it is clear that the ECB intends to use other indicators to assess its monetary policy stance to achieve its medium term price stability objective. This is underlined by the fact that it sets a broad monetary aggregate as a 'reference value', not as a 'target value'.

Background studies

Using a monetary aggregate as a reference value to signal future inflation can be useful to a central bank in achieving price stability provided that: (1) there exists a stable relationship between growth of the money supply and inflation; (2) the central bank is able to control the money supply; and (3) the money supply growth is a leading indicator of inflation. Whereas the second and third conditions are usually satisfied, such is not the case over time and space for the first condition. The stability of this money–prices link depends on the properties of the aggregate demand for money in the economy. The first condition has been verified at the national level of EU countries and at the aggregate European-area level by the European

Monetary Institute (EMI), the precursor of the ECB, the European Commission (McMorrow 1998), the IMF (Kremers and Lane 1990) and others. A stable relationship for most of the major European Union Member States and for the eurozone itself is confirmed in a survey study conducted by the EMI (Browne *et al.* 1997). The authors looked at the results of some 45 studies of the money demand function at the country level in the EU and of some 14 studies of the area-wide money demand in the EU. Their conclusions are that the estimated equations for the individual countries, paying particular attention to the case of Germany, have estimated parameters consistent with the sign, if not always the magnitudes, predicted by economic theory. In most cases, the evidence points to the existence of a long-run equilibrium relation between money and a few determining variables, such as real income, prices and interest rate. The size of the adjustment coefficients indicates that deviations from the steady state may be of long duration. Where stability tests are conducted, the equations generally confirm that the estimated relationships are stable over the sample period from the mid-1970s to the early 1990s.

The area-wide equations often yield results that are better than comparable national equations. Both statistical and theoretical reasons have been advanced to explain this phenomenon. If the instability of national money demand functions is due to country-specific shocks, the averaging-out of shocks across countries will give better results for the area-wide money demand equation. If shifts in EU residents' liquidity preferences between different EU currencies contributes to the instability of the national money demand function (i.e. there exists currency substitution between European currencies), then an area-wide money demand equation will eliminate this source of instability by neutralising the currency substitution effect. However, it is important to note that if the single currency area brings about more synchronised shocks, then the stability of area-wide money demand functions estimated on the basis of data from pre-monetary union time series may not be valid for the post-monetary union period. In conclusion, the authors of the survey paper stress that the empirical results obtained by aggregating national data from the mid-1970s to the early 1990s may not be representative of the situation that will prevail in the single currency area, since a 'regime change' and ongoing financial liberalisation may give rise to new sources of instability in the behaviour of monetary aggregates. These caveats may explain the decision of the ECB to adopt a monetary policy strategy that is not exclusively based on targeting a broad monetary aggregate in its pursuit of maintaining price stability.

ECB's broad monetary aggregate of M3

According to the analysis conducted by the ECB and by its predecessor, the EMI, (European Central Bank, *Monthly Bulletin*, February 1999;

Coenen and Vega 1999), a broad monetary aggregate normally shows higher stability in terms of the money demand function and better leading indicator properties for the price level than a narrow monetary aggregate. Of course, in terms of controllability by the central bank, the broad money aggregate is inferior to the narrow monetary aggregate. In the eurozone, for the period 1984–98, the M3 growth rate, defined as the percentage change for a given quarter over the same quarter in the previous year, smoothed by means of an eight-quarter moving average, leads by six quarters the percentage change of prices, also smoothed by means of an eight-quarter moving average. For these reasons, the ECB Governing Council decided to use a broad monetary aggregate, M3, to define the monetary reference value. M3 consists of currency in circulation (which in December 1998 represented 7 per cent of M3), overnight deposits (33 per cent), deposits with an agreed maturity of up to two years (20 per cent), deposits redeemable at notice up to three months (28 per cent), repurchase agreements (4 per cent), debt securities with maturity of up to two years (2 per cent), money market funds and money market paper (7 per cent).

The reference value for monetary growth was based on the relationship between money, on the one hand, and prices, output, and velocity, on the other (the so-called 'Fisher equation'). More specifically, the medium term rate of inflation is estimated to be equal to the growth rate of the broad money supply, adjusted for the estimated growth in velocity, less the trend growth rate of output. On the basis of an estimated real GDP trend growth rate for the eurozone in the range 2–2.5 per cent per annum (see European Central Bank, *Monthly Bulletin*, July 1999: 40) and an estimated trend decline of broad money velocity in the range of 0.5–1 per cent per annum, setting the reference value for M3 growth at 4.5 per cent per annum results in a medium term rate of inflation in the range of 1–2 per cent per annum, which is consistent with the Governing Council's announced objective of maintaining the upper bound of the inflation target at 2 per cent per annum. Moreover, on the basis of these numbers given by the ECB, it appears that the ECB has implicitly defined a lower bound of 1 per cent, not 0 per cent, for the medium-term increase of the HICP.

The Governing Council monitors developments against the M3 reference value on the basis of a three-month moving average of the monthly 12-month growth rates for M3. This ensures that erratic monthly outturns in the data do not unduly distort the information contained in the monetary aggregate. Each December, from 1999 to 2001, the ECB's Governing Council reaffirmed this reference value for calendar years 2000, 2001 and 2002, respectively. According to the ECB, the trend growth rate of GDP in the eurozone could be higher in the future if necessary structural reforms in labour and product market were realised (see, for example, European Central Bank 2001c). Moreover, the ECB does not observe in the eurozone the productivity gains witnessed in the US over the period

1995–2000: 2.6 per cent per year in the US versus 0.7 per cent per year in the EU. The ECB emphasises that its monetary policy strategy does not use conventional monetary targeting; it uses M3 as a 'nominal anchor' and guidepost in executing its monetary policy, which explains the reason for qualifying the M3 growth rate as a 'reference value', and not as a 'target rate'. The ECB believes that even announcing a 'reference range' might be falsely interpreted by the public as implying that interest rates would be changed automatically if monetary growth were to move outside the boundaries of the range. While the basic long-run relationship between money and prices has be shown to be robust across a wide range of policy regimes, the ECB believes that during the transition to the new single currency, the relationship is subject to greater than usual uncertainty. In such a situation, responding in a mechanical way to deviations from the pre-announced monetary target would be unwise.

The relationship between actual monetary growth and the pre-announced reference value is regularly and thoroughly analysed by the ECB Governing Council. That analysis is communicated to the public whenever the central bank decides to ignore the deviations of monetary growth from its reference value so that the markets may understand the underlying reasons for its decision. For instance, in the early months of the launch of the single monetary policy, the three-month moving averages of the monthly 12-month growth rates of M3 were consistently above the reference value of 4.5 per cent (e.g. the growth rate of M3 for the period February–April 1999 over the period February–April 1998 was 5.4 per cent; see Figure 3.2). Yet each time, the ECB President reported at his monthly press conferences that, according to the Governing Council, the monetary developments were in line with the maintenance of price stability over the medium term, and that the upward deviation of M3 from its reference value 'did not constitute a signal of future inflationary pressures considering that it may to some extent mirror the specific environment related to the start of Stage Three [high pace of growth of overnight deposits related to the introduction of the euro]' (Duisenberg 1999a). The low level of opportunity costs of holding overnight deposits, the uncertainty relating to the introduction of the euro and the economic upturn in the eurozone that took place in 1999 (from a year-over-year rate of 1.9 per cent in the first quarter to 3.1 per cent in the final quarter) may partly explain the increase of money demand for transaction purposes. In 1999, M3 grew on average by 5.7 per cent, compared with 4.9 per cent in 1998 and 4.1 per cent in 1997. The broad monetary aggregate M3 continued to grow above its reference value throughout 2000 but the growth rate began to decline in mid-2000, approaching 5 per cent by the end of 2000 and 4.7 per cent by the beginning of 2001. Unlike the Bundesbank's target band for the M3 growth rate that was to be respected over a calendar year, the M3 reference value of the Eurosystem is a medium-term concept. It is not to be construed as a reference value for a calendar year but rather as a value to be attained over several years. In early May 2001, the ECB announced that the data on M3 growth rates were distorted upwards by about 0.5 percentage point per annum, owing to evidence that the data incorrectly included money market fund shares/units held by non-residents. In late 2001, with the release of the October M3 figures, the ECB again corrected the broad monetary aggregate variable by eliminating further distortions, due to the inclusion of non-resident holdings of other negotiable instruments, such as money market paper and debt securities issued with an initial maturity of up to two years. This adjustment reduced the eurozone annual M3 growth by about 0.7 percentage points, at an annual rate (European Central Bank, *Monthly Bulletin*, May 2001 and November 2001). With these adjustments, the revised M3 figures indicated that the three-month moving average of the annual growth rate of M3 had been at, or below, the reference value of 4.5 per cent from mid-2000 to May 2001 (see Fig. 3.2). From approximately mid-2001 to the end of 2001, the strong rise of the adjusted M3 growth rate, which reached a peak of 8 per cent per annum by the end of that year, was not seen by the ECB as signalling a risk to price stability in the medium term. The Governing Council argued that the increase was explained by temporary factors. The rise in energy and food prices increased the demand for transaction balances. The increased uncertainty owing to the decline in the stock market and to the effects of the terrorist attacks of 11 September created a portfolio shift

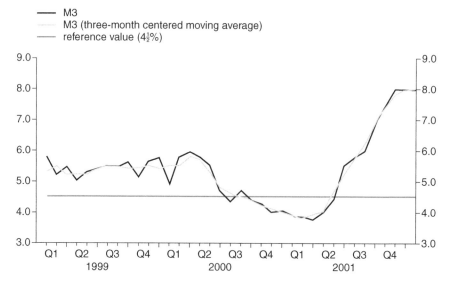

Figure 3.2 M3 growth and the reference value (annual percentage changes; adjusted for seasonal and calendar effects): 1999–2001.

Source: ECB.

away from risky long-term assets to an increase in the demand for more liquid assets that are included in the definition of M3.

Second pillar: analysis of a large number of economic and financial variables

The assessment of inflation (or deflation) in the eurozone is forward looking. Since it is not mechanically linked to the broad money supply growth rate in relation to the M3 reference value set by the ECB Governing Council, the assessment of future inflation is made by analysing a wide array of economic and financial variables, including survey data of future consumer and business confidence in the eurozone and institutional forecasts of future inflation and GDP growth rate (see Table 3.1). The formal analysis of this broadly-based assessment of future inflation is encapsulated in the ECB's twice-yearly projections of future inflation. These results are informally adjusted each month to take into account new information, the impacts of a change in monetary policy and of the euro exchange rate, and judgemental considerations. The ECB Governing Council underlines that the inclusion of the inflation projections calculated by the ECB staff in the 'second pillar' is not to be interpreted as a monetary policy strategy of 'inflation targeting', which uses an inflation-forecast. Those inflation projections are just one of many variables included in the 'second pillar' of its monetary policy strategy.

To assess the underlying tendencies on future inflation, the ECB examines the eurozone output gap, which is reflected in the underlying dynamics of the overall demand and supply conditions. A positive output gap (i.e. aggregate demand greater than potential output) may be used as an indicator of future upward inflationary pressures.

On the demand side, the ECB examines and assesses the evolution of the eurozone real GDP growth rate and its components, which are the estimated structural budgetary balances of the governments in the eurozone, investment expenditures, exports minus imports and consumption expenditures. The eurozone structural budgetary balance tries to capture the exogenous impact of the eurozone budgetary policy on aggregate demand. The evolution of investment and consumption expenditures is assessed by examining the business and consumer confidence indexes and the long-term real interest rates. The European Commission's Business and Consumer Surveys of industrial and consumer confidence, published monthly for the eurozone, are continually monitored by the ECB. A number of timely privately published indexes of business activity and sentiment are also closely watched by the ECB, such as the Reuters–NTC Research monthly purchasing managers' index for the eurozone and Germany's IFO Institute's monthly business climate index, which is based on a survey of 7,000 enterprises in both West and East Germany and which includes both the current and expected business climate (IFO

Table 3.1 The major macroeconomic indicators, with release frequency*, used in the framework of the ECB's broadly based assessment of future price developments in the eurozone

Indicators	Comments
Harmonised Index of Consumer Prices (HICP) and its components (M-1*): Overall index of which:	Released by Eurostat 18 days following the end of the reference month; since November 2001, Eurostat releases a flash estimate, based on German and Italian data and energy prices, on the last day of the reference month.

Goods
  Food
    Processed food (12.6% weight)
    Unprocessed food (8.2%)
  Industrial goods prices
    Non-energy industrial good (32.6%)
    Energy (9.0%)
Services (37.5%)
	ECB assesses recent trend of overall index; also examines its components to distinguish between one-off impacts and more permanent impacts on inflation rate; exogenous price shocks, such as changes in VAT rates, in the price of crude oil, in the prices of unprocessed food owing to an outbreak of 'mad cow' or foot and mouth disease, are examples of one-off price shocks that have a 'temporary' impact on the underlying movement of the inflation rate; however, under certain macroeconomic conditions, such as during a period of excessive aggregate demand, these one-off effects can lead to 'second round effects', owing to changing inflationary expectations.
	Governing Council also examines staff's projections of future trend of HICP, as well as external forecasts provided by public and private organisations.

Other price and cost indicators Industrial producer prices (M-1) Unit Labour costs (Q-3) Compensation per employee (Q-3) Labour productivity (Q-3) Oil prices (EUR per barrel) (M) Commodity prices (EUR) (M-1)	All of these variables, available on a monthly or quarterly basis, may, under certain macroeconomic conditions, be leading indicators of variations of the HICP

Category	Variables	Description

Output and demand developments	Real gross domestic product and its major components (Q-2.3)
	Industrial production excluding construction of which:
	  Manufacturing (M-2)
	  by main industrial groupings:
	  Intermediate goods (M-2)
	  Capital goods (M-2)
	  Consumer goods (M-2)
	  Construction (M-3)
	
	Capacity utilisation (Q-1)
	Economic sentiment index (M-1)
	Consumer confidence indicator (M-1)
	Industrial confidence indicator (M-1)
	Construction confidence indicator (M-1)
	Retail sales, constant prices (M-3)
	New passenger car registrations (M-2)
	Long-term nominal interest rate (D)
	General Government budgetary position (Y, estimates for year *t* released by Member States in October of year *t* − 1 and updated in April of year *t*)
		These variables reflect demand/output conditions in the eurozone. An important component of overall output is industrial production. Although it amounts to no more than one-third of the total, in cyclical terms it is the most sensitive component of output and data available at a monthly frequency with a relatively small time lag. Further evidence of developments in the industrial sector can be derived from surveys on industrial confidence, which are produced by the European Commission and available with an even shorter time lag and exhibit a close relationship with actual industrial production. Similarly, there is a relationship between real GDP growth, private consumption growth and the consumer confidence index, which is available before the other two variables.
		
		Increases in marginal cost of production and hence pressure on output prices may be indicated by an increase in capacity utilisation. ECB argues that there is, in general, a positive relationship between capacity utilisation and industrial producer prices in the Euro area.
		
		Discretionary budgetary policy can have an impact on the cyclical position of the economy in the short run. Over the medium term, a policy of maintaining a balanced budget can have positive effects by fostering consumer and industrial confidence, while confidence would be adversely affected if budgetary policies were not considered sustainable.

continued

Table 3.1 Continued

Indicators	Comments
External Sector	
Exchange rates:	
Effective exchange rate	Effective exchange rate index is composed of the currencies of 12 major trading partners with weights derived from the euro area's manufacturing trade with these countries, averaged over the period 1995–97. For real effective exchange rate index, CPIs or other price indexes are used as deflators. The weights are US 24.72%, UK 23.92%, Japan 14.78% and Switzerland 8.71%. Economic activity in the rest of the world affects exports of the eurozone and is therefore an important assessment of total demand. A change in import prices measured in foreign currency or by a change in the exchange rate of the euro affects consumer prices both directly and indirectly. The impact of exchange rate movements on the HICP is estimated to be 0.6 of a percentage point for each 10% change in the effective euro exchange rate.
Nominal (D)	
Real (M-1)	
World economic environment	
Exports of eurozone (M-2)	
Labour market developments	
Employment growth in industry (M-3); Variation of the unemployment rate (M-1.2)	Indicators of demand and supply conditions in the labour sector and consequently labour market tightness.
Trend growth rate of real GDP	Indicator of aggregate supply, which is compared to aggregate demand to signal price pressures. Also partly determines the 'reference value' of the nominal growth rate of M3 set by ECB Governing Council
Internal projections and external forecasts of inflation and growth rate	Twice-yearly projection range of inflation and GDP growth rates for the current year and the following year prepared by ECB staff; at the behest of the European Parliament and others, and in line with the long-standing custom of the US Federal Reserve System, the ECB Governing Council began in late 2000 to publish twice a year the staff's macroeconomic projections on

inflation and real GDP growth rates for the eurozone. These projections are prepared by the ECB staff, in conjunction with the staff of the National Central Banks to ensure that the eurozone results are consistent with the individual eurozone countries' projections. The two-year out projections are made on the basis of a set of assumptions, two of which are an unchanged monetary policy and a constant euro exchange rate. The staff projections combine the use of econometric models with judgemental inputs, to capture exceptional factors not incorporated into the model. An example of an econometric model used by the ECB staff for calculating its projections is the relatively small quarterly estimated structural macroeconomic model for the eurozone developed by Fagan et al. (2001); ECB also considers external forecasts of inflation and growth rates released by public and private organisations, such as

- the twice-yearly European Commission, IMF World Economic Outlook, and OECD Economic Outlook forecasts;
- the private forecasts, including the Survey of Professional Forecasters, obtained by the ECB from questionnaires submitted to some 83 private financial and research institutions across the EU. Since December 1999, the ECB publishes the results of these surveys.

Source: European Central Bank, *Monthly Bulletin*, April 1999, December 1999: 40; and author.

Note
*Data frequency is indicated in parentheses: D = daily, M = monthly, Q = quarterly, Y = yearly; for monthly or quarterly data, the number following the symbol indicates the lag in months from the end of the reference month or quarter to the time of the first release of the data. For example, quarterly eurozone GDP figures are released with a 70-day lag (2.3 months) from the end of the last month of the three-month period covered. Since most national data are released prior to the Eurostat data, the national data from the large eurozone states can be used as a leading indicator of the eurozone data (see Box 3.1 for time lags of national data release pertaining to the three principal eurozone Member States).

78 *Monetary policy*

Box 3.1 Timeliness of four major economic indicators released by the three largest eurozone Member States (Germany, D; France, F; and Italy, I), the eurozone (EUR-12), and the US

Time lag: number of days after (+) the end of reference Month (M) t or Quarter (Q) t

Consumer Price Index (M) – provisional
D $t-5$ [based on data from the 6 largest Länder]
F $t+12$
I $t-8$ [based on data from 12 large Italian cities]
EUR-12 $t+18$ [flash estimate available with $t+0$]*
US $t+16$

Gross Domestic Product (Q) – first release
D $t+53$
F $t+53$
I $t+45$
EUR-12 $t+70$**
US $t+30$

Unemployment (M)
D $t+7$
F $t+30$
I   only available every 3 months
EUR-12 $t+35$ (lacks data on I and NL)
US $t+5$

Industrial Production (M)
D $t+41$
F $t+60$
I $t+46$
EUR-12 $t+61$
US $t+14$

Sources: Eurostat (Luxembourg), statistical bureaus of Member States and of US.

Notes:
* Beginning with the reference month of November 2001, Eurostat releases each month a flash estimate of the eurozone inflation rate on approximately the last day of the reference month. This flash estimate is based on early inflation data released by Germany and Italy and on early information about energy prices.
** Only available with this time lage since 8 June 2001, date of the release of the data for the reference period of the first quarter of 2001. Additionally, Eurostat intends to start publishing in the near future a flash estimate of GDP within 45 days of the end of the quarter (see European Commission 2000c).

Institute for Economic Research 2001). Although a national index and therefore not officially recognised by the ECB, the IFO index – which is released 21 days after the end of the reference month and which refers to the country that represents 30 per cent of the eurozone GDP – is more timely than the eurozone business confidence index released by the Commission. The evolution of exports and imports is assessed by examining the global environment, as well as the nominal effective exchange rate of the euro against 12 currencies, with a weight of approximately 25 per cent for the US dollar, 24 per cent for the pound sterling, 15 per cent for the Japanese yen, and 9 per cent for the Swiss franc. The recent pattern of industrial production, order books, retail sales and employment growth is also examined by the ECB to assess the aggregate demand side of the economy.

On the supply side, the ECB, using indicators such as the percentage point change of the unemployment rate[3] and the percentage change of unit labour costs, examines the labour component of the production process to assess the evolution of production costs and their current and future impact on prices. It also examines the capital component of the production process by looking at the capital utilisation rate. To determine the overall gap between aggregate demand and supply, the ECB looks at the gap between the actual real GDP growth rate and the trend growth rate of eurozone real GDP, estimated to be between 2 and 2.5 per cent per annum. The trend growth rate, which is a proxy for the potential level of output, is subject to revision in light of the implementation by Member States of structural changes in the labour and product markets, as well as any yet-to-be observed impact of the new technology (TMT, or telecommunications, media and technology) on labour productivity.

For assessing future price developments, the ECB also uses key financial indicators such as the movement from month to month of the average long-term bond yield of ten-year government bonds in the eurozone. Properly interpreted, the movement in the government long-bond yield incorporates, for a constant risk premium and a constant real rate of interest, the change in the expected rate of inflation over that time horizon, as measured by an aggregate of the expectations of the economic agents participating in that bond market. Another long-term expected inflationary indicator considered by the ECB is the spread between the yield on a price index-linked bond and the yield on a comparable nominal bond. The yield on an index-linked bond provides a measure of the long-term real interest rate required by investors. For a given inflationary risk premium, the spread between the two yields captures inflationary expectations. The only government in the eurozone that issues an index-linked bond is the French Treasury, which issues a 10-year index-linked bond, linked to the French Consumer Price Index (excluding tobacco).

To summarise, the ECB's monetary policy strategy to maintain price stability in the medium term rests on two pillars: the first pillar is based on the 'reference value' for the growth rate of the broad monetary aggregate;

80 *Monetary policy*

the second pillar is an assessment of the risks to price stability based on an analysis of a wide range of financial, economic, and survey data (see Table 3.1). According to the ECB, the high degree of uncertainty of attempting to implement a monetary policy in the uncharted territory of the new single currency zone based solely on the first pillar, requires a broader assessment using additional information – thus, the reason for the existence of the second pillar:

> Overall, the assessment of the outlook for price developments for the Euro area is subject to considerable uncertainty, which means that a number of caveats must be borne in mind [e.g. the changing relative importance of 'domestic' as opposed to external developments and the increased competitive pressures within the Euro area, following the introduction of the single currency]. These have to be addressed by analysing as wide a range of indicators as possible. The aim is to produce an assessment of the future outlook for prices by constructing an overall picture taking into account monetary developments [first pillar], financial market information, inflation forecasts and survey data, as well as a thorough assessment of price developments on the basis of the available short-term economic indicators.
> (European Central Bank, *Monthly Bulletin*, April 1999: 29)

The monetary policy strategy, with its primary objective of maintaining eurozone 'price stability' is eclectic in the sense that the Governing Council has adopted neither a conventional *monetary targeting strategy* of the pre-euro Bundesbank (see below) nor a *direct inflation targeting strategy* used by the Bank of England and the Sveriges Riksbank in Europe and the Bank of Canada in North America[4] (see Mishkin and Posen 1997). Critics (e.g. Gros *et al.* 2000, Favero *et al.* 2000) argue that the eclectic nature of the ECB strategy creates confusion for the market in terms of assessing both the timing and direction of monetary policy changes. The 'two pillar' system is open to an ad-hoc justification for any monetary policy change or for keeping the monetary policy constant. One can either place more weight on the broad money supply variable in relation to the monetary reference value and less weight on the other economic and financial variables, or vice versa, to signal that the monetary policy should be changed or should remain constant to achieve the medium-term inflation definition of price stability set by the Governing Council. Only in rare cases do all the variables in the 'two pillar' system move together and thus clearly indicate to the market the course of monetary policy. In all other cases, the critics argue that the market will be confused by such a policy strategy.

OPERATIONAL INSTRUMENTS OF THE EUROSYSTEM

A description of the instruments used by the Eurosystem to implement its monetary policy is given below. Knowledge of these instruments is necessary to understand the section on monetary policy. A summary of these instruments is given in Table 3.2.

Open market operations of the Eurosystem

Open-market operations are carried out by the Eurosystem to steer interest rates, to manage the liquidity situation in the market and to signal the stance of monetary policy. Although all the policy decisions with respect to open market operations are taken at the level of the ECB Governing Council/Executive Board, the actual execution of these operations is decentralised at the level of the NCBs. The counter-parties in these open market operations are the credit institutions in the eurozone. The framework described below is very similar to the one that existed prior to 1999 in Germany. This is in contrast to the Federal Reserve System framework, which has centralised open market operations with bond dealers, not credit institutions, as the main counter-parties. The principal open market operations of the Eurosystem can be divided into three categories: main refinancing operations, longer term refinancing operations and fine-tuning operations (see Table 3.2).

Main refinancing operations

The most important open market operation is the main refinancing operation. These operations are regular weekly liquidity-providing reverse transactions with a maturity of two weeks.[5] The operations are executed normally every Tuesday by the NCBs (and settled on Wednesday) on the basis of fixed rate or variable rate tenders. A reverse transaction is an operation, in this case, whereby the central bank buys a security from the credit (banking) institution with an agreement to sell it back two weeks later. The price differential between the buying and selling price of the security is the interest charged by the central bank for providing the liquidity. In a *fixed rate* tender, the credit institutions indicate to their local NCBs how much money they wish to transact at the fixed interest rate ('repo rate') announced by the ECB Governing Council. In the allotment of a fixed rate tender, the bids received from the credit institutions are added together. If the aggregate amount bid exceeds the total amount of liquidity to be allotted decided by the ECB Executive Board, the submitted bids will be satisfied pro rata, according to the ratio of the amount to be allotted to the aggregate amount bid. For example, if the total amount allotted is 30 per cent of the total amount bid by all credit institutions, a particular credit institution will only receive 30 per cent of its request for

Table 3.2 Monetary policy instruments of the Eurosystem, the pre-euro Bundesbank and the Federal Reserve System

Central Bank	Types of transactions		Maturity	Frequency	Procedure
Monetary policy operations	Provision of liquidity	Absorption of liquidity			
OPEN MARKET OPERATIONS					
Eurosystem					
Main refinancing operations with credit institutions	Reverse transactions ('repos')	–	Two weeks	Weekly	Standard tenders, fixed or variable (Dutch or American) rate tenders
Longer-term refinancing operations with credit institutions	Reverse transactions (represents about 20% of total open market operations)	–	Three months	Monthly	Standard variable rate tenders
Fine-tuning operations	Reverse transactions or outright purchases	Reverse transactions or outright sales	Non-standardised	Rarely executed	Quick tenders or bilateral procedures
Pre-euro Bundesbank					
Main refinancing operation with credit institutions	Repurchase agreements with depository institutions	–	Two weeks	Weekly	Standard tenders, fixed or variable (Dutch or American) rate tenders
Fine-tuning operations with credit institutions	Reverse operations, including foreign exchange swaps	Reverse operations, including foreign exchange swaps	Non-standardised	Irregular	Quick tenders or bilateral procedures
Federal Reserve System					

	Open-market operations with bond dealers in government securities	Repurchase agreements	Matched sale and purchase agreements			
				Seven days on average	Very frequently; sometimes more than once in a given day	Variable (American style) rate tenders; no minimum bid rate
	Outright purchases		Outright sales	—	Infrequently; represents a very small percentage of OMO	Variable (American style) rate tenders; no minimum bid rate
STANDING FACILITIES						
Marginal lending facility						
Eurosystem		Reverse transactions with NCBs	—	Overnight	Access at the discretion of the credit institutions (counter-parties)	
Pre-euro Bundesbank		Lombard loans by Land Central Banks	—	Overnight	Emergency lending to credit institutions to satisfy temporary reserve requirements, at a rate which formed the upper limit to overnight interbank rate	
		Discount loans by Land Central Banks	—	Overnight	Preferential lending to credit institutions at a rate which formed the lower limit to overnight interbank rate	
Federal Reserve System		Discount loans by Federal Reserve Banks	—	Short-term	Loans to depository institutions for adjustment credit, seasonal credit and extended credit at a rate below the federal funds rate	
Deposit facility						
Eurosystem		—	Deposits	Overnight	Access at the discretion of the credit institutions (counter-parties)	
(Available neither at the Land Central Banks of pre-euro Bundesbank nor at the regional Federal Reserve Banks of the FRS)						

Sources: European Central Bank (1998a: 8); Deutsche Bundesbank (1995); Federal Reserve System (1994).

liquidity. It should be underlined that these liquidity-providing open market operations are made available to each credit institution on the basis of the amounts requested by each credit institution and of the overall allotment quota. Under the main refinancing operation, credit is not allocated on the basis of regional or national considerations. The allotments are based on estimates of the liquidity needs of the eurozone as a whole, consistent with the monetary policy guidelines adopted by the Governing Council. The Executive Board's estimations are made on the basis of the aggregation of the national liquidity deficits forecast by the individual participating national central banks.

In a *variable rate* tender, the credit institutions must indicate both the amounts of money and the interest rate at which they wish to transact. Bids are listed in diminishing order of offered interest rates. Bids with the highest interest rate levels are satisfied as having priority and bids with successively lower interest rates are accepted until the total liquidity to be allotted is exhausted. A variable rate tender allows market-demand for liquidity to determine the refinancing rate. The variable rate tender is considered to have the advantage of fairness to participants in the money market, as those financial institutions that bid a high interest rate are served first whereas those that bid too low an interest rate may not receive any refinancing.

There are two different types of variable rate tenders: the *Dutch-style auction* and the *American-style auction*. In the Dutch auction, a single interest rate is applied to the allotment of liquidity to the credit institutions. The single rate is equal to the marginal interest rate, where the total bids for funds is equal to the volume of liquidity decided by the central bank to be allocated. The Dutch-style auction, with a minimum interest rate bid, was the preferred type of variable rate tender of the pre-euro Bundesbank before the end of 1988. The American auction is a multiple rate auction whereby the allotment at each interest rate is equal to the amount requested by each individual bid and is satisfied in a descending order by the central bank until the total allotment of liquidity is exhausted. After 1988, the Bundesbank used the American-auction variable rate tender, with no minimum bid interest rate. The Federal Reserve System also uses this type of auction to carry out its 'repo' operations.

Main refinancing operations of the ECB

The Eurosystem launched its main refinancing operations in January 1999 with a fixed rate tender procedure, which it maintained until the end of June 2000 when the Governing Council decided to switch to a variable rate tender, American-style, with a minimum interest rate bid. A fixed rate tender sends a signal to the market what the Governing Council of the ECB considers the appropriate level of the short-term (two-week) interest rate. A total of 944 banks participated in the Eurosystem's first main refinancing operation, which took place on 5 January 1999 at the fixed interest rate of 3.0 per cent. The credit institutions submitted bids to their NCBs for an amount of €482 billion. The ECB Executive Board decided to allocate a total amount of liquidity to the banking system equal to €75 billion, representing an allotment quota of 15.57 per cent of the amount requested by each credit institution. This was an unusually high allotment ratio. In 1999, the average allotment volume was €69 billion, representing an average allotment ratio of 10.8 per cent. The ECB Executive Board's allotment decision is based on the liquidity needs of the banking system so as to ensure that the average interbank overnight rate is close to the tender rate of the main refinancing operations.

When the Governing Council decided in early June to switch to a variable rate tender for the main refinancing operation effective as of 28 June 2000, it chose the American-style auction with a pre-announced minimum bid interest rate (4.25 per cent) to signal to the market what it considered the appropriate interest rate on its main refinancing operation. This minimum rate plays the role performed by the pre-announced interest rate in the fixed rate tender procedure. The ECB adopted a variable rate tender procedure with a minimum bid rate simply because, under the fixed rate tender procedure, there existed a severe overbidding of funds on the part of large credit institutions, resulting in allotment ratios in late April and May 2000 of less than 1 per cent. The consequence of such small allotment ratios is that small credit institutions that are reluctant to overbid for funds at the fixed rate do not receive enough liquidity at reasonable rates. The variable rate tender procedure with multiple rates (i.e. American-style auction) eliminates this anomaly since credit institutions are provided with the liquidity requested at each interest rate bid, in descending order of the interest rate bid, until the total amount of liquidity funds has been allocated by the central bank.

Longer-term refinancing operations

The second most important liquidity-providing open market operation is the longer-term refinancing operation. These operations are also reverse transactions, but with a maturity of three months. The operations take place once a month, normally on the first Wednesday of each reserve maintenance period (and are settled on the following business day). Since the Eurosystem does not, as a rule, intend to send signals to the market by way of these operations, the longer-term refinancing operation is a variable rate tender, whereby the banks must specify in the tender the amounts of funds desired at various different interest rates. The ECB Executive Board decides on an overall allotment of credit, which is pre-announced. Allotment up to the end of March 1999 took place at a single rate, which is the marginal interest rate at which the demand for funds is equal to the supply of funds (a Dutch auction). Since the end of March 1999, the allotment has been at multiple rates, whereby the accepted bids are allotted in descending order of the interest rate bids (an American auction). In the American auction, successful bidders pay the rate they bid. The main reason initially for using the Dutch auction was to assist smaller credit institutions to bid for funds without being penalised for potentially knowing less about the market than larger institutions. Throughout 1999, with the exception of the last three months – for reasons related to the potential liquidity problem of the Y2K-probem – the pre-announced allotment amount was €15 billion. Since the start of 2001, the allotment amount has been at €20 billion per month, which represents about 20 per cent of the total amount allotted every week at the main refinancing operation.

Fine-tuning operations

Fine-tuning operations, which can either provide or absorb liquidity, are executed on an ad hoc basis in order to smooth the effects on interest rates caused by unexpected liquidity fluctuations in the market. A fine-tuning operation can be executed as either a reverse transaction or an outright transaction, where the central bank buys or sells a security in the market without an agreement to reverse the transaction at some later date. Fine-tuning operations are normally executed by the NCBs through quick tenders (announced and completed within an hour) or on a bilateral basis, whereby the national central bank deals directly with a bond dealer without any tender procedure. Although not used to date, 'regional' fine-tuning operations could be used to provide or absorb liquidity on a national basis, whenever an asymmetric liquidity fluctuation occurs between two or more eurozone Member States. From January 1999 to January 2002, the Eurosystem engaged in eight fine-tuning operations, three of which were:

1 a (reverse) liquidity-absorbing operation on 5 January 2000 to drain excess liquidity previously created as a safeguard mechanism in anticipation of the Y2K problem, with an intended allotment of €35 billion of seven-day fixed-term deposits at a variable rate with a maximum rate of 3 per cent, which only resulted in bids in the amount of €14.42 billion;
2 a (reverse) overnight liquidity-providing operation on 21 June 2000 at a variable rate tender with a minimum rate of 4.25 per cent, undertaken to prevent short-term interest rates from rising above the minimum rate just prior to the launch of the first main refinancing operation with a variable rate; and
3 a (reverse) overnight liquidity-providing operation on 12 September 2001 at a fixed rate tender of 4.25 per cent with no pre-specified allotment amount (i.e. the supply of funds lent by the Eurosystem is equal to the amount of funds requested by the eurozone credit institutions), following the terrorist acts of 11 September 2001.

Standing facilities

In addition to open market operations, the Eurosystem has two other monetary policy instruments, the *marginal lending facility* and the *deposit facility*, to provide or absorb overnight liquidity at the discretion of the credit institutions. These two facilities are administered in a decentralised manner by the NCBs.

Marginal lending facility

The credit institutions can use the marginal lending facility (equivalent to the Lombard facility of the pre-euro Bundesbank) to obtain overnight liquidity from their NCB against eligible assets. Under normal circumstances, there are no credit limits to access the facility. The only requirement is to present sufficient collateral. However, the interest rate on this facility, set by the ECB Governing Council, is higher than the main refinancing rate (the 'repo rate') and sets a ceiling on the interbank overnight market interest rate, measured by EONIA (Euro OverNight Index Average).

Deposit facility

The credit institutions can use the deposit facility to make overnight deposits with their NCB. The interest rate on the deposit facility provides a floor for the interbank overnight market interest rate. Since April 1999, the width of the corridor defined by the rate on the marginal lending facility and the rate on the deposit facility is 2.0 percentage points (see Fig. 3.3). However, for the first three weeks of 1999, the interest rate corridor was temporarily narrowed to 50 basis points, to limit the volatility in money market rates at the start of the single monetary policy. The rates on the standing facilities follow the movement of the main (minimum) refinancing rate, which is usually set at the mid-point of the corridor. Over the year 1999, the daily average use of the marginal lending facility (liquidity providing) amounted to €1 billion, while the daily average use of the deposit facility (liquidity absorbing) amounted to €0.8 billion.

These two facilities are used more intensively at the end of the reserve maintenance period when the averaging mechanism of the reserve requirements can no longer be used, as is described in the next section.

Reserve requirements in the Eurosystem

The Governing Council of the ECB decided to impose reserve requirements on credit institutions established within the eurzone.[6] In recent years, many central banks have eliminated required reserves, such as the pre-euro Banque Nationale de Belgique, Danmarks Nationalbank, Sveriges Riksbank, the Bank of England and the Bank of Canada. Prior to their integration in the Eurosystem in 1999, both the Deutsche Bundesbank and the

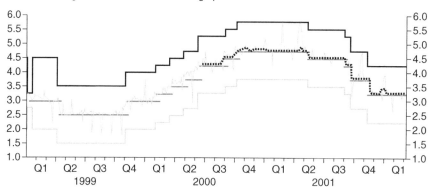

Figure 3.3 ECB interest rates and money market rates (percentages per annum; daily data)

Source: ECB.

Note: The rate for main refinancing operations is the rate applicable to fixed rate tenders for operations settled before 28 June 2000. Thereafter, the rate reflects the minimum bid rate applicable to variable rate tenders.

Banque de France still maintained required reserve ratios, although the ratios had been declining over time so as to reduce the incentives for financial disintermediation (e.g. banks becoming insurance companies) and delocalisation (a venue change) towards jurisdictions with no reserve requirements. By mid-1995 to the end of 1998, the Bundesbank's minimum required reserve ratios for sight liabilities and for savings deposits were 2 per cent and 1.5 per cent, respectively – a reduction from an average of 11 per cent on sight deposits, 4.95 per cent on time deposits and 4.15 per cent on savings deposits at the beginning of the 1990s (Deutsche Bundesbank 1996:58). The Board of Governors of the Federal Reserve System still maintains required reserve ratios on transaction deposits of member banks and, since 1980, has extended this requirement to all depository institutions (see below).

Like the pre-euro Bundesbank, the ECB Governing Council sees a minimum required reserve system as a way of contributing to the stabilisation of short-term interest rates, therefore reducing the need for frequent central bank interventions to fine tune short-term interest rates. The averaging provision of the minimum reserve requirements described in the next section aims to contribute to the stabilisation of money market interest rates by giving institutions an incentive to smooth the effects of temporary liquidity fluctuations. For instance, if banks find themselves with excess liquidity, they will absorb it as reserves to be used to offset a shortage of reserves on some other days during the reserve maintenance period. Thus, by not trying to lend out the excess liquidity, which would temporarily push interest rates down, the banks keep short-term interest rates constant, such as the overnight interest rate or EONIA. This precludes the frequent use of open market operations for fine-tuning purposes, which the ECB believes is not desirable for executing monetary policy, as central bank signals become blurred whenever markets have difficulty in distinguishing policy signals from technical adjustments, i.e. fine-tuning (Bindseil 1997, European Central Bank, *Annual Report 1999*: 51).

Reserve calculation

A eurozone credit institution must hold a minimum of reserves equal to 2 per cent of its reserve base, less a lump-sum allowance of €100,000 of reserves, which effectively excludes the very smallest institutions from the obligation to hold reserves. Reserves must be held at the NCB in the country where the institution is located, even if it is incorporated elsewhere (no cross-country pooling of reserves). For example, the German branch of a French bank and a German branch of a US bank must both hold reserves with the Bundesbank. The 'reserve base' comprises all deposits and debt securities issued with a maturity of up to two years, including foreign-currency denominated liabilities but excluding any balances owed to other institutions subject to eurozone minimum reserves. Where a credit institution could not prove the proportion of its debt securities (e.g. Certificates of Deposit) that are held by other eurozone credit institutions, and which are therefore exempt from reserve requirements, they were originally allowed to exclude a flat 10 per cent of debt securities issued. Effective from 24 January 2000, they are allowed to exclude a flat 30 per cent of debt securities issued.

The reserve base used to calculate the reserve requirement in any given maintenance period is derived from the balance sheet as at the end of the preceding month. Reserve holdings are calculated as the average of an institution's end-of-day balances over the maintenance period, which starts on the 24th of each month and ends on the 23rd of the following month. For instance, the reserve maintenance period starting on 24 February 1999 and ending on 23 March 1999 is based on the value of the reserve base as of 28 February 1999. Averaging allows an institution to decide at which point in the maintenance period it wishes to hold the required reserves. A financial institution may, for instance, legally hold an insufficient amount of reserves on a given day provided that the amount of reserves held on other days during the maintenance period offsets the reserve gap. The required reserves are remunerated ex post at the *average*

90 *Monetary policy*

of the ECB's repo rate over the period, so there is little scope for speculation. Reserve holdings exceeding the required reserves are not remunerated. Excess reserves of financial institutions can always be held in the overnight deposit facility available at the NCBs, which is usually the case during the last four days of the reserve maintenance period, when there appears to be an increased use of this facility. Averaging of reserve requirements means that an institution need rarely use the marginal lending facilities available at its local NCB. In the event that it needs funds to satisfy the reserve requirements, the marginal lending facility is available at a rate above the repo rate.

MONETARY POLICY DECISIONS OF THE EUROSYSTEM

We now examine the monetary policy decisions of the ECB from 1999, when the single currency area was launched, to the beginning of 2002, when the euro coins and bills were introduced and the national coins and bills were withdrawn from circulation. The next section examines the convergence of monetary policy decisions of the EU Member States from late 1997 to the end of 1998 in the run-up to the launch of the single currency area.

Monetary policy actions of the euro-designated NCBs prior to the advent of the single currency

A single currency area with a single monetary policy requires a single administered short-term interest rate set by the central bank. Although, prior to January 1999, each Member State's national central bank retained legal control over its monetary policy, short-term interest rates had to converge by the time the single eurozone monetary policy was launched. Throughout 1997 and the early part of 1998, in the run-up to the decision to designate the Member States that would participate in the first wave of countries composing the eurozone as of 1 January 1999, Italy, Spain, Portugal and Ireland all had significantly higher market-determined short-term interest rates than the 'core countries' – Germany, France, the Benelux countries, Austria and Finland. In the case of Italy, Spain and Portugal, this fact was partly explained by the risk associated with the possibility that these three Member States would not satisfy the convergence criteria necessary to qualify for entry into the eurozone. As it became clear that they would fulfil the entrance requirements, their market short-term interest rates gradually fell. In the case of Ireland, it was clear that the Irish punt was overvalued against the currencies of the 'core countries' and would have to enter the eurozone at a significantly lower rate. The expected depreciation of the Irish punt maintained the positive interest rate spread with the 'core countries'.

Key official short-term interest rates

In early May 1998, when 11 Member States were designated to participate in the future single currency area, the official central bank short-term interest rates of four designated Member States – Italy, Spain, Portugal and Ireland – were still significantly higher than the key official short-term interest rates set by the central banks of the 'core' Member States, namely, the Deutsche Bundesbank (3.3 per cent), the Banque de France (3.3 per cent), De Nederlandsche Bank (3.3 per cent), the Banque Nationale de Belgique (3.3 per cent), the Oesterreichische Nationalbank (3.2 per cent), and the Suomen Pankki (3.4 per cent), as shown in Table 3.3. In the peripheral Member States of Spain, Portugal and Ireland, the exceptionally strong performance of these three economies, with a real GDP growth rate in 1997 of over 3 per cent for Spain (3.8 per cent), Portugal (4.1 per cent) and Ireland (10.7 per cent), and the associated inflation risks, precluded a rapid reduction in official short term interest rates that would have brought them in line with the benchmark of the core countries. The NCBs of Spain and Portugal made one small reduction in their official short-term interest rate soon after those two countries were designated to join the eurozone, and waited until the fourth quarter of 1998 to reduce further the official short-term interest rates. In Italy, the broad monetary aggregate M2 growth rate of 10 per cent clearly exceeded the central bank's reference ceiling of 5 per cent annual growth rate. This, along with increases in prices and unit labour costs of above the euro area average, prevented the Banca d'Italia from rapidly reducing the official short-term interest rate to the level existing in the core countries, despite a 1.5 per cent real GDP growth rate in Italy in 1997. On 22 April 1998, when it became clear that Italy would be a founding member of the eurozone, the Banca d'Italia reduced its discount rate by 50 basis points. In the fourth quarter of that same year, it further reduced its discount rate by 100 basis points at the end of October, by 50 basis points on 3 December and, finally, by 50 basis points on 23 December. The Central Bank of Ireland only began to reduce its short-term official interest rates as of the fourth quarter of 1998. Consequently, just prior to the launch of the single monetary policy, all the NCBs of the future eurozone aligned their key official short-term interest rate at 3 per cent. The President of the ECB announced that the joint reduction in interest rates was to be seen as a 'de facto decision on the level of interest rates with which the ESCB [Eurosystem] will start Stage Three [1 January 1999] of Monetary Union and which it intends to maintain for the foreseeable future' (European Central Bank 1998c).

ECB Monetary Policy Actions: January 1999 to end 2001

The Eurosystem's monetary policy was launched with an interest rate on the main refinancing operations equal to 3.0 per cent, i.e. equal to the level of interest rate set on 3 December 1998 in a coordinated reduction of the

Table 3.3 Convergence of key official short-term interest rates, in per cent, of eurozone National Central Banks, from mid-1997 to end of 1998

Eurozone National Central Bank (first wave)	Key official short-term interest rate	By the end of 1997 (date set)	As of 1 May 1998 (date set)	By the end of November 1998 (date set)	By the end of December 1998 (date set)
Banque Nationale de Belgique	Securities repurchase rate	3.3 (9 Oct)	3.3	3.3	3.0 (3 Dec)
Deutsche Bundesbank	Securities repurchase rate	3.3 (9 Oct)	3.3	3.3	3.0 (3 Dec)
Banco de España	10-day repurchase rate	4.75 (15 Dec)	4.5 (13 Feb)	4.25 (5 May) 3.75 (6 Oct) 3.5 (4 Nov)	3.0 (3 Dec)
Banque de France	intervention rate	3.3 (9 Oct)	3.3	3.3	3.0 (3 Dec)
Central Bank of Ireland	short-term lending facility	6.75 (1 May)	6.75	5.75 (9 Oct) 3.69* (6 Nov)	3.0* (3 Dec)
Banca d'Italia	Discount rate	5.5 (23 Dec)	5.0 (22 Apr)	4.0 (26 Oct)	3.5 (3 Dec) 3.0 (23 Dec)
Banque centrale du Luxembourg**	same as Belgique	3.3 (9 Oct)	3.3	3.3	3.0 (3 Dec)
De Nederlandsche Bank	rate on special advances	3.3 (9 Oct)	3.3	3.3	3.0 (3 Dec)
Oesterreichische Nationalbank	repurchase rate	3.2 (9 Oct)	3.2	3.2	3.0 (3 Dec)
Banco de Portugal	repurchase rate	5.3 (18 Nov)	5.1 (19 Jan) 4.9 (26 Feb) 4.7 (18 Mar)	4.5 (11 May) 3.75 (4 Nov)	3.0 (3 Dec)
Suomen Pankki	tender rate	3.25 (15 Sep)	3.4 (19 Mar)	3.4	3.0 (3 Dec)

Note
*14-day repo rate
**Prior to 1 June 1998, the nominal central bank of Luxembourg was called the Institut Monétaire Luxembougeois.

key interest rates of the NCBs of the designated eurozone Member States. In addition, the interest rate for the marginal lending facility was set at 4.5 per cent and the interest rate for the deposit facility at 2.0 per cent, creating a corridor of 2.5 percentage points for the market-determined overnight interest rate (EONIA).[7]

April 1999 – reduction of main refinancing rate by 50 basis points

The first change of the monetary policy stance in the eurozone occurred on 8 April 1999, when the ECB Governing Council decided by a consensus to lower the interest rate of the Eurosystem's main refinancing operations by half a percentage point to 2.5 per cent, the interest rate on the marginal lending facility by one percentage point to 3.5 per cent and the interest rate on the deposit facility by half a percentage point to 1.50 per cent, in order to place the main refinancing rate in the middle of a two percentage point corridor bounded by the rates on the two standing facilities. According to the ECB Governing Council, the decision to lower the key interest rates was based on a perceived risk of deflation in the eurozone in the medium term. Over several months up to February 1999, the eurozone annual rate of inflation was 0.8 per cent, as measured by the year-on-year HICP (see Figure 3.4). The possible upward bias in the measurement of inflation, combined with the recent indicators of economic activity in the eurozone pointing to a sizeable overall slowdown in the fourth quarter of 1998, convinced the Governing Council to lower the key interest rates – despite the fact that M3 was still growing at a rate above its 'reference value' (see Figure 3.2) – for fear of deflation, not inflation. The three-month moving average of the 12-month growth rate of M3 covering the period ending December 1998–February 1999 (the latest available three months when the decision was taken) was 5.1 per cent, a figure to be compared with the reference value of 4.5 per cent. However, the Governing Council believed that the M3 growth rate was to be interpreted with caution as the broad money supply was affected by special factors at the start of Stage Three of EMU. Consequently, the Governing Council gave less importance to the first pillar of the monetary policy strategy until more observations were available to assess the trend growth rate of M3 in the new single currency area. In the eurozone, the first estimates of quarter-on-quarter real GDP growth for the fourth quarter of 1998 were 0.2 per cent (since then, revised to 0.13 per cent, with Germany and Italy each registering a negative growth rate) compared with a quarter-on-quarter growth rate of 0.7 per cent (revised to 0.54 per cent) for the third quarter of 1998. Industrial production in the manufacturing sector was registering a decline of almost 1 per cent in the fourth quarter of 1998 compared with the previous quarter and, according to the February release of the European Commission Business Survey, industrial

94 Monetary policy

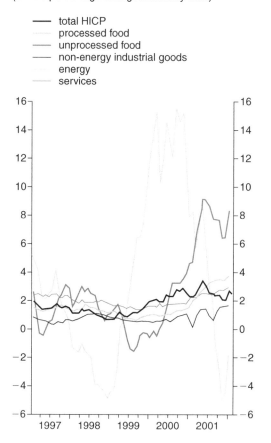

Figure 3.4 Breakdown of HICP inflation in the euro area by component.
Source: Eurostat.
Note: For periods prior to 2001, HICP data do not include Greece.

confidence continued to deteriorate in January 1999. The external environment was not favourable to Europe. The Russian debt default, with the accompanying liquidity crisis of summer–autumn 1998, was feared to have negative impacts on some European banks, especially the German banks whose exposure to Eastern Europe was significant. The NATO bombing campaign of Kosovo and Serbia, launched in late March 1999, was also expected to produce a negative shock on output, notably in Italy.

November 1999 – increase of main refinancing rate by 50 basis points

The expansionary stance of monetary policy, combined with a depreciation of the euro of about 10 per cent against the US dollar or against a weighted average of 13 currencies, was maintained until the beginning of November 1999. Then, on 4 November 1999, after having signalled to the market since mid-July 1999 that the next move of the ECB would be to increase interest rates, the ECB Governing Council decided – again by a consensus – to raise the interest rate on the main refinancing operations of the Eurosystem by 0.5 percentage point to 3 per cent, taking back the entire reduction of that key short-term interest rate set at the beginning of April 1999. At the same time, the ECB Governing Council raised the interest rates on the marginal lending facility and the deposit facility by 0.5 percentage points each to 4 per cent and 2 per cent, respectively (see Figure 3.3). According to the ECB Governing Council, the reasoning behind this increase in interest rates was that, from around the beginning of summer of 1999, the balance of risks to medium-term price stability had gradually been moving upwards for two principal reasons.

- Although the inflation rate measured by the HICP for the year-on-year period ending September 1999 was only 1.2 per cent, the inflation rate was expected to increase gradually in the months ahead, mainly because the increase in energy prices earlier that year was working its way through to consumer prices. The Governing Council looked at the industrial producer prices and noted that they increased by 0.6 per cent in the 12-month period ending August 1999, the first year-on-year increase since April 1998. Since the industrial goods have a weight of 41.2 per cent in the Harmonised Index of Consumer Prices, there appeared to be significant risk in the medium term of an increase in the consumer prices as a result of the pass-through effect of industrial prices. Moreover, the data released at that time for the eurozone suggested an acceleration of real GDP growth rates in the second half of 1999, as indicated by the industrial confidence index, which had increased from −12 in March 1999 to −5 in September 1999, and by the month-to-month increases in the eurozone industrial production from April to August 1999. Furthermore, the rise in the long-term bond yields in the eurozone and the associated pronounced steepening of the yield curve were considered by the Governing Council as a sign indicating that the financial markets were expecting increased economic growth in the near future. Finally, Germany's most important business climate index, the Munich-based monthly IFO Institute index, had consistently increased since its turnaround in June 1999.
- The monetary data up to September 1999 reinforced the view that M3 was on a rising trend. The 12-month growth rate of M3 from the period July–September 1998 to July–September 1999 was 5.9 per cent,

which was almost 1.5 percentage points above the reference value of 4.5 per cent. This deviation from the reference value had steadily increased during 1999. The strong growth rate of the most liquid components of M3 were of particular importance to the Governing Council since these developments indicated a generous liquidity situation in the eurozone and added to the risk of an increase of the inflation rate in the medium term.

February to April 2000 – three increases of the main refinancing rate by 25 basis points each

With the Y2K problem out of the way and the economic and financial data continually pointing towards the clear risk that the 2 per cent ceiling of inflation may be breached in the near future, the Governing Council increased the rates on the main refinancing operations, and on the two standing facilities, in three successive steps of 25 basis points in early February, mid-March and late April. The principal economic and financial data included the increasing energy prices and the continuing depreciation of the euro against the major currencies, and both of these facts, coupled with a strong cyclical upswing of output in the eurozone, placed substantial risk on an increasing underlying rate of inflation. On each occasion, the President of the ECB and the 'Editorial' in the *Monthly Bulletin* (i.e. the so-called 'minutes' of the ECB Governing Council) guided the market to interpret the increase of the key official interest rates as just one of a number of increases to come in the context of the tightening monetary policy cycle begun in November 1999. The decision to increase the rates in early February 2000 was based primarily on the following monetary (the first pillar), economic and financial (the second pillar) data.

- The three-month moving average growth rate of M3 for the period October/December 1998 to October/December 1999 was 6.1 per cent, signalling increased risks to price stability in the future as M3 remained persistently above its reference value of 4.5 per cent.
- The nominal effective exchange rate of the euro had depreciated by 12 per cent since the beginning of 1999, causing concern for future price stability because of the increasing prices for imported goods.
- The upswing of output in the eurozone from a quarter-to-quarter growth rate of 0.5 per cent (later revised to 0.6 per cent) in the second quarter of 1999 to a growth rate of 1.0 per cent the third quarter of 1999 as confirmed by the second release in mid-January 2000 of the real GDP figures.
- The continuing decline of the unemployment rate from 10.5 per cent in December 1998 to 9.6 per cent in December 1999.
- The US real GDP growth rate for the fourth quarter of 1999 had just been released, indicating a growth rate of 1.8 per cent over the third

quarter of 1999, which indicated an extremely favourable external environment for economic expansion in the eurozone with its associated risk to inflationary threats.
- The wage negotiations launched in Germany by a trend-setting union, which provided the ECB with an opportunity to signal that wages should not incorporate the temporary increases of energy prices and of imported goods observed in the HICP.

In mid-March 2000, the ECB Governing Council decided once again to increase its key official interest rates, on the basis of information that confirmed all the trends indicated above: the effective exchange rate of the euro continued to decline by approximately 1.7 per cent over the course of one month and, in particular, the euro continued its decline below parity against the US dollar; the eurozone GDP figures released by Eurostat (2000) for the fourth quarter of 1999 showed the same quarter-to-quarter growth rate of 1 per cent (later revised to 0.8 per cent) as in the previous quarter, confirming a sustained turnaround in the economic activity; and finally, the headline 12-month inflation rate for the period ending January 2000 was reported as 2 per cent, the first time the upper limit of the ECB's medium-term objective for price stability was reached.

In late April 2000, when the Governing Council increased its main refinancing interest rate for the fourth time since November 1999, the European Commission (2000a) had already released its Spring 2000 Economic Forecasts showing an anticipated real GDP growth rate in the eurozone of 3.4 per cent in calendar year 2000, which was a growth rate of aggregate demand significantly higher than the long-run potential eurozone growth rate of 2 or 2.5 per cent estimated by the ECB. The positive output gap was interpreted by the ECB as contributing to the risk of the medium term inflation rate breaching the 2 per cent ceiling. The Commission also published an inflation forecast of 1.8 per cent for calendar year 2000 against 1.1 per cent for calendar year 1999.

June to October 2000 – another three increases of the main refinancing rate

In early June 2000, as expected, the Governing Council again increased its main interest rates. The only surprise was that it increased its interest rate on refinancing operations by 50 basis points to 4.25 per cent instead of the expected 25 basis points. However, the larger-than-expected increase had to be seen in the context of the simultaneous announcement that, effective late June, the Governing Council would be switching from a fixed-rate tender procedure to a variable rate tender procedure, as explained below. Moreover, the Governing Council signalled to the market that no further rate increase was to be considered until mid-September 2000. This larger than expected increase was based on information indicating that the risk of the HICP breaching the 2 per cent ceiling in the medium term remained, owing to (1) the strong rise of oil prices in May 2000; (2) the sustained decline of the euro that had just reached a low of $0.88; (3) the 6.3 per cent annual growth rate of M3 for the three-month moving average covering the period February–April; and (4) the acceleration of the output recovery in the eurozone. Although not publicly mentioned by the Governing Council, in view of its unwritten rule never to cite any Member State by name, the recent data that had been released by Germany indicated that the unemployment rate had fallen to a four-year low in May 2000, industrial production in April had risen by a higher-than-expected 1.5 per cent over the previous month, and manufacturing orders in April had risen by the highest rate since reunification in 1990. It was clear that Germany, which then represented 32 per cent of the eurozone GDP, was converging with the strong growth rate of France, which represented 22 per cent of eurozone GDP. Moreover, the growth indicator published by the *Financial Times/Financial Times Deutschland/Les Echos* showed that the eurozone recovery was progressing at a rapid rate, suggesting that the eurozone economy had grown at a quarterly rate of 1.2 per cent in the first quarter of 2000 (*Financial Times*, June 9, 2000). In late summer and early fall, the monetary, economic and financial indicators were all pointing towards the risk that the future medium-term inflation rate would breach the 2 per cent ceiling. By mid-August, the 12-month inflation rate ending July 2000 was already at 2.4 per cent. The ECB did not anticipate an early reversal either of the euro exchange rate (see Box 3.2 for further details) or of the energy prices. These expectations coupled with the strong output growth indicators at the time led the ECB Governing Council to increase the minimum bid rate on the main refinancing operations of the Eurosystem by 25 basis points on 31 August 2000 and again on 5 October 2000. From November 1999 to October 2000, in the face of strong growth in the eurozone and accelerating inflation that breached the upper end of its definition of price stability, the ECB Governing Council raised its key interest rate seven times, taking the main refinancing rate from 2.50 per cent to 4.75 per cent.

By the end of 2000, the release of the weak German GDP growth rate, released for the third quarter (0.6 per cent over the previous quarter), and the significant decline in the widely reported German IFO index of business confidence, pointed to a softening of the growth rate in the eurozone. The IFO business climate index had peaked in May 2000. At the same time, the US data seemed to indicate a convergence of growth rates between the US and the eurozone, thus providing favourable conditions for a reversal of the euro exchange rate. Under those conditions, the ECB decided to leave its key interest rate unchanged. The ECB would now 'wait [to] see' whether the inflationary pressures reversed themselves.

Box 3.2 The declining euro from 1999–2000: a possible explanation

Figure 2.1(a) plots the time series of the euro against the US dollar from 1975 to early 2000. Since the euro was only launched in 1999, Figure 2.1(b) shows the value of the 'synthetic euro', defined as the weighted average value of the 11 currencies, against the US dollar, of the countries composing the initial eurozone, for the period prior to 1999. It is clear that the 'synthetic euro' had been declining against the US dollar since 1995. In other words, the US dollar had been on a rising trend against the 'synthetic euro' since early 1995, a trend partly explained by the extraordinary investment occurring in the technological sector in the US, leading to a gap in productivity increase between the US and the rest of the world – see Economic Report of the President (2001: Chapter 1) on the US 'New Economy'; Roeger (2001) on the contribution of information and communication technologies (ICT) to growth in Europe and in the US; McMorrow and Roeger (2001: Section 4); and Hansen and Roeger (2000) for a theoretical explanation of how positive supply shocks may appreciate the real value of a currency in the medium term.

The belated recognition in early 1998 by the market that the European Union was actually going to launch – and not just discuss, plan and delay indefinitely the future launch of – a single currency area in 1999, arrested the decline of the 'synthetic euro' against the US dollar throughout 1998. 'Euro-phoria' – the belief that the creation of a monetary union would provide a quick impetus to the elimination of regulations in the goods and labour markets and of the remaining structural barriers to capital mobility and labour mobility between Member States, combined with the belief that the euro would eventually be able to challenge the dominant position of the US dollar as the primary international reserve currency[a] – temporarily reversed the declining trend of the 'synthetic euro', taking the newly created currency in early January 1999 to its highest level since 1995. However, the new currency quickly reversed itself and continued along the trend that had begun in 1995 to hit a low of $0.82 in late 2000 (see Figure 2.1(b)), a decline of some 30 per cent from January 1999. Historically, since the breakdown of the post-war Bretton Woods system in 1971, movements on such a scale over such a time period between major currencies are not unprecedented. In fact, during the first half of the 1980s, the component currencies of the euro fell by 55 per cent against the dollar, before recovering most of this ground in the remainder of the 1980s and early 1990s. The decline of the euro over the period 1999–2000 must be looked at with the perspective that, in 1985, the 'synthetic euro' had fallen to an historic low of $0.68.

Some explanations of the decline of the euro since its launch are given below (see also Gros *et al.* 2000: Part II.2; and International Monetary Fund 2001: Chapter II: 66–75).[b]

1. Capital outflows from the eurozone to North America and Britain

In 1999, the net direct investment and portfolio investment flows recorded large net outflows from the eurozone in the amounts of €120.6 billion and €41.7 billion, respectively. In calendar year 2000, the comparable figures were €23.0 billion and €120.4 billion. Without a one-off inflow of a large direct investment in the eurozone against the exchange of shares (Vodafone of the UK purchasing Mannesmann of Germany), the net outflow from the eurozone would have been much larger during calendar 2000. The net capital outflows from the eurozone can be explained by the relatively higher growth rates in the US compared with the eurozone during the period 1998 to 2000 (see point 2 below), and by the globalisation trend of large European firms that saw the necessity to acquire a 'foothold' in the large US market in order strategically to maintain a competitive edge (see Box 3.3 for examples of the more visible cases). Although cross-border mergers and acquisitions are entered as capital flows in the balance of payments accounts, those flows do not necessarily give rise to immediate foreign exchange transactions, and therefore should not affect the exchange rate. However, to the extent that a eurozone company issues its own shares to buy or merge with the American company, the American shareholders, who now are too heavily-weighted in euro-denominated assets, may wish at some later date to sell them, which may lead to a depreciation of the euro (see Fender and Galati 2001).

2. The relative GDP growth rates favouring the US over the eurozone

Euro weakness during 1999–2000 was largely a story of dollar strength. The euro was driven down by repeated US GDP quarterly growth surprises on the upside throughout 1999 and the first nine months of 2000. The acceleration in productivity growth in the US raised, at least temporarily, prospective corporate real earnings growth, thus attracting long-term capital inflows. The quarter-to-quarter US real GDP growth rate at an annual rate was about twice the rate of the eurozone for the period beginning the third quarter of 1998 and ending the first quarter of 2000. This significant growth gap is one of the reasons for the large outflow of funds from the eurozone to the US, creating the conditions for the declining and weak euro.

3. Biased market perceptions owing to the lack of timely eurozone economic data

In general, the release of eurozone economic data lacks timeliness. This is true whether the comparison is made with the release of comparable data from the US or from Germany (see Box 3.1 for a few examples). Currently, the first estimate of the eurozone quarterly GDP is released by Eurostat with a 70-day lag after the end of the reference quarter. In the US and Germany, the lags are 30 and 53 days, respectively. The time gap in the release of comparable data between the US and the eurozone makes concurrent comparisons of the relative performance of the two blocs difficult, and may have contributed to an amplified unfavourable market judgement towards the eurozone, as the latter's expansionary phase from mid-1999 to the end of 2000 was lagging the US business cycle.

The evolving unfavourable analysis of the eurozone economic performance relative to the US performance during 1999–2000 was compounded by the fact that the market tended at the outset to focus on German macroeconomic data to obtain a eurozone view, because German data are well-known by the market and are released prior to the eurozone data and to the other national macroeconomic data (see Box 3.1). Since the German economic performance from 1998 through 2000 was below the eurozone average, the market's initial judgement of the eurozone was consistently based on worse data than the later-released Eurostat figures, which were quickly eclipsed by the following batch of relatively unfavourable numbers from Germany. It is noted, for example, that the German real GDP growth rates were 2.0 per cent in 1998, 1.8 per cent in 1999 and 3.0 per cent in 2000 against 2.9 per cent, 2.7 per cent and 3.4 per cent, respectively, for the eurozone (see Table 4.2).

102 *Monetary policy*

4. Portfolio shift linked to the start of the single currency area

The introduction of the euro in 1999 led to a significant increase of international bonds issued in euro, both by private corporations and international organisations (i.e. World Bank). The European Commission estimates the increase in 1999 to be of the order of 250 per cent over the combined amount of issuance in euro legacy currencies (European Commission 2001c). The increase in the supply of euro-denominated bonds, combined with the decrease in the demand by eurozone investors of euro-denominated assets so as to diversify into other currencies, led to a decline in the euro. The need for diversification arose because the assets denominated in two different legacy currencies (e.g. French franc and Deutsche mark) became assets denominated in a single currency (euro).

5. Fear of a possible economic policy-making vacuum at the eurozone level in the event of a major economic or financial crisis

In the event of a major crisis, market regulators, banking supervisors and fiscal authorities are still decentralised at the national level (see Chapter 4). The market fear is that, as a major crisis looms, the eurozone will lack the means to take decisive action. The European institutional culture based on 'comitology' and on the requirement of unanimity in the Council for important economic issues will lead to procrastination. At the end of this process, and after a long delay allowing the crisis to spin out of control, the fear is that the 'national interest' will eventually prevail, with a lack of coordination of economic policies. The only truly supra-national institution is the European Central Bank, but it will not be able to play the role of 'lender of last resort' in a financial crisis. In short, the market is uneasy about the lack of an 'economic government' in the event of a major crisis. The early problems encountered by the lack of a single voice to speak for the beleaguered euro were seen as a precursor of more serious coordination problems between eurozone governments in the event of a grave economic crisis. In fact, ministers tend to address their own constituency and at times contradict each other, or their national Central Bank Governors (see Box 3.4 for examples). Lack of progress towards the establishment of a eurozone 'economic government' reflects uncertainty of direction regarding political integration. With the exception of the current Belgian and German governments (see Verhofstadt 2000 and Schröder 2001), European Union governments increasingly emphasise intergovernmental cooperation as opposed to wider role for supra-national institutions. The result is that whenever worldwide events occur, which increase the degree of financial risk, the euro is not the currency of choice as a 'safe haven'; the currency of choice remains the US dollar, which paradoxically may sometimes rise even as the relative economic performance of the US declines.

Notes:
a See, for example, Hoffman and Schröder (1997), Illmanen (1997), Owens (1996) and Luce (1998). The latter reports that the strength of the euro came with the realisation that the eurozone will have a large structural trade surplus equivalent to 1.5 per cent of the eurozone's gross domestic product. Moreover, the fund managers believed that the ECB was expected to take a more hawkish stance on inflation than the US Federal Reserve.
b Among the various explanations, we do not include the international interest rate spread between the euro and dollar deposits. The open-economy uncovered interest rate parity condition cannot explain by itself the exchange rate movement for two reasons:
  i the uncovered interest rate parity condition only suggests that the currency with the lower interest rate, as was the case of the euro until mid-2001, is *expected* to appreciate in the future, which could lead either to an immediate depreciation of the currency or, assuming a variable risk premium, to an immediate appreciation or no change of the currency; and
  ii the uncovered interest rate parity condition affects only international deposit flows and cross-border transactions of bonds denominated in different currencies with equivalent credit risk; these transactions for the period 1999–2000 were not the significant cross-border flows determining the euro exchange rate–equity-related flows were more important.

May 2001 to November 2001 – four reductions of the main refinancing rate

In the face of short-term inflationary pressures stemming from the lagged effects of the increases in both the imported prices in 2000 and the prices of unprocessed food, the ECB was reluctant to relax its monetary policy stance during the first quarter of 2001, lest the rise in the inflation rate, which was already at approximately 3 per cent year-over year, create a more permanent impact through the second-round effects stemming from wage settlements that would incorporate these higher inflation rates. When the ECB received confirmation that the three-month moving average growth rate of the broad monetary aggregate was moving towards the reference value of 4.5 per cent growth per year, combined with the confirmation that the previously calculated M3 figures were distorted and

104 *Monetary policy*

biased upwards due to the inclusion of non-euro area residents' holdings of short-term negotiable paper, the ECB Governing Council was willing to announce in early May 2001 a reduction of 25 basis points of its key interest rate. The first pillar of its monetary policy strategy was signalling lower risks to price stability in the medium term, notwithstanding that fact that the lagged effects of the recent transitory inflationary pressures would still show up in the current inflation figures. By the middle 2001, as the global economy was slowing down, all the forecasts – including the Eurosystem's staff projections – were indicating a reduction of the eurozone's GDP growth rate close to its trend potential growth rate of 2–2.5 per cent per annum. The second pillar was also signalling less medium-term risk to the price stability objective. Thus, the ECB Governing Council once again reduced its key interest rate by 25 basis points in late August 2001.

The next two interest rate reductions of 50 basis points each in September and November 2001 were influenced, in terms of both timing and magnitude, by the consequences of the terrorist attacks in the United States on 11 September 2001. As the evidence mounted that the US had entered a recession even before the terrorist attacks (US real GDP quarter-over-quarter growth rate for the third quarter of 2001 was -1.3 per cent at an annual rate), the events of 11 September only reinforced the prevailing slowdown in the world economy. The external demand in the eurozone would decline further. The second pillar of the monetary policy strategy indicated further reduced risks to price stability. Although the growth rate of the monetary aggregate M3 was again accelerating, this observation was assessed as just reflecting a shift in private investors' portfolios from equity towards safer liquid assets as a result of the increased uncertainty after the terrorist attacks. In fact, an analysis of the components of M3 showed that the annual growth of credit to the private sector was declining. By the end of 2001, with expectations that a recovery in the eurozone would take place in 2002, the ECB held its key interest rate at 3.25 per cent.

No 'fine tuning' and 'no surprises' by the ECB?

When the eurozone National Central Banks coordinated a reduction in their key interest rates in December 1998, just prior to the launch of the single currency, the ECB President indicated that the ECB Governing Council would maintain this level of interest rate for the 'foreseeable future' from the start of Stage Three of the monetary union (Duisenberg 1998; European Central Bank 1998c). In early April 1999, the ECB Governing Council decided, in a move that surprised the markets, to lower its key interest rate by 50 basis points (see Table 3.4). At his press conference, the ECB President emphasised that the market could not expect another reduction by quipping, 'this is it'. The ECB was signalling to the market that a monetary policy change is not to be viewed as a

Box 3.3 Some recent large takeovers resulting in Foreign Direct Investment (FDI) outflows* from the eurozone, 1999–2001

1. French utilities and communications group Vivendi acquires in June 2000 for €36 billion Seagram, the Canadian entertainment and drink company that owns Universal, the Hollywood movie studio.
2. Unilever, the Anglo-Dutch food and detergent group, purchases in 2000 the large US food firm, Bestfoods, for $20.3 billion.
3. Spain's Terra Networks takes over American internet access and portal company Lycos, in a transaction worth $4.5 billion.
4. France Telecom acquires Orange, UK's largest mobile operator owned by Vodafone in a transaction worth €40.3 billion.
5. Deutsche Telekom purchases British One2One.
6. Chemical giant BASF AG purchases agro-chemical maker American Cyanamid Co.
7. Alcatel of France purchases Newbridge Networks of Ottawa.
8. Daimler-Benz of Germany merges with Chrysler Corp. in 1998.
9. Deutsche Bank acquires US National Discount Brokers for $1 billion.
10. Deutsche Telekom purchases US VoiceStream Wireless for $45 billion.
11. ING, the Dutch banking-assurance group, purchases the financial services operations of Aetna, the US insurance group, and ReliaStar Financial Corp. (US) for a total of $13.8 billion cash.
12. Dublin-based drug company Elan purchases Dura Pharmaceuticals of California for €2.1 billion.
13. ASM Lithography of the Netherlands purchases Silicon Valley Group for €1.8 billion.
14. Allianz, the German insurer, buys Pimco and Nicholas Applegate, two US asset management firms, in deals worth $4.3 billion.
15. UniCredito Italiano, a large Italian bank, buys Pioneer Group, a US asset management firm, in a deal worth $1.3 billion.
16. E.ON AG, formed in 1999 by the merger of German utilities Veba and Viag, in 2001 buys PowerGen, Britain's second largest generator of electricity, in a deal worth €15 billion.
17. Société Générale, the second largest bank in France, purchases in April 2001 51 per cent of TCW Group, a US asset manager, in a deal amounting to $800 million.

106 *Monetary policy*

18 BNP Paribas, France's largest bank, purchases, in May 2001, 55 per cent of BancWest, a large US bank, in a deal worth $2.45 billion.
19 Seat Pagine Gialle, the Italian yellow pages directory company and internet service provider, purchases (in 2001) Eniro, the Swedish yellow pages directory company, for €3 billion.
20 Alcatel of France proposes in 2001 a merger with (a purchase of) Lucent Technologies of the US in a deal that would lead to the French telecommunications company controlling Lucent; Lucent shareholders would receive Alcatel shares in an amount equal to $23.5 billion; two weeks later, the negotiations collapse owing to Lucent's claim that the Alcatel proposal would not create 'a merger of equals', but rather a takeover of Lucent by Alcatel.
21 Vivendi Universal of France, the world's second largest media group, purchases (in 2001) in a cash and stock offer, MP3.com, a leading US online music platform company, in a deal worth $372 million.
22 Vivendi Universal of France acquires (in 2001) Houghton Mifflin, the Boston educational book publisher, for about $1.8 billion.
23 RWE AG, Germany's second largest power company, purchases in 2000 Thames Water plc, a British utility, for $9.8 billion.

Note:
*Although all FDI flows appear in the capital account of the balance of payments, some of these transactions do not necessarily have a direct impact on the exchange rate, as they do not go through the foreign exchange market; they simply involve an exchange of shares (see International Monetary Fund 2001: 70–73). Notwithstanding this observation, it is still valid to consider that these FDI transactions may have an impact on the euro exchange rate. If the target company's shareholders, who receive shares from the acquiring company, do not wish to hold euro-denominated assets, these transactions may lead to downward pressure on the euro exchange rate, as these shareholders sell their newly acquired euro assets.

'Konjunkturgetriebene Politik' (a cyclically-inspired policy), but rather as a policy change that takes a 'forward-looking perspective focusing on the medium-term trends in inflation' (Duisenberg 1999a), in line with the conventional image that the pre-euro Bundesbank had established for itself. Similarly, in early November 1999, the Governing Council of the ECB also indicated that the 50 basis-point increase in the main refinancing rate was to be maintained for the foreseeable future. Under normal circumstances, the ECB did not plan to have periodic small changes in interest rates in response to new economic data that are clearly of a cyclical nature. In

Table 3.4 Key ECB interest rate, the main refinancing rate: 1999–2001

Announcement date (effective date)	Rate (%)	Type of tender
22 December 1998 (4 January 1999)	3.00	Fixed rate
8 April 1999 (14 April 1999)	2.50	Fixed rate
4 November 1999 (10 November 1999)	3.00	Fixed rate
3 February 2000 (9 February 2000)	3.25	Fixed rate
16 March 2000 (22 March 2000)	3.50	Fixed rate
27 April 2000 (4 May 2000)	3.75	Fixed rate
8 June 2000 (15 June 2000)	4.25	Fixed rate
(28 June 2000)	4.25 minimum bid rate	Variable rate, American-style auction with minimum bid rate*
31 August 2000 (1 September 2000)	4.50 minimum bid rate	Variable rate, American-style auction with minimum bid rate
5 October 2000 (11 October 2000)	4.75 minimum bid rate	Variable rate, American-style auction with minimum bid rate
10 May 2001 (15 May 2001)	4.50 minimum bid rate	Variable rate, American-style auction with minimum bid rate
30 August 2001 (5 September 2001)	4.25 minimum bid rate	Variable rate, American-style auction with minimum bid rate
17 September 2001 (19 September 2001)	3.75 minimum bid rate	Variable rate, American-style auction with minimum bid rate
08 November 2001 (14 November 2001)	3.25 minimum bid rate	Variable rate, American-style auction with minimum bid rate

Source: European Central Bank, *Monthly Bulletin*, various issues.

Note
*In a variable rate, American-style auction with a minimum bid rate, the eurozone credit institutions, wishing to borrow short-term funds (two weeks), must quote both a rate equal to, or above, the minimum bid rate set by the ECB and an amount of funds they wish to borrow from the central bank at that quoted rate. The bids with the highest interest rate level are satisfied with priority and successively lower bids are accepted until the exhaustion of the total liquidity decided by the ECB is allotted. Thus, an American-style auction is a multiple rate auction, whereas a Dutch-style auction is a single rate auction whereby the allotment of funds is done at a single rate equal to the marginal interest rate (i.e. the interest rate at which the total allotment of funds is exhausted).

short, the ECB did not wish the market to interpret its policy changes as 'short-term economic management' or 'fine tuning' of the economy. This explains the ECB's initial preference for relatively large increases in its key interest rates. An interest rate change of 50 basis points, instead of 25 basis-point, would avoid giving the impression that the ECB was trying to 'micro manage' the economy. The ECB strategy was to set its official short-term interest rates at a level consistent with maintaining the medium-term inflation outlook below its 2 per cent ceiling. This strategy would reduce the uncertainties regarding the future course of monetary policy and thus contribute to reducing any risk premium embodied in long-term real interest rates. The ECB argued that, by reducing such risk premia in the real long-term interest rate, the monetary policy can contribute to improving the allocative efficiency of the capital market and, as a result, improve overall economic welfare (European Central Bank, *Monthly Report*, November 1999: 5).

In a reversal of strategy, the ECB Governing Council began, in its second year of implementing the eurozone's monetary policy, to change its key interest rates in steps of 25 basis points, and at the same time continued to provide to the market some indication of the future movement of its key rates, as it had begun to do prior to the November 1999 rate increase. This additional information on the next probable move of the ECB was provided at the monthly press conference and in the *Monthly Bulletin*'s 'Editorial' as a means of reducing the risk premium incorporated in the real interest rates.

In early June, the Governing Council increased its main refinancing rate by 50 basis points instead of the expected 25 basis points. This larger than expected increase was not necessarily to be interpreted as yet another reversal of strategy, but had to be seen in the context of the announcement, made at the same time, that effective late June, the ECB would switch from a weekly fixed-rate tender to a variable-rate tender for its main refinancing operations. If the ECB had increased rates by only 25 basis points in early June while simultaneously announcing its intention to move to a variable rate tender in late June, the financial markets, anticipating a further 25 basis-point increase at the next monetary policy meeting scheduled for mid-July, would have taken this expected increase into account when bidding for funds at the weekly variable-rate auctions starting in late June. In effect, the auction market would have increased the rate on the ECB's behalf. This is what the President of the ECB meant when he declared at his press conference in early June that the 50-basis point increase 'cleared the horizon' until September 2000 (Duisenberg 2000a). The following two increases in the main refinancing minimum bid rate were each kept to 25 basis points (see Table 3.4). Similarly, when the ECB began to lower its key interest rate as of mid-2001, the May and August 2001 reductions were kept to 25 basis points each. The two 50 basis point reductions, one in September 2001 and the other in November 2001, have to be seen in the context of the altered global economic environment following the terrorist acts of 11 September 2001. In fact, at its regularly scheduled monetary policy-making meeting of 13 September 2001, the ECB Governing Council decided to keep the main refinancing minimum bid rate unchanged. Only two business days later and taking its cue from the FOMC's 50-basis point reduction of the federal funds target rate, the ECB Governing Council, in a hastily convened teleconference on 17 September 2001, decided to lower its key interest rate by 50 basis points.

While conducting monetary policy by implementing small changes of interest rates may be optimal for a risk-averse policy maker, operating in an uncertain environment, as a way of avoiding large policy errors (Brainard 1967), it creates more uncertainty for the market, which is constantly trying to anticipate the next policy move of the monetary policy committee during the two-week period or month between meetings of the committee. To that extent, the long-term interest rates may embody a risk premium, reflecting the uncertainty of future monetary policy changes. Informal information about the future policy bias announced after a policy meeting is designed to reduce some of that market uncertainty. After each meeting, the FOMC of the Federal Reserve System systematically releases this type of information (see Table 3.5). The pre-euro Bundesbank's Central Bank Council never released information about the future policy bias but had a preference for large changes of its official Lombard and discount interest rates, of the order of 50 to 100 basis points. The Lombard/discount rates of the pre-euro Bundesbank formed a ceiling and floor, respectively, for the main refinancing rate of the pre-euro Bundesbank, the 'repo rate'. Of the 18 changes made between 1979 and 1987, all were of either 100 or 50 basis points, and of the 12 changes made in the 1990s, between February 1994 and April 1996 – date of the last change before the integration of the Bundesbank in the Eurosystem – all were of the order of 50 basis points, except in two cases, in April 1994 (see Figures 3.6(a) and 3.6(b)).

The ECB's first 30 months: an overall evaluation

Most observers of the new European Central Bank agree that the Governing Council did not commit any major errors in the monetary policy decisions taken during the first two years of its operation. Admittedly, the decisions taken during the first two years were relatively simple, with small risks of making errors. In the first quarter of 1999, the eurozone quarter-over-quarter GDP was growing at around 2 per cent per annum, which was at the low end of the growth range of the long-run trend (potential) growth rate of output in the eurozone, and the rate of inflation was running at about 1 per cent per annum, well below the ECB's 2 per cent ceiling that defines price stability in the medium term. Under those circumstances, reducing the key interest rate by 50 basis points in early April 1999 was not a difficult

Table 3.5 FOMC's target ('intended') federal funds rate, future policy bias and disclosure policy: 1990–2002

Date of FOMC meeting	Target federal funds rate*	Comments on future policy bias and disclosure policy
2–3 July 1990	8.25% 8.00, as of 13 July	Unchanged from previous decision, but policy guidelines for the inter-meeting period is biased towards 'easing' ('a *slightly* lesser degree of reserve pressure *would* be acceptable')** so that as of mid-July federal funds rate is at 8.00%; recession begins in July 1990. *Disclosure policy:* since mid-1976, all FOMC monetary policy decisions, including the inter-meeting policy bias, are only disclosed in the official minutes that are released to the public two or three days after the next scheduled meeting (a total of approximately 45 days); from mid-1967 to early 1975, a publication delay of approximately 90 days from the date of the meeting was in effect; until 1994 (see below), no statement is released immediately following an FOMC meeting.
2 October 1990	8.00 7.75, as of 29 October	Inter-meeting policy guideline is biased towards significant easing ('a *somewhat* lesser degree of reserve pressure *would* be acceptable') so that as of end of month federal funds rate is at 7.75%
13 November 1990	7.50 7.25, as of 7 December	Inter-meeting policy guideline is biased towards significant easing ('a *somewhat* lesser degree of reserve pressure *would* be acceptable') so that as of early December federal funds rate is at 7.25%
18 December 1990	7.00 6.75, as of 9 January 1991 6.25, as of 1 February 1991	Inter-meeting policy guideline is biased towards significant easing ('a *somewhat* lesser degree of reserve pressure *would* be acceptable') so that as of early January 1991 federal funds rate is at 6.75% and as of early February 1991 the rate is at 6.25%
5–6 February 1991	6.25 6.00, as of 8 March	Inter-meeting policy guideline is biased towards significant easing ('a *somewhat* lesser degree of reserve pressure *would* be acceptable') so that as of 8 March the federal funds rate is

26 March 1991	6.00	6.00%
	5.75, as of 30 April	Inter-meeting policy guideline is symmetric ('a somewhat greater or somewhat lesser degree of reserve pressure *might* be acceptable') but as of 30 April the federal funds rate is at 5.75%; recession ends in March 1991
14 May 1991	5.75	Inter-meeting policy guideline is symmetric ('a somewhat greater or somewhat lesser degree of reserve pressure *might* be acceptable')
2–3 July 1991	5.75	Inter-meeting policy guideline remains symmetric ('a somewhat greater or somewhat lesser degree of reserve pressure *might* be acceptable') but as of 6 August the federal funds rate is at 5.50%
	5.50, as of 6 August	
20 August 1991	5.50	Changes its inter-meeting policy guideline from symmetric to a significant easing bias ('a somewhat lesser degree of reserve pressure *would* be acceptable') so that as of 13 September the federal funds rate is at 5.25%
	5.25, as of 13 September	
1 October 1991	5.25	Inter-meeting policy guideline is biased towards easing ('a slightly lesser degree of reserve pressure *would* be acceptable') so that as of 31 October the federal funds rate is at 5.00%
	5.00, as of 31 October	
5 November 1991	4.75	Inter-meeting policy guideline is biased towards easing ('a slightly lesser degree of reserve pressure *would* be acceptable') so that as of 6 December the federal funds rate is at 4.50%
	4.50, as of 6 December	
17 December 1991	4.50	Inter-meeting policy guideline is biased towards significant easing ('a somewhat lesser degree of reserve pressure *would* be acceptable')** to be taken in the context of the twin objectives of price stability and sustainable economic growth
20 December 1991 (unscheduled)	4.00	Telephone conference
4–5 February 1992	4.00	Inter-meeting policy guideline is biased towards easing ('slightly lesser reserve restraint *would* be acceptable')

continued

Table 3.5 Continued

Date of FOMC meeting	Target federal funds rate*	Comments on future policy bias and disclosure policy
31 March 1992	4.00 3.75, as of 9 April	Inter-meeting policy guideline is biased towards easing ('slightly lesser reserve restraint *would* be acceptable') so that as of 9 April federal funds rate is at 3.75%
19 May 1992	3.75	Inter-meeting policy guideline is changed to symmetric ('slightly greater or slightly lesser reserve restraint *might* be acceptable')
30 June–1 July 1992	3.25	Inter-meeting policy guideline is changed towards an easing bias ('slightly lesser reserve restraint *would* be acceptable')
18 August 1992	3.25 3.00, as of 4 September	Inter-meeting policy guideline is biased towards easing ('slightly lesser reserve restraint *would* be acceptable') so that as of 4 September 1992, federal funds rate is 3.00%
6 October 1992	3.00	Inter-meeting policy guideline is biased towards easing ('slightly lesser reserve restraint *would* be acceptable'), but changed to a symmetric guideline at the meeting of 22 December 1992.
3–4 February 1994	3.25	Inter-meeting policy guideline is symmetric ('slightly greater reserve restraint or slightly lesser reserve restraint might be acceptable'). *Disclosure policy:* Beginning in 1994, FOMC releases an immediate statement *whenever a policy change occurs*; the policy change statement is phrased in terms of a target federal funds rate, but the immediate press release does not include the inter-meeting policy bias, which continues to be released with the minutes.
22 March 1994	3.50	Inter-meeting policy guideline remains symmetric
18 April 1994 (unscheduled)	3.75	Telephone conference
17 May 1994	4.25	Inter-meeting policy guideline remains symmetric

5–6 July 1994	No change, but	Inter-meeting policy guideline is changed towards a tightening bias ('slightly greater reserve restraint *would* be acceptable')
16 August 1994	4.75	Inter-meeting policy guideline is changed towards symmetry
27 September 1994	No change, but	Inter-meeting policy guideline is changed towards a tightening bias
15 November 1994	5.50	Inter-meeting policy guideline is changed towards symmetry
20 December 1994	No change, but	Inter-meeting policy guideline is changed towards a tightening bias
31 January–1 February 1995	6.00	Inter-meeting policy guideline is changed towards symmetry
28 March 1995	No change, but	Inter-meeting policy guideline is changed towards a tightening bias
23 May 1995	No change, but	Inter-meeting policy guideline is changed towards symmetry
5–6 July 1995	5.75	Inter-meeting policy guideline is changed towards an easing bias
22 August 1995	No change, but	Inter-meeting policy guideline is changed towards symmetry
19 December 1995	5.50	Inter-meeting policy guideline is still towards symmetry
31 January 1996	5.25	Inter-meeting policy guideline is still towards symmetry, but starting with the meeting of 3 July 1996, the inter-meeting policy guideline is each time maintained towards a tightening bias
25 March 1997	5.50	Inter-meeting policy guideline is changed towards symmetry; starting with the meeting of 19 August 1997, the FOMC's monetary policy directive addressed to the New York Fed, heretofore phrased in terms of the degree of pressure on reserves, is phrased in terms of a target federal funds rate.
29 September 1998	5.25	Inter-meeting policy guideline is towards an easing bias ('a *somewhat* lower federal funds rate *would* be acceptable')
15 October 1998 (unscheduled)	5.00	Inter-meeting telephone conference
17 November 1998	4.75	Inter-meeting policy guideline is towards symmetry

continued

Table 3.5 Continued

Date of FOMC meeting	Target federal funds rate*	Comments on future policy bias and disclosure policy
18 May 1999	No change, but	Inter-meeting policy guideline is towards a tightening bias. *Disclosure policy*: Effective as of this meeting, FOMC releases to the public an immediate statement after each meeting, *even when there is no change in policy*. Moreover, the immediate statement includes the inter-meeting policy tilt, which heretofore had only been released with the minutes.
30 June 1999	5.00	Inter-meeting policy guideline is symmetric
24 August 1999	5.25	Inter-meeting policy guideline is symmetric
5 October 1999	No change, but	Inter-meeting policy guideline is towards a tightening bias
16 November 1999	5.50	Inter-meeting policy guideline is symmetric
21 December 1999	No change, and	Inter-meeting policy guideline is symmetric
2 February 2000	5.75	*Disclosure policy*: Effective as of this meeting, FOMC replaces the inter-meeting policy guideline with a statement about the 'future risks of inflation vs output weakness'; Future risks are weighted mainly towards inflation, i.e. future policy is biased towards 'tightening'
21 March 2000	6.00	Future risks are weighted mainly towards inflation, i.e. 'tightening'
16 May 2000	6.50	Future risks are weighted mainly towards inflation, i.e. 'tightening'
28 June 2000	No change, but	Future risks are weighted mainly towards inflation, i.e. 'tightening'
22 August 2000	No change, and	Same as above
3 October 2000	No change, and	Same as above
15 November 2000	No change, and	Same as above
19 December 2000	No change, but	Future risks are weighted mainly towards economic weakness, i.e. 'easing'
3 January 2001 (unscheduled)	6.00	Future risks are weighted mainly towards economic weakness, i.e. 'easing'

30–31 January 2001	5.50	Same as above
20 March 2001	5.00	Same as above (Recession begins in March 2001)
18 April 2001 (unscheduled)	4.50	Same as above
15 May 2001	4.00	Same as above
26–27 June 2001	3.75	Same as above
21 August 2001	3.50	Same as above
17 September 2001 (unscheduled; as a result of events of 11 September)	3.00	Same as above
2 October 2001	2.50	Same as above
6 November 2001	2.00	Same as above
11 December 2001	1.75	Same as above (Recession ends at about this time)
30 January 2002	1.75	Same as above
19 March 2002	1.75	Future risks are balanced with respect to goals of price stability and sustainable economic growth. *Disclosure policy*: FOMC decides to release immediately the roll call of the vote on the federal funds target rate decision, including the preferred policy choice of any dissenters.
7 May 2002	1.75	Same as above
25–26 June 2002	1.75	Same as above

Notes:
*Up until 1994, the 'target' federal funds rate is the New York Fed Trading Desk's determination of the federal funds rate consistent with the FOMC's directive regarding the preferred 'degree of reserve pressure'. As from 1994, the Committee indicates explicitly the 'target' federal funds rate in its immediate press release addressed to the public. As from August 1997, the Committee also phrases its monetary policy directive addressed to the New York Fed's Trading Desk in terms of a 'target' federal funds rate. Shaded sections in table indicate a period of declining target federal funds rate.
**Prior to the December 1991 meeting, the implementation by the New York Fed Trading Desk of the FOMC's inter-meeting policy bias was based on certain factors that the New York Fed Trading Desk had to consider. Those factors constituted the objective of price stability, the trends in economic activity, the behaviour of the monetary aggregates, and the developments in foreign exchange and domestic financial markets. From December 1991 to December 1999, the inter-meeting policy bias addressed to the Trading Desk in New York had to be considered in the context of the Committee's long-run objectives for price stability and sustainable economic growth. As of 2000, the FOMC no longer addresses an inter-meeting policy bias to the New York Fed Trading Desk: the target federal funds rate remains unchanged from meeting to meeting, which has been the case, *de facto*, since 1994.
Source: Federal Reserve System, *Annual Report of the Board of Governors of the Federal Reserve System*, various issues; the target federal funds rate is obtained from the Federal Reserve website at www.federalreserve.gov/fomc

116 *Monetary policy*

decision to make. The only sour note came from the M3 growth rate that was increasingly deviating from the 4.5 per cent reference value set in the first pillar of the ECB's monetary policy strategy to maintain price stability in the medium term (see Figure 3.2). However, the ECB had warned the public that the 'monetary pillar' of its monetary policy strategy was only to be used as a reference value, not a target value, because of the risk of instability posed to the eurozone demand function for money by the launch of the single currency area. Indeed, two years later, the ECB announced that the three-month moving average annual growth rate of M3 had been overestimated, owing to the inclusion of money market fund shares, money market paper and debt securities held by non-eurozone residents.

Similarly, the decision to increase the key two-week main refinancing interest rate by a total of 2.25 percentage points over a one year period, starting in November 1999 and ending in October 2000, was again not a difficult and risky monetary policy change to face. The risks, in the medium term, were clearly biased towards the rate of inflation breaching the 2 per cent ceiling. The evidence was clear that the inflation risks were coming from all sides: from the increase in energy prices and food prices, from the almost continuous depreciation of the euro that had begun soon after the launch of the single currency area, from the robust eurozone GDP growth rate exceeding the eurozone's long-run trend or potential growth rate of 2–2.5 per cent per annum (see European Central Bank 2000: 37–48), and from the signals given by the growth rate of the monetary aggregate M3. In other words, the first and the second pillars of the monetary policy strategy were signalling inflationary pressures in the medium term. From the third quarter of 1999 to the end of the second quarter of 2000, each quarter-over-quarter real GDP growth rate registered 3.6 per cent per annum, on the basis of the GDP data released at that time. The external environment, with even stronger growth in North America, with strong growth in the United Kingdom and with a depreciating euro, reinforced the view that the eurozone GDP growth rate above its long-term trend rate was going to be maintained. The three-month moving average growth rate of the broad monetary aggregate had reached a peak of approximately 6.5 per cent per annum – some 2 percentage points above its reference value – in the second quarter of 2000. The eurozone inflation rate, measured by the Harmonised Index of Consumer Prices over a 12-month period, breached the 2 per cent ceiling as of the second quarter of 2000 – registering 2.4 per cent for the 12-month period ending June 2000. Choosing a more restrictive monetary policy under those circumstances did not pose a dilemma to the ECB Governing Council.

The difficult monetary policy decision faced by the ECB appeared in early 2001 when the two pillars of its monetary policy strategy were indicating a diminished inflation risk in the medium term while the current year-over-year inflation rate was clearly above the 2 per cent ceiling. As of early 2001, the eurozone economy was slowing down and the broad monet-

Monetary policy 117

ary aggregate M3 was moving back towards, and even below, its reference value – all pointing towards a diminished inflation risk in the medium term. On the basis of its two pillars defining its monetary policy strategy, the ECB could have considered relaxing its monetary policy stance during the first quarter of 2001. Yet, in view of the then current price developments observed in the eurozone, the ECB did not want the so-called temporary factors of price inflation to be embedded in wage increases, which would then lead to second-round and more permanent effects on inflation. Consequently, it decided to wait until the second quarter of 2001 before starting to relax its monetary policy in small steps. The less favourable external growth environment, the risk of Germany – which represents about one third of the eurozone GDP – sliding into a recession, and the lower growth rate of M3, all pointed to lower inflation in the medium term. However, the then-current inflation rate in early 2001 staying above 2 per cent, combined with the expectation that the year-over-year eurozone inflation would not fall below 2 per cent for at least the next six months, posed a timing problem for the ECB Governing Council. The ECB wanted to relax its monetary policy stance without giving the impression to the price and wage setters that its commitment to the medium-term price stability objective was being compromised. The timing problem was compounded by the external pressures placed on the ECB. The ECB Governing Council may have decided to delay the reduction in its key interest rate to assert its institutional independence from the Eurogroup Finance Ministers. A newspaper article (Nayeri 2002), based on interviews of two ECB Governing Council members, stated that the ECB decision of 11 April 2001 to leave its benchmark interest rate unchanged, only to reduce it the following month, may have been prompted by undue political pressure. The 'insiders' claim that the strong pressure to lower the interest rate from the Belgian Finance Minister, the then-Eurogroup President who attended the ECB Governing Council meeting of 11 April 2001, irritated the Governing Council, leading the ECB President to say 'I hear, but I do not listen' to those who argued for an interest rate cut (see Box 3.4 for further details). This ECB reaction to political pressures was very much in line with the pre-euro Bundesbank's modus operandi of sending signals to the political authorities that external pressures to influence monetary policy decisions would be counterproductive.

MONETARY POLICY STRATEGY AND INSTRUMENTS OF THE PRE-EURO BUNDESBANK

Monetary targeting

Monetary targeting as a strategy to achieve its primary objective of 'safeguarding the currency' was not implemented by the Bundesbank until the

Box 3.4 Statements of eurozone officials and key events, January 1999–November 2001

14 January 1999: Oskar Lafontaine, German Finance Minister and his French counterpart, Dominique Strauss Kahn, warn against an excessive *appreciation* of the euro.

9 February 1999: Bundesbank forecasts 0.4 per cent GDP decline in Germany for fourth quarter 1998 over third quarter 1998 (important because market still focuses on timely German data to obtain an overall 'picture' of the eurozone, despite the fact that Germany only represents 32 per cent of eurozone GDP).

11 March 1999: Oskar Lafontaine, German finance minister, resigns after continually criticising the ECB for failing to cut interest rates, in what one market analyst described as 'monetary terrorism'.

15 March 1999: European Commissioners, expecting to be sacked by the European Parliament after the release of a fraud report, resign *en masse;* the EU only has a care-taker Executive.

24 March 1999: Nato begins bombing of Kosovo and Serbia.

25 March 1999: Duisenberg, ECB President: 'The possibility cannot be excluded that increased uncertainty about the political support for a stability-oriented monetary and fiscal policy has contributed to the weakening of the euro.'

11 May 1999: Domingo-Solans, member of ECB Executive Board: 'I think we're giving too much importance to the exchange rate level'.

26 May 1999: first crack in the economic Stability and Growth Pact when Amato, the then newly appointed Italian finance minister, forces EU colleagues to change his country's 1999 budget deficit target from 2.0 per cent to 2.4 per cent.

2 June 1999: ECB monthly press conference:

Reporter's question: 'Mr. Issing (member of ECB Executive Board), the other night, was speaking at the University of Cologne and said that he saw no risk, with the euro at its current level ($1.03), that inflation would be imported into the eurozone. That implied that he was not particularly worried about the current level of the exchange rate. Indeed, the euro at this level might have some advantages, because it would stimulate activity and exports outside the eurozone. Do you share that view that in some ways the current level of the euro is actually beneficial to the eurozone economy, that it may in some ways be a good thing?'

Duisenberg's reply: 'It is not something we strive for. But that it has the effect you mentioned cannot be denied. As always, I see no reason whatsoever to disagree with what my esteemed colleague Issing has said.'

3 June 1999: Tietmeyer (the then President of the Bundesbank): 'Clearly, the decline in the euro's external value over the last few days has not been good news.'

21 June 1999: Prodi (President-designate of Commission): 'If we (Italy) continue to have costs that diverge from other European countries, it will be more difficult to remain in the euro'. Addressing an Italian audience, Prodi is suggesting that membership in the eurozone may not be an irreversible decision.

4 November 1999: Duisenberg: 'Does the actual movement (of eurodollar exchange rate) give rise to concern? The answer is no. It doesn't matter very much.'

Early May 2000: As the euro continues to slide and breaches the $0.90 level, comments from French Prime Minister Jospin, who calls for 'a collective response from the large monetary blocs', from ECB President Duisenberg, from Banque de France Governor Trichet, who declares that 'market participants will realise with our help that the present rates are out of line with fundamentals...', and from the French and German Finance Ministers all fuel speculation that the ECB may intervene in the foreign exchange market; however, Bundesbank President Welteke plays down the effectiveness of intervention: '...(intervention) is always problematic and it is very doubtful whether it can be successful against the market trend'.

8 May 2000: As the Eurogroup Finance Ministers issues a statement about the need for fiscal consolidation to boost the euro, the display of unity collapses as the German and French Finance Ministers differ in public over whether the then-forthcoming revenues from the sale of 3G mobile phone licences should be used to reduce government debt.

29–30 May 2000: In a wish to reverse the perception that eurozone officials contradict each other, the eurozone political leaders and central bankers attempt to speak with one voice regarding the possibility of foreign exchange intervention, as the euro hovers around the $0.90 level: Bundesbank President Welteke: 'Intervention is part of the tool-kit of central bankers'; French Prime Minister Jospin again suggests joint action by the ECB and the US and Japanese central banks to arrest the fall of the euro: 'Current developments in the euro ... call for joint reflection and maybe even joint action by the ECB and Euro 11, as well as better coordination between major monetary zones'.

4 September 2000: German Chancellor Schröder tells a Berlin audience that a weak euro is good for German exports and should be a cause for satisfaction, not consternation.

16 October 2000: In an interview with *The Times* newspaper, Duisenberg takes the unusual step of openly discussing ECB intervention strategy and dampens hopes of imminent intervention to support the euro by acknowledging that the timing of action by the Group of Seven central banks in September had been influenced by the US presidential elections.

25 October 2000: At a Group of 20 meeting in Montreal, the ministers of finance and central bank governors of the G7 and the President of the ECB fail to mention the euro in their press release, signalling to the market that the US was not enthusiastic about participating in a concerted intervention to halt the decline of the euro.

31 October 2000: Welteke, President of the Bundesbank, says that the ECB remained ready to intervene in the currency markets again if necessary. 'But part of the success of intervention is that one doesn't announce it ahead of time' (in an indirect criticism of the Duisenberg interview with *The Times*).

22 March 2001–7 April 2001: *Muddled communication to the public about possible cut in the main ECB refinancing rate:*
On 22 March 2001, Issing (ECB chief economist and member of Executive Board) says the central bank must lower its estimates for growth and inflation (the projections that had been released in December 2000); the next day Trichet (Governor of the Banque de France) says the ECB is no longer worried about future inflation (although current 12-month rate ending February 2001 was 2.6 per cent and had been above 2.0 per cent every month since June 2000); the same night, Issing retracts his previous comments.

On 29 March 2001 at its regular fortnightly meeting, the Governing Council does not change main refinancing rate; on 30 March 2001, Trichet reads a statement to the press that the central bank has a 'wait and see' approach about relaxing monetary policy; on 4 April 2001, Welteke states, 'we (members of the Governing Council) have agreed to write down a formula on a piece of paper about what we say in response to indiscreet questions journalists ask us time and again about where rates are headed' (the script became public only after Trichet read from it at a press conference in Rouen, France on

30 March 2001); Welteke, who seemed to resist an early reduction in interest rate, adds that most members wanted to keep the statement secret.

On 4 April 2001, Eichel, the German Finance Minister, makes it plain that he hopes the ECB would cut rates: 'I think ... that the world economy in general is in a phase when it is slowing in all areas, the central banks should ... think about that in monetary policy'.

11 April 2001: Following the recommendations from the IMF, the OECD, and the Presidency of the Eurogroup Finance Ministers (Belgian Finance Minister Reynders) to lower interest rates and the hints that it was ready to reduce its key interest rate by 25 basis points, the Governing Council decides to hold the interest rate constant at its regular meeting of 11 April 2001, without providing any indication when, if ever, it would reduce its key interest rate. 'I hear but I don't listen', says Duisenberg in response to the argument that the eurozone needs lower interest rates in the face of an economic slowdown in the US. On 6 April, 11 of the 19 economists surveyed by Bloomberg News expected the ECB to lower its key rate by 25 basis points and two economists expected a 50 basis point reduction. Some eight months later, it is revealed (Nayeri 2002) that the Governing Council's decision to hold the interest rate fixed at that meeting was taken partly to spurn Reynders, who attended the meeting and pressured the Governing Council to reduce interest rates.

26 April 2001: The central bank has convinced the financial markets that it will not reduce its key interest rate in the near future since risks are weighted more towards inflation remaining above 2 per cent in the near future and less towards GDP growing below potential (estimated by the central bank at 2.5 per cent growth rate). For example, Welteke states 'Monetary policy is not an instrument of cyclical policy-making ... the tasks and strategy of ECB are different from Fed ... we cannot cite markets and the economy (as did the Fed) to justify changes in monetary policy ... we have a primary mandate to maintain inflation below two per cent in the medium term.' Issing and Duisenberg disclose on 27 April that the ECB expects to overshoot its 2 per cent ceiling for annual inflation in early 2002. However, French Finance Minister Fabius, at a G7 meeting on 30 April, says in an interview that the ECB should loosen its monetary policy.

3 May 2001: The financial markets are still convinced that the ECB will not lower its key interest rate at the meeting of 10 May;

however, Issing adds some confusion on the occasion of a speech in London, indicating that the eurozone medium term inflation outlook has improved and that the threat only comes from the second round effects of wages (not energy and food prices or the euro exchange rate) due to the present levels of inflation. However, he adds that there is 'little room for fine-tuning the economy and controlling the economic cycle (with monetary policy)'.

10 May 2001: ECB takes markets by surprise in announcing a 25 basis point cut in its key interest rate, citing that the first pillar indicates that a 'corrected' M3 no longer poses a threat to price stability, while Duisenberg denies during his press conference that the ECB decision was influenced by the fact that on 7, 8 and 9 May, German data released on industrial output and unemployment indicated and confirmed a trend of a significant slowdown of the German economy: on 7 May, it is reported that manufacturing orders in Germany declined 4.4 per cent in March; on 8 May, unemployment in Germany is reported to have increased for the fourth consecutive month in April; on 9 May, German industrial output data show a decline of 3.7 per cent in March. Market observers conclude that ECB was prepared to cut interest rates prior to this date, but could not do it lest ECB should appear to lose its independence, in the face of 'outside' pressures from EU finance ministers and international organisations; a few days later, Welteke reveals that the Governing Council was split on the question of the 25 basis point reduction in the interest rate.

31 May 2001: As the euro is sliding to a six-month low, owing to the slowing growth and rising inflationary pressures in the eurozone, Duisenberg, speaking to reporters, suggests that he sees no need to consider central bank intervention to rescue the currency: 'It (the exchange rate) only becomes important if it no longer supports our inflation target in a serious way – and that's not the case'. That comment sent the euro falling one cent against the dollar to $0.844. The ill-timed Duisenberg comment seemed to contradict the concerns of a weak euro on inflation, expressed by Bundesbank President Welteke a week earlier.

September 2001: Two days after the terrorist attacks in the US, the ECB Governing Council decided at its regularly scheduled meeting of 13 September to keep the minimum main refinancing short-term interest rate unchanged, only to reduce it by 50 basis points on the 17 September at a hastily convened teleconference meeting, a few hours after the US Fed announced a 50 basis point reduction of the target federal funds rate, thus giving the impression to the markets that the ECB was pressured by the Fed; some two weeks later, Issing (member of the ECB Executive Board) states that the ECB would have reduced its key interest rate by 50 basis points at its regularly scheduled meeting of 27 September had it not already done so at its special meeting of 17 September, trying to dispel the idea that the ECB was reacting to the events of 11 September.

October 2001: In the face of growing evidence that the eurozone growth rate will be significantly lower than had earlier been anticipated, the Ministers of Finance from Austria, Belgium, France, Germany and Luxembourg openly criticise the ECB for its reluctance to cut interest rates aggressively. Even the German Chancellor reacts to the ECB's decision not to cut the interest rate on 11 October by questioning whether the Bank had yet 'reached the peak of common sense'. In addition, it is publicly revealed that several NCB officials disagreed with Duisenberg's remarks of 11 October 2001 that the ECB had 'very little room for manoeuvre' (to reduce interest rates further) and that his remarks did not reflect accurately the discussions held in the Governing Council on that date. Then, on 18 October, the ECB suggests in its October monthly report to indicate that it may cut interest rates in the very near future. Yet, on 25 October, at its regular meeting, the Governing Council fails to act, with the market interpreting this postponement of a reduction of interest rates as the ECB's reaction to the improper political pressure placed on it during the previous week at the Ghent European Council meeting. In a statement reminiscent of the position of the pre-euro Bundesbank, ECB Governing Council member Welteke, President of the Bundesbank, says in an interview with the German daily *Die Welt* that 'the independence of a young institution such as the ECB should not be called into question ... we will change interest rates as and when we consider it the right time, not when politicians want ... we do not regard it as any particular incentive when politicians demand that we cut interest rates.'

November 2001: In the run-up to the ECB's meeting of 8 November, the market is expecting a 50 basis point reduction of the main refinancing rate in response to mounting evidence that the eurozone economy is in its worst state since 1993 and that the inflation rate is expected to fall below 2 per cent by early 2002. However, a few days prior to the meeting, the Bundesbank President warns publicly that

> he and his ECB colleagues do not want to build up long-term inflation expectations by cutting interest rates too aggressively. These comments change market expectations towards a 25 basis point cut on 8 November, only to be surprised by the ECB's decision to cut its key interest rate by 50 basis points.

mid-1970s when, with the collapse of the Bretton Woods fixed exchange rate regime against the US dollar, the nominal anchor of the international monetary system disappeared. By the mid-1970s, inflationary expectations in Germany, as well as in many other industrialised countries, had changed. By the end of 1973, the annual inflation rate in Germany had reached a peak of 8 per cent, in contrast to an average annual rate of inflation of 2.6 per cent from 1958 to 1971. From December 1971 to December 1972, that inflation rate increased to 6.5 per cent. The worldwide boom, which began at the end of 1971, was accompanied by inflation rates exceeding 6 per cent in Canada, France, Germany, Italy, Japan and the United States. During the first half of 1973 the economies of most industrialised countries grew rapidly, with the German annual real growth rate reaching close to 6 per cent. This rapid growth of demand, together with poor harvests and cutbacks in world oil production, created particularly strong upward pressures on the prices of food and some key raw materials.

With the decline in aggregate demand and the subsequent recession of 1974–75, the Bundesbank was determined to lock-in medium-term inflationary expectations as inflation declined from its peak. It wanted to provide a simple, yet credible framework for the market to be assured of the central bank's long-term commitment to achieve its price stability objective. Thus, in December 1974, the Bundesbank announced a new monetary policy strategy that would use an aggregate monetary target as its central feature.

Every year since 1975 – and until the launch of the single currency – the Bundesbank derived its monetary target by using a basic formula – the same formula now used by the ECB to set its monetary reference value – that could easily be understood by the general public. At the end of each year, it announced a growth rate of the potential real GDP, to which it added a medium-term inflation rate. Adding together these two percentages gave the nominal growth rate of production potential. By adding the long-term percentage change in the 'velocity of circulation' of money, it obtained the growth rate of the money stock consistent with the production potential.[8] From 1975 to 1985, the medium term inflation assumption embedded in the basic formula was designated by the Bundesbank as the 'unavoidable inflation rate', to take into account the fact that price increases that had already entered into the decisions of the economic agents could not be eliminated immediately. For example, the 'unavoidable inflation rate' was set for 1975 at 4.5 per cent, which was lower than the actual rate of inflation prevailing in 1974, or the 5.6 per cent rate of inflation realised in 1975 (see Table 3.6). As the realised annual rate of inflation fell to 2 per cent and below, the Bundesbank renamed, in 1985, the 'unavoidable inflation' rate as the 'normative price increase', which was defined as a maximum annual rate of 2 per cent in the medium term.

The pre-euro Bundesbank, like the current ECB today, underlined that its monetary policy strategy to achieve its defined price stability objective was not to be interpreted as an inflation targeting strategy. The Bundesbank argued that the length and complexity of the links between the instruments of monetary policy (the short-term key interest rates) and the final objective of maintaining a low inflation rate, precluded such a 'direct' monetary policy strategy for two reasons. First, given the long and variable time lags between the change in the short-term key interest rates and its impact on the inflation rate, the monetary authorities have to react *before* they actually observe the rate of inflation breaching its target value. Thus, the change in the monetary policy stance cannot simply be based on the current rate of inflation, but must necessarily be based on the analysis of a large number of indicators used to project the future inflation rate, so that the monetary policy decision can occur well in advance of the future inflation problem. Secondly, a monetary policy strategy based on a complex analysis of multi-indicators results in a lack of transparency for the general public to determine whether the monetary authorities are credible in their commitment to their final goal. The consequence of this lack of transparency/credibility may lead to undesirable changes in inflationary expectations once the actual inflation rate (or risks to the actual inflation rate) deviates from the presumed target. Thus, the Bundesbank decided to use an 'indirect' monetary policy strategy to reach its final objective. It had to find an intermediate target that satisfied two prerequisites: (i) a stable link between the intermediate target and the final goal (the inflation rate), and (ii) the medium-term controllability of the intermediate target by the Bundesbank. The Bundesbank argued that targeting a monetary aggregate satisfied these two prerequisites. Such a relatively simple monetary policy strategy would allow the general public to monitor whether the Bundesbank was committed to its final goal. The resulting transparency would result in a more credible monetary policy, allowing the central bank to anchor the inflationary expectations of the private economic agents (see Deutsche Bundesbank 1995).

The pre-euro Bundesbank's monetary targets

From 1975 to 1987, the Bundesbank formulated its monetary target in terms of the central bank money stock, which was defined as currency held outside of banks and the required minimum reserves on bank deposits calculated at constant reserve ratios in effect as at January 1974 (16.6 per cent

Table 3.6 Bundesbank monetary targets, inflation objective and the outcomes (with eurozone and US memorandum data)

Year	Target: growth of the central bank money stock or the money stock M3 (from 1988) (%)	Actual growth rate (%)	Monetary target achieved?	Inflation objective ≦ (%) (c)	Actual inflation (%)	Memo item: actual US inflation (%) (d)
1975	8 (a)	10 (a)	no	4.5	5.6	9.1
1976	8 (a)	9 (a)	no	4.5	4.4	5.8
1977	8 (a)	9 (a)	no	3.5	3.6	6.5
1978	8 (a)	11 (a)	no	3.0	2.7	7.6
1979	6–9	6	yes	3.0	4.2	11.3
1980	5–8	5	yes	4.0	5.4	13.5
1981	4–7	4	yes	3.8	6.3	10.3
1982	4–7	6	yes	3.5	5.3	6.2
1983	4–7	7	yes	3.5	3.3	3.2
1984	4–6	5	yes	3.0	2.4	4.3
1985	3–5	5	yes	2.0	2.2	3.6
1986	3.5–5.5	8	no	2.0	−0.6	1.9
1987	3–6	8	no	2.0	1.0	3.6
1988	3–6	7	no	2.0	1.9	4.1
1989	about 5	5	yes	2.0	3.0	4.8
1990	4–6	6	yes	2.0	2.7	5.4
1991	3–5 (b)	5	yes	2.0	4.2	4.2
1992	3.5–5.5	9	no	2.0	3.7	3.0
1993	4.5–6.5	7	no	2.0	4.5	3.0
1994	4–6	6	yes	2.0	2.7	2.6
1995	4–6	2	no	2.0	1.7	2.8
1996	4–7	8	no	2.0	1.4	3.0
1997	3.5–6.5	4.7	yes	2.0	1.9	2.3

	ECB M3: reference growth rate (%)	Eurozone M3: actual growth rate (%)	ECB: inflation objective < (%)	Eurozone: actual inflation rate (%)
1998	3–6	5.5	2.0	1.0
		yes		1.6
1999	4.5	5.6	2.0	1.1
2000	4.5	4.9	2.0	2.3
2001	4.5	5.5	2.0	2.5
2002	4.5		2.0	
				2.2
				3.4
				2.8

Sources: Deutsche Bundesbank 1995; Deutsche Bundesbank, *Annual Report* [year], various issues; *Economic Report of the President* 2001: Table B-63; European Central Bank, *Monthly Bulletin* [month, year], various issues.

Notes:
a   As an annual average growth rate from the previous year to the current year; other monetary figures refer to growth rates from the fourth quarter of the previous year and the fourth quarter of the current year.
b   From 1991 figures for Germany as a whole; target indicated was in accordance with the adjustment of July 1991.
c   Change from previous year in percentage. From 1975–85, the implicit objective was called the 'unavoidable inflation rate'; from 1985–98, it was called the 'normative price increase'.
d   CPI-U; change from previous year in percentage.

128 *Monetary policy*

for sight deposits, 12.4 per cent for time deposits and 8.1 per cent for savings deposits). In 1988, the Bundesbank switched to a broad definition of money, M3, when setting its monetary target. The money stock components of M3 were generally the same – but in different proportions – as those constituting the definition of central bank money. The Bundesbank argued that, by the late 1980s, the heavy weight of currency (50 per cent) in the definition of central bank money combined with the high sensitivity of the demand for currency with interest rates, led to an unreliable relationship between the growth rate of central bank money stock and nominal production potential. The monetary aggregate M3 did not suffer from this shortcoming since the currency component only represented a weight of 11 per cent.

For the period 1975–78, the Bundesbank fixed and announced an annual *point* target growth rate, from December of one year to December of the following year, as its central bank monetary aggregate. As of the end of 1978, the monetary target was fixed and announced at the end of each year as a fourth-quarter to fourth-quarter growth rate (see Table 3.6 and Figure 3.5). The procedure was also changed by targeting an annual fixed growth range of its monetary aggregate, defined as a band of three percentage points (later narrowed to two percentage points as of 1984). A target band instead of a point was chosen to capture the reality that the monetary aggregate is subject to fluctuations that are difficult to control in the short run or that should not be controlled, since velocity may temporarily deviate from trend.

Although it would appear from the above description that the pre-euro Bundesbank monetary policy strategy was to target a monetary aggregate to achieve its primary objective, a recent article by Bernanke and Mihov (1997) shows that the Bundesbank's strategy was closer to inflation-targeting. Until 1990, the Bundesbank record 'indicates a clear negative relationship between deviations of money growth from target and deviations of inflation from target ... [suggesting] its willingness to deviate from money growth targets to offset unexpected inflation' (Bernanke and Mihov 1997: 1044).

Operational instruments

The Bundesbank had available a variety of policy instruments to achieve its monetary target. The principal instruments were the Lombard rate, the discount rate and the 'repo' rate. The relative use and importance of each instrument evolved over time.

The Lombard rate, which formed the upper limit to the overnight interbank rate, was the rate at which the Bundesbank lent on an emergency basis to credit institutions (see Figure 3.6(b)). By the mid-1980s, the Lombard facility became a marginal source of funds for credit institutions that needed emergency overnight liquidity to satisfy their reserve requirements. Lombard

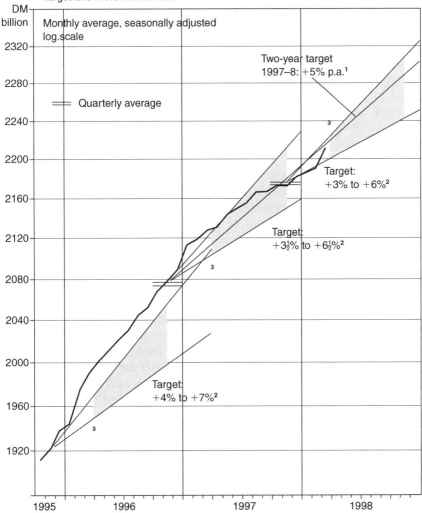

* Average of five bank-week return days; end-of-month levels included with a weight of 50%.
1 Between the fourth quarter of 1996 and the fourth quarter of 1998.
2 Between the fourth quarter of the preceding year and the fourth quarter of the current year.
3 The target corridor has been left unshaded until March because M3 is normally subject to major random fluctuations around the turn of the year.

Figure 3.5 Pre-euro Bundesbank targets of M3: 1995–98.

Source: Deutsche Bundesbank.

loans represented an insignificant percentage of the total funds lent by the Bundesbank (see Figure 3.6(a)). The discount rate, which formed the lower limit to the overnight interbank rate, was the rate at which the Bundesbank granted regular short-term collaterised loans to credit institutions (see Fig. 3.6(b)). Security Repurchase Agreements were purchases of securities by the Bundesbank from the credit institutions that, in turn, repurchased them from the Bundesbank some two weeks later. The interest rate, called the 'repo rate', on this short-term (two-week) loan provided by the Bundesbank to the credit institution, was the difference between the 'purchase' and 'repurchase' price of the security. Starting in the mid-1980s, the securities repurchase agreements ('repos') became an important vehicle for liquidity management (see Deutsche Bundesbank 1985 and Figure 3.6(a)). While rediscounting credit at the discount rate constituted about 84 per cent of the total credit institutions' refinancing provided by the Bundesbank in 1980, by 1993 it represented only 30 per cent of the total refinancing, while the securities repurchase transactions represented about 70 per cent of the total refinancing provided by the Bundesbank. The weekly repurchase tender operations consisted of either *volume tenders* at a fixed interest rate announced by the Bundesbank with an allotment ratio (i.e. the ratio of volume of funds demanded by credit institutions to volume allotted by the Bundesbank) for funds determined by the Bundesbank Directorate, or *variable rate tenders* with either a Dutch-style auction or an American-style auction. Until late 1988, the Bundesbank used only the Dutch-style auction for variable rate tenders, for which the allotment of funds is made at a single rate equal to the marginal interest rate, i.e. the rate of interest at which the volume of funds bid by the credit institutions is equal to the volume allotted by the Bundesbank Directorate. In this Dutch-style auction, the credit institutions were forced to bid for funds at a minimum rate announced by the Bundesbank. After 1988, the Bundesbank used the American-style auction for variable rate tenders, whereby allotments were made in accordance with the credit institutions' bidding requests starting with the highest rates until the total liquidity allotment decided by the Bundesbank Directorate was distributed. Although no minimum bid rate was set in this type of auction, all the bids had to lie necessarily within the corridor set by the Lombard rate and the discount rate. Between February 1996 and December 1998, the Bundesbank conducted only fixed rate tenders since it wanted to provide guidance to short-term market interest rates in the period prior to the launch of the monetary union. The rate was fixed in the corridor defined by a ceiling equal to the Lombard rate and a floor equal to the discount rate, a corridor whose width could typically be between one and two percentage points (see Figure 3.6(b)).

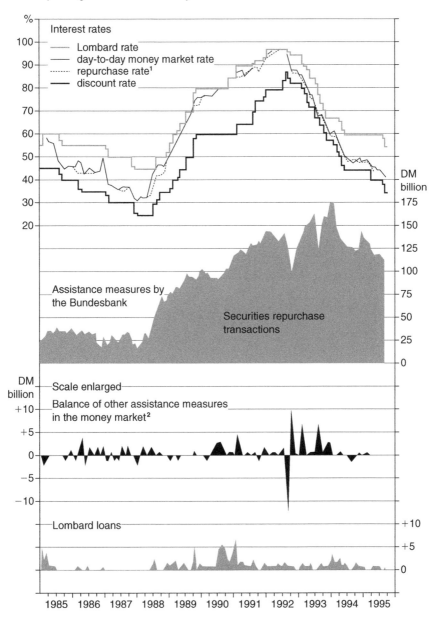

1 Average monthly interest rate for securities repurchase transactions with one-month maturities and, from October 1992, with two-week maturities: uniform allotment rate (fixed-rate tenders) or marginal allotment rate (variable-rate tenders).
2 Quick tenders, foreign exchange swap and repurchase transactions, short-term Treasury bill sales and shifts of Federal balances under section 17 of the Bundesbank Act.

Figure 3.6(a) Pre-euro Bundesbank's Lombard, Discount and Repo rates: 1985–95.
Source: Deutsche Bundesbank.

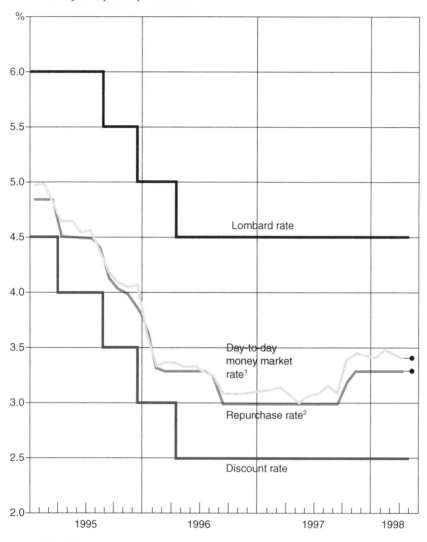

1 Monthly averages.
2 Average rate during the month applied to securities repurchase agreements with two-week maturities; uniform allotment rate (fixed-rate tender) or marginal allotment rate (variable-rate tender). ● = Latest position: 14 May 1998.

Figure 3.6(b) Pre-euro Bundesbank's Lombard, Discount and Repo rates: 1995–98.
Source: Deutsche Bundesbank.

THE FED'S MONETARY POLICY STRATEGY

From the mid-1970s to the end of the 1980s, the Federal Reserve System used some form of monetary targeting as part of its monetary policy strategy to achieve its two principle objectives of price stability and sustainable rate of growth of output. The monetary policy strategy was never conducted by simply setting a monetary target on its own. The strategy combined a monetary target with a target value for an operating instrument such as the federal funds rate, or the borrowed or non-borrowed reserves.[9] From 1975 to 1978 the monetary policy used monetary targets combined with a federal funds (i.e. the overnight interbank rate) target rate; from 1979 to 1989, the monetary policy strategy used monetary targets combined, at first, with a non-borrowed reserve target and, later, with a borrowed reserve target; from 1990 to the present, the monetary policy strategy de-emphasises, and eventually eliminates the monetary target bands and substitutes an analysis of a large body of economic, financial, and survey data to set, at first, a target level of reserves as the operating instrument and, later, a target federal funds rate as the operating instrument.

The period 1975–78: monetary targets combined with the federal funds rate target

In accordance with a Congressional Resolution adopted in March 1975, the Federal Open Market Committee began, in May 1975, to set and to publicly announce ranges of tolerances of annual growth rates of the various definitions of money supply (M1, M2, M3),[10] and of bank credit for the next 12 months. This change in strategy was adopted against the background of accelerating inflation (see Table 3.6). The Chairman of the Board of Governors appeared every quarter before the banking committees of Congress to explain the FOMC's projected 12-month monetary growth ranges. Every three months, the defined annual target ranges were calculated from quarterly average base periods that were moved ahead one quarter at each reporting. This procedure resulted in what is known as an upward 'base drift' of the target zones, a procedure that was often criticised by outside observers. In addition to the target monetary growth rates, the FOMC's discussion in formulating its directive to the New York Fed's Trading Desk included a target range of the federal funds rate. Given the narrow limits of between one-half to one percentage point on the range allowed for changes in the federal funds rate during the inter-meeting periods of the FOMC, and the reluctance to allow large variations of the federal funds target band from meeting to meeting, the monetary target growth rates were often not respected. In many cases, the allowed adjustments in the federal funds rate were inconsistent with the monetary target annual growth rate bands defined by the FOMC, with the consequence that the variations in federal funds rate lagged the movements of the short-term interest rates.

The period 1979–89: monetary targets combined at first with a non-borrowed reserve target (1979–82), and then with a borrowed reserve target

With the acceleration of inflation throughout the 1970s, from 5.7 per cent in 1970 to 11.3 per cent in 1979, and with the new emphasis of price stability objective given to the Federal Reserve System under the Federal Reserve Reform Act (16 November 1977) and the Full Employment and Balanced Growth Act (27 October 1978),[11] the then-recently appointed Chairman of the Board of Governors, Paul Volcker (August 1979–August 1987), decided in October 1979 to change the operating strategy used by the FOMC throughout the 1970s. The Federal Reserve had lost credibility in controlling inflation, with the consequence that the actual rate of inflation was now embedded in the inflationary expectations of economic agents. On 6 October 1979, the Federal Reserve announced a major shift in the technique of implementing monetary policy. As mentioned above, it had attempted to maintain the expansion of monetary aggregates within the target bands by adopting a target for the federal funds rate. Under the new approach, open market operations would control non-borrowed bank reserves consistent with the target rates of monetary growth. At this time, the Federal Reserve continued to have confidence in the longer-term relationship between growth in the monetary aggregates, especially M1, and the rate of inflation. Thus, the monetary growth rate bands were defined to bring about a reduction in the inflation rate. From Autumn 1979 to Autumn 1982, the new operating strategy of the FOMC, designed to maintain the monetary aggregates within the publicly announced target bands, set open-market operation directives in terms of achieving a target path of non-borrowed reserves; namely, the reserves of the banking system not supplied through the discount window. Under the new approach, the federal funds rate varied over a wide range. It is widely believed that the new strategy played an important role in the disinflationary process of the early 1980s.

The usefulness of targeting a non-borrowed reserve path as a means of reducing the inflation rate depended critically on the existence of a predictable, reliable relationship between the monetary aggregates and nominal economic activity. By late 1982, frequent and unpredictable money demand shifts were observed, due in large part to financial deregulation and innovation, which, in particular, affected the demand for the narrowly defined money, M1. For instance, the widespread use of NOW accounts – i.e. interest-bearing chequable deposits included in M1 but considered by their holders, in part, as savings rather than transactions balances – lowered the M1 velocity. On the other hand, the rapid growth of general purpose and broker/dealer money market mutual fund balances, which are included in M2 but not in M1, tended to raise M1 velocity and to lower M2 velocity. Although most money market mutual fund balances were subject to transfer by cheque, the average turnover of these accounts was relatively low. The demand for money, especially M1, was deemed to have become 'unstable' or, in other words, the velocity of money had become unstable. The operating procedure of targeting non-borrowed reserves without taking into account the shifts that may have occurred in the demand for money meant that a given level of non-borrowed reserves would have an unintended effect on the real or nominal aggregate demand by way of an interest rate change. For instance, a sudden decline in the demand for narrow money stock M1, holding constant the level of non-borrowed reserves would result in a decrease in the federal funds rate, as depository institutions found themselves with excess reserves. The decline in interest rates would have an impact on output or prices or both. Consequently, the relationship between the growth rate of the monetary aggregate M1 and the inflation rate was no longer stable.

For these reasons, in late 1982, the FOMC modified once again its operating strategy, placing primary emphasis on borrowed reserves in drafting its directive. The directive referred to the degree of 'pressure on reserve positions'. This procedure enabled the Federal Reserve to be more responsive and accommodative to perceived changes in the demand for money. Unlike the operating procedure of focusing on non-borrowed reserves, any change in the demand for total reserves, due to an exogenous change in the demand for money, could be accommodated by adjusting the non-borrowed reserve path in order to achieve a borrowed reserve objective so as to maintain a constant level of federal funds rate. Again, following the example given above, in the face of a sudden decline in the demand for M1, the New York Fed Trading Desk could maintain the same 'degree of reserve pressure' – i.e. the same borrowed reserve objective – by reducing the non-borrowed reserve path, and thus maintain the same level of federal funds rate. It was argued that this operating strategy implied targeting an associated federal funds rate with the defined degree of 'reserve pressure' (Gilbert 1994). The new procedure also resulted in ignoring the defined target growth rate for the narrow money supply M1 and in officially abandoning the requirement, as of 1986, of defining an annual target growth rate of M1.

Time period 1990–present: the use and analysis of a large array of economic and financial variables to assess future output gap and inflation rate, with a de-emphasis, and eventually an elimination, of monetary target bands; the operating instrument becomes simply a target federal funds rate

In light of the increased uncertainty surrounding the link between a narrow definition of money and nominal economic activity, the Federal Reserve had not set an annual target range for M1 since 1986 and had widened the annual target growth ranges of M2, M3 and total domestic non-financial debt so as to be less binding than in the past. In the 1990s, the FOMC was able to change its monetary policy stance (i.e. the target federal funds rate and/or the discount rate) even when the monetary aggregates were well within their targeted range, or vice-versa. For instance, in 1994, the FOMC's directives sought to increase significantly the 'existing degree of pressure on reserve positions' (i.e. increase the target federal funds rate), even though the growth rates of M2 and M3 were growing at a rate in the lower half of its target range of 1–5 per cent and 0–4 per cent, respectively. To forestall inflation, the Federal Reserve placed pressure on reserve positions so as to raise the federal funds rate by 25 basis points in February 1994. Monetary policy was tightened further in five subsequent policy actions over the course of the year and, by the end of December 1994, the federal funds rate stood 2.5 percentage points higher than in January 1994 (see Table 3.5). On the other hand, in 1998 when M2 and M3 expanded very rapidly, placing those two monetary aggregates well above the upper bound of the 1–5 per cent growth range of M2 and the 2–6 per cent growth range of M3, the FOMC maintained a constant target federal funds rate and even decided to reduce it in the fourth quarter of 1998 (see Table 3.5 and Figure 3.7). Beginning in the 1990s, the Fed's monetary policy strategy responded more to signals relating to the expected future course of output relative to its potential and to the expected future course of prices, than to signals relating to monetary aggregates. In the last quarter of 1998, the FOMC focused more on the potential impact of the Russian debt default and the Asian crisis on US financial markets and the subsequent impact on aggregate demand than on the growth rates of the monetary aggregates. In the final quarter of 1998, the FOMC cited the growing caution by lenders, the 'unsettled conditions' in global financial markets, the risk of commodity price deflation, and fears of a significant slowdown of output growth below its potential in the US to explain the reduction of the federal funds target rate. The easing of monetary policy was not a reaction to any observed weakness of economic activity (the quarter-on-quarter real GDP growth rate of the fourth quarter of 1998 was at an annual rate of 5.9 per cent) but rather a forward-looking action intended to sustain the economic expansion in the face of external shocks. The cumulative 75 basis point reduction in the federal funds rate bought the rate back to its level of September 1994 (see Table 3.5).

Under the Federal Reports Elimination and Sunset Act, passed by Congress in 1995, certain sections of the Full Employment and Balanced Growth Act of 1978 (the 'Humphrey–Hawkins Act') were no longer effective as of mid-2000. In particular, the FOMC is no longer required to set yearly target ranges for the broad monetary aggregates and to present them at the obligatory Congressional hearings held twice a year, at which time the Fed Chairman used to explain any deviations of these monetary aggregates from the announced bands. Accordingly, since July 2000, the

Monetary policy 137

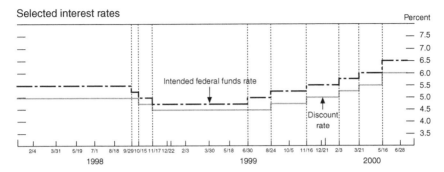

Note: The data are daily. Vertical lines indicate the days on which the Federal Reserve announced a change in the intended funds rate. The dates on the horizontal axis are those on which either the FOMC held a scheduled meeting or a policy action was announced. Last observations are for 17 July 2000.

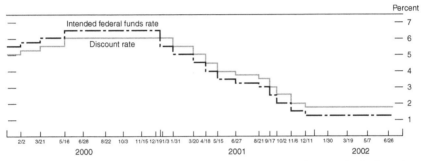

Note: The data are daily and extend through 10 July 2002. The dates on the horizontal axis are those of scheduled FOMC meetings and of any intermeeting policy actions.

Figure 3.7 US discount rate and targeted intended federal funds rate: 1998–2002.
Source: Federal Reserve System.

Federal Reserve no longer defines monetary target ranges as part of its monetary policy strategy, arguing that

> these ranges for many years have not provided useful benchmarks for the conduct of monetary policy. Nevertheless, the FOMC believes that the behavior of money and credit will continue to have value for gauging economic and financial conditions.
> (See Federal Reserve System 2000b: 62)

In the early 1990s, the operating instrument changed from placing an emphasis on borrowed reserves to targeting the federal funds rate. The link between borrowed reserves and the federal funds rate was weakened as a result of the significant reduction in required reserves, the disappearance of routine discount window borrowing, and the public concerns about the financial health of depository institutions. Against the background of the savings and loan associations' difficulties, many depository institutions feared that the public would interpret borrowing at the discount window as an indication of financial problems. Thus, depository institutions changed their behavioural pattern in the use of the discount window. The Fed could no longer control the federal funds rate by targeting a borrowed reserve level. In this new environment, the Federal Reserve gradually attempted to control the federal funds rate rather than a targeted quantity of borrowed reserves. However, the FOMC would continue to phrase its directive in terms of the 'degree of reserve pressure', with the Trading Desk at the New York Fed responsible for interpreting the Committee's preference in terms of an associated federal funds rate (see Federal Reserve Bank of New York 1991: Table 2). It was not until the meeting of August 1997 that the FOMC directive addressed to the New York Fed Trading Desk was explicitly written in terms of a federal funds target rate. However, since 1994, the FOMC has mentioned the federal funds target rate in its public announcement issued immediately following the conclusion of its meeting, thus underlining the importance of that overnight interest rate in formulating its monetary policy operating strategy. The degree of 'reserve pressure' indicated in the FOMC's directive was translated in the press release for the public into a target federal funds rate.

Does the FOMC's monetary policy strategy follow a Taylor rule?

In a well-known paper, Taylor (1993) showed that the monetary policy strategy of the FOMC over the period 1987–92 could be characterised as a simple reaction function (equation) based on a small number of variables. Such a monetary policy strategy is now called a 'Taylor rule'. On the basis of his analysis of the data over that five year period in the US, the policy actions of the FOMC seem to adjust the real short-term interest rate on the basis of the current value of the output gap and the current deviation of inflation from its target rate. For instance, if the current output gap (the difference between aggregate demand and potential output) is positive and/or the current inflation rate is higher than the target inflation rate, the FOMC increases the nominal interest rate sufficiently so as to obtain an increase in the real interest rate from its long-run equilibrium value. The long-run equilibrium value of the real interest rate, called the 'neutral rate', is the real rate prevailing when both the output gap is zero and the rate of inflation is equal to the target rate of inflation. Algebraically, the 'Taylor rule' can be written as follows:

$$r_t = r^* + \alpha(y_t - y^*) + \beta(\pi_t - \pi^*)$$

Monetary policy 139

where r_t is the current real interest rate, defined as the nominal interest rate less the target rate of inflation, i.e. $(i_t - \pi^*)$ where i is the nominal interest rate, which is the policy instrument of the Fed;
r^* is the long-run equilibrium value of the real interest rate (the 'neutral rate');
y_t is the current real value of aggregate demand;
y^* is the potential level of output;
π_t is the current rate of inflation;
π^* is the Fed's target rate of inflation
α and β are the coefficients representing the weights placed by the FOMC on its two policy objectives, namely on maintaining a sustainable growth rate of output and price stability (i.e. a low rate of inflation π^*).

According to this monetary policy strategy, the Fed manipulates the short-term nominal interest rate so as to raise or lower the real interest rate variable (the left-hand side of the equation) above or below its neutral rate, depending on whether the sum of the output gap and inflation gap $(\pi_t - \pi^*)$, each weighted by its appropriate coefficient, is positive or negative, respectively. Thus, when the current real interest rate is below r^*, the Fed has an expansionary monetary policy stance, and conversely when the current real interest rate is above r^*, the Fed has a restrictive monetary policy stance.

THE FED'S PRINCIPAL OPERATIONAL INSTRUMENTS

A brief description of the currently available monetary policy instruments of the Fed is given below. A comparative summary with the monetary policy instruments used by the ECB and the pre-euro Bundesbank is presented in Table 3.2. It is recalled here that, with the exception of the discount rate mechanism, all the monetary policy instruments of the Fed are centralised in the hands of the Trading Desk of the Federal Reserve Bank of New York and all open-market operations conducted with the major bond dealers in New York are entered in the System Open Market Account (SOMA) held at the New York Fed. This is in contrast to the existing organisation of the Eurosystem where all the eurozone NCBs participate in the execution of open-market operations (i.e. the main refinancing operations) conducted with the credit institutions located in their respective country.

Repurchase agreements (RPs); matched sale-purchase transactions (SPs)

The principal operating instrument of the Federal Reserve System is open-market operations to target an announced federal funds rate. The federal funds rate is the overnight interest rate on funds that depository institutions lend to, or borrow from, each other in order to maintain a certain level of reserves necessary to satisfy both the required reserve and the excess reserve balances of depository institutions, the latter used for settlement and clearing purposes. Since the passage of the Monetary Control Act in 1980, the Board of Governors of the Federal Reserve System requires all depository institutions – commercial banks regardless of membership in the Federal Reserve System, savings banks, savings and loan associations, credit unions, branches and agencies of foreign banks, and Edge Act and agreement corporations[12] – to hold a percentage of their deposits as required reserves. The Federal Reserve pays neither interest on required reserves nor on excess reserves held by depository institutions in accounts at the district Federal Reserve Banks, or indirectly on a pass-through basis in accounts at other approved depository institutions.[13]

The federal funds rate is a market-determined short-term interest rate. Whenever it rises above or falls below the target rate announced by the FOMC, the Federal Reserve System engages in open-market operations to provide indirectly liquidity to, or absorb liquidity from, the depository institutions. The Federal Reserve Bank of New York is the District Bank authorised by the FOMC to execute those operations. When the Federal Reserve System wishes to provide liquidity to the depository institutions, the System Trading Desk at the Federal Reserve Bank of New York engages in short-term repurchase agreements (RPs) with authorised counter-parties, who are the major bond dealers in US government and Federal Agency bonds. The System Open Market Account (SOMA) buys securities from dealers who agree to repurchase them by a specified date at a specified price. Whenever a bond dealer engages in a RP agreement with the System Trading Desk, the initial transaction increases the reserves in depository institutions as the System credits the reserve account of each dealer's bank. The System determines the total amount of RPs that are needed to meet reserve objectives necessary to maintain the target federal funds rate. The auction for RPs is a decision taken by the Federal Reserve System (open-market desk at the Federal Reserve Bank of New York) on a daily basis, based on the market conditions and the general policy directive received from the FOMC. These operations are usually conducted several times a week. Repurchase agreements for the SOMA account may have a maturity term ranging from one to 90 days, but most mature within seven days. The securities negotiated in these transactions are primarily outstanding US Treasury bills with a maturity of one year or less. The Federal Reserve Bank of New York arranges all the offers of the bond dealers in descending order and then accepts those offers with the highest rates until the total designated amount of funds has been allocated to the bond dealers. This is the so-called 'variable rate, American-style' auction of repurchase agreements, with no minimum bid rate.

Monetary policy 141

Whenever the Federal Reserve System wishes to absorb reserves from depository institutions, it engages with the authorised bond dealers in matched sale–purchase transactions (SPs). These transactions involve a contract for the immediate sale of securities to, and a matching contract for subsequent purchase from, each participating dealer. Matched SP agreements are less frequently used than RPs since reserves can be automatically drained whenever maturing RPs are not renewed.

Outright purchases and sales

In addition to the repurchase agreements or the matched sale–purchase transactions, the Federal Reserve System may engage in outright purchases or sales of government securities (US Treasury securities and Federal Agency Obligations). These transactions are another type of open market operation to provide liquidity to, or absorb liquidity from, depository institutions. In contrast to the temporary provision or absorption of liquidity with the repurchase/matched sale–purchase agreements, the outright transactions are of a permanent nature since they do not involve any reverse transaction at some later date. Outright transactions represent a small percentage of the total open market operations conducted by the System. For example, in 1998, outright purchases of US Treasury securities and Federal Agency Obligations amounted to $3.5 billion, whereas repurchase agreements amounted to some $797 billion (Federal Reserve System 1998: 321).

Discount rate

The Federal Reserve's lending at the discount rate, which is set by the Board of Governors upon the request of each individual district Federal Reserve Bank, primarily facilitates the balance sheet adjustments of individual banks that face temporary, unforeseen changes in their asset-liability structure. Although both lending at the discount window and open-market operations with bond dealers have comparable effects on the availability of liquidity, discount window operations are better suited to fulfil the liquidity needs of individual depository institutions.

The role of the discount rate has changed over the years. In the 1920s, the discount window was the primary instrument to implement monetary policy. Federal Reserve Bank lending represented a large part of the total reserves of banks, with the discount rates as the principal monetary policy indicators of the Federal Reserve Banks. Today, with a well-developed financial market in US securities, a well-developed inter-bank loan market, and a single financial market over the entire territory of the US, open market operations with bond dealers provide depository institutions with the necessary liquidity to maintain the inter-bank overnight interest rate (the federal funds' rate) close to the target rate announced by the

System. Given the relatively small volume of borrowing at the discount window (the total outstanding Federal Reserve Bank loans at month-end varied between $13 million and $1 billion in 1998), the discount rate changes today are either to bring that official rate in line with market rates or to use it as an announcement effect regarding monetary policy stance. Since the passage of the Monetary Control Act of 1980, all depository institutions holding deposits subject to reserve requirements have access to the discount window. Prior to that, only banks that were members of the Federal Reserve System had access to the discount window.

The three types of discount window credit are short-term adjustment credit, seasonal credit and extended credit. In all cases, the Federal Reserve Bank provides credit to depository institutions at its own discretion. The discount window is to be used as a safety valve in the reserve market. Since the basic discount rate, the rate charged on loans to depository institutions for short-term adjustment credit, is usually below short-term money market rates, including the federal funds rate, there is a pecuniary incentive on the part of credit institutions to fund their reserve needs at the discount window, which explains the need for discretionary allocation of discount window lending by the Federal Reserve Banks. The short-term adjustment credit provided by the Federal Reserve Banks may be related to the liquidity needs of depository institutions arising from unexpected loss of deposits, which are usually beyond the institution's control. The seasonal credit loans are primarily directed towards the small credit agricultural institutions that face strong loan demand during the planting and growing seasons. Extended credit loans by Federal Reserve Banks are usually provided in the context of loans to depository institutions that have financial difficulties but also have reasonable prospects of resolving these difficulties in an orderly fashion, such as the process of being acquired by another healthy depository institution. The discount rates related to the seasonal credit and the extended credit are higher than the basic discount rate and closer to market-related rates.

4 Economic policy coordination in the eurozone

Monetary policy in the eurozone is made by one supranational body, the European Central Bank; the other principal economic policies in the eurozone are made by the governments of each Member State composing the eurozone. While there is a single monetary policy for the entire eurozone, there are as many different macroeconomic and microeconomic policies as there are Member States. In order to understand the coordination of economic policies between the governments of the eurozone Member States, this chapter describes the economic policy framework that has evolved in the European Union to coordinate policies between Member States that essentially retain all their national powers in most economic policy areas. Since the macroeconomic policies taken by all the eurozone Member States have an impact on the monetary policy decisions taken by the ECB, we also describe the institutional channels that have been set up for the communication between the ECB and the Community bodies responsible for the coordination of the Member States' economic policies. This entire economic policy framework, composed on the one hand of 12 national governments and the Community bodies responsible for the coordination of their policies, and on the other hand, of these Community bodies interacting with the one central bank, is complex and bureaucratic, a criticism often levelled by expressing the view that the eurozone is an economic space with a single central bank and no single 'economic government'. As shown below, this is an exaggeration. However, the fear of a possible economic policy-making vacuum at the eurozone level in the event of a major financial crisis is justified since the European Central Bank has not been given the power to play the role of the 'lender of last resort'. We therefore also describe in this chapter the role of the national governments, Community bodies and the Eurosystem in the prudential supervision of financial institutions and in the maintenance of stability of the financial system.

THE ECONOMIC POLICY FRAMEWORK

Since the creation of the European Economic Community in 1957, provisions for economic policy coordination between Member States have been incorporated into the Treaties and implemented by the adoption of Community secondary legislation, known as Decisions, Regulations and Directives. For example, Article 105.1 of the Treaty establishing the European Economic Community (also known as the Treaty of Rome [1957]) stipulated:

> In order to facilitate the attainment of the objectives [of each Member State] stated in Article 104 [balance of payment equilibrium, stable exchange rate, high level of employment, price stability], Member States shall *coordinate* their economic policies.

Key Council Decisions of July 1969, March 1971, February 1974 and March 1990[1] were all adopted with a view to implement the notions of economic policy coordination between the Member States, stipulated in various articles of the Treaty of Rome.

The July 1969 Council Decision required the Member States to hold prior consultations with the Commission and the Council, regarding important short-term economic policy measures that may substantially affect the economies of the other Member States. The March 1971 Council Decisions, resulting from the Resolution (political agreement) to launch the process to achieve progressively an Economic and Monetary Union by 1980, strengthened the coordination of short-term economic policies of the Member States and the cooperation between the central banks of the Member States. The February 1974 Council Decision, which superseded one of the March 1971 Decisions, called on Member States to attain a high degree of convergence of their economic policies. The March 1990 Council Decision, which in turn superseded the February 1974 Decision, required the attainment of progressive convergence of economic policies and performance during Stage I of the Economic and Monetary Union, with twice-yearly multilateral surveillance by the Commission and the Council of each Member State's policies and performance in the areas of price stability, public finances, interest rates and exchange rates. Some 35 years after the ratification of the Treaty of Rome, Article 99 of the Maastricht Treaty, which came into force in November 1993, still stipulates the requirement for the Member States to coordinate their economic policies:

> Member States shall regard their economic policies as a matter of common concern and shall coordinate them within the Council...
> (Article 99.1 of the 'Treaty')

One of the criticisms levelled at the eurozone economic policy framework is the lack of coordination between monetary policy and other aspects of macroeconomic policy, which may lead to an undesirable 'policy mix' between the two. While monetary policy is centralised in a supranational institution and must be formulated and executed without any pressure from either national governments or Community institutions, the Maastricht and Amsterdam Treaties do not provide for a centralised economic policy framework for budgetary/fiscal policy, employment policy or microeconomic structural reforms. These responsibilities remain at the national level. The Community bodies, such as the Ecofin Council composed of Finance Ministers from all EU Member States, only provide the guidelines to be followed by each Member State in order to achieve the goals set by the Community in these areas. Compounding the coordination problems for the eurozone is the fact that, according to the 'Treaty', the group of Finance Ministers from the eurozone Member States (the Eurogroup) is not even legally recognised as a Community body authorised to adopt measures to coordinate economic policies within the eurozone. There is clearly no 'economic government' at either the EU or eurozone level. However, it is important to realise that the Maastricht Treaty and the Amsterdam Treaty have considerably increased the degree of coordination of economic policies among the Member States and have led to an on-going dialogue between the European Central Bank and the Community bodies composed of the representatives of the eurozone Member States. This section provides an overview of the EU economic policy framework, with special emphasis on the roles of the European Council, the Commission, the Ecofin Council and the Eurogroup in the area of economic policy coordination and on the communication links between the European Central Bank and the Eurogroup.

The broad economic policy guidelines

The responsibilities for budgetary/fiscal policy, employment policy and microeconomic structural reforms remain at the national level, although the Community institutions formulate and adopt – according to a formal procedure involving the Commission, the Ecofin Council and the European Council – Broad Economic Policy Guidelines (BEPGs) that each Member State is expected to follow. The Community institutions also examine and assess through a multilateral surveillance procedure whether the Member States' policies and performance are in line with the goals set by the Community. The Ecofin Council, acting on a recommendation from the Commission, can make individual recommendations to Member States that perform poorly in these areas.

According to the provisions of Articles 98 and 99 of the 'Treaty', the Broad Economic Policy Guidelines lie at the heart of the economic policy coordination procedure between the EU Member States. Article 98 provides that:

Member States shall conduct their economic policies with a view to contributing to the achievement of the objectives of the Community, as defined in Article 2,[2] and in the context of the broad guidelines referred to in Article 99.2...

Article 99.2 stipulates:

The [Ecofin] Council shall, acting by a qualified majority on a recommendation from the Commission, formulate a draft for the broad guidelines of the economic policies of the Member States and of the Community, and shall report its findings to the European Council.

The European Council shall, acting on the basis of the report from the [Ecofin] Council, discuss a conclusion on the broad guidelines of the economic policies of the Member States and of the Community.

On the basis of this conclusion, the [Ecofin] Council shall, acting by a qualified majority, adopt a recommendation setting out these broad guidelines. The [Ecofin] Council shall inform the European Parliament of its recommendation.

The BEPGs contain overall and country-specific policy recommendations that are drawn up annually by the Commission after the Spring European Council meeting (March of each year) and submitted to the Ecofin Council. Acting by a qualified majority on the Commission *recommendation*,[3] the Council formulates a draft for the European Council, which in turn discusses a conclusion on the BEPGs. The BEPGs are formally adopted in June by the Ecofin Council, in the form of a recommendation to the Member States. Although an Ecofin Council recommendation addressed to a Member State is not legally binding on the Member State, the 'Implementation Report' of the BEPGs, written by the Commission (see, for example, European Commission 2002c), 'praises and shames' each Member State, as a way of forcing peer pressure on the Ministers not to ignore their political commitment to implement the BEPGs. When the Irish budgetary plans for 2001 were considered expansionary and pro-cyclical and therefore inconsistent with the 2000 BEPGs adopted in the previous year, the Commission recommended the Ecofin Council address to the Irish government a recommendation to immediately take measures to deal with the inconsistency. The Commission recommendation was adopted by the Ecofin Council, acting by qualified majority, at its meeting of 12 February 2001 (Council 2001). The Ecofin Council also decided to make its recommendation public. As from 2003, in line with the decision taken at the Barcelona European Council meeting of March 2002, the Commission and the Ecofin Council will focus more on the implementation by the Member States of the BEPGs, which will be elaborated as medium term guidelines rather than yearly ones.

The three principal areas covered in the BEPGs are the budgetary (fiscal) policies, the employment policies and the microeconomic structural reforms in the goods, services and financial markets. The legal basis for including each policy area in the BEPGs is somewhat different. The budgetary/fiscal policy guidelines are covered under Article 104 of the 'Treaty' (paragraphs 2–8, 10 and 12–13 became effective as of the beginning of Stage 2 of EMU in 1994; the other paragraphs entered into force as of the beginning of Stage 3 of EMU in 1999) and further developed and extended by the Stability and Growth Pact as described below and in European Commission 1999b: Sections F3 and F4. The Stability and Growth Pact principally deals with the annual surveillance of each EU Member State's medium-term budgetary balance, which is to be close to zero or positive over the economic cycle, and with the implementation of the excessive deficit procedure, which is set off whenever the ratio of a Member State's budgetary deficit to GDP exceeds the 3 per cent reference value.

The employment policy guidelines are included in the BEPGs in accordance with the employment section of the Treaty of Amsterdam (Articles 125–130 of the EC Treaty), which states that

> Member States, through their employment policies, shall contribute to the achievement of the objectives referred to in Article 125 [to develop a coordinated strategy for employment to achieve objectives defined in Article 2] in a way consistent with the broad guidelines of the economic policies of the Member States and of the Community adopted pursuant to Article 99.2.
>
> (Article 126.1)

The main features and methods of coordinating the employment policies of the Member States have been dubbed the 'Luxembourg process', named after the city where an Extraordinary European Council meeting on Employment was held in November 1997 to launch the application of the employment section of the Treaty of Amsterdam (1997). The procedure, which must respect the principle of subsidiarity (decentralised approach) enshrined in Articles 5 and 127.1 of the EC Treaty, is as follows. Each year, on a *proposal* from the Commission, the Council (Employment and Social Policy) draws up guidelines that the Member States must take into account in their employment policies to promote a skilled, trained and adaptable workforce, and a flexible labour market. Each Member State then provides to the Commission and the Council a multi-annual 'National Action Plan', which is a detailed presentation of the measures that it plans to implement within the framework of the Employment Guidelines established by the Community. These Plans may be revised each year in order to be in line with the revised Community employment guidelines. The implementation of the Plans is later examined in an annual Joint Commission and Council 'Employment Report', which contains a comparative overview of Member States' performance, some examples of good practice, and possible recommendations to any Member State that falls short of its National Action Plan. The Council recommendations on employment policy are neither binding, nor accompanied by legal or financial sanctions. However, annual multilateral surveillance, which includes comparative results among the Member States, such as benchmarking relative to the best practice, places peer pressure on the Member States to force them to comply with their commitments in this area.

The microeconomic structural reforms in the goods, services and capital markets, begun in the late 1980s with the ratification of the Single European Act (1986), are aimed at improving competitiveness and the functioning of the markets in goods, services and capital across all the EU Member States. This structural reform goal, known as the 'Cardiff process' after its endorsement at the Cardiff European Council meeting of June 1998, is integrated in the annual formulation of the BEPGs as a means to complete the single market. The Cardiff process was first proposed by the Ecofin Council when the 11 Member States were designated to compose the initial eurozone (see European Commission 1999b: section E2, paragraphs 8 and 9). Each year, the annual BEPGs take into account the Commission's Cardiff report, which includes a scoreboard of indicators of effective market integration.

Community oversight of budgetary policies of Member States

When the EMU provisions of the Maastricht Treaty were drafted, the German government and Bundesbank insisted on the necessity that the governments of Member States participating in the monetary union comply with some basic rules regarding their budget deficits, lest the loose budgetary policies of undisciplined governments should have spillover effects on the overall level of interest rates in the eurozone. A large eurozone Member State or a few small Member States running persistent structural deficits may increase the risk premium incorporated in all Member States' government bond yields. Thus, not only would the Member States have to satisfy certain budgetary criteria before joining the monetary union, but the Member States would also have to respect certain budgetary rules once admitted into the monetary union. Sanctions and, as a last resort, fines would be imposed on the violators. Given the political commitment made by the EU as of mid 1995 to target 1999 as the start of Stage 3 of EMU, the Ecofin Council decided in 1997 to use the already existing multilateral surveillance provision of the coordination of economic policies under Article 99.3 of the Maastricht Treaty as a means to impose medium-term budgetary guidelines on all Member States. Furthermore, the Ecofin Council decided, at the same time, to clarify the implementation of the excessive deficit procedure, described in Article 104, with particular reference to (1) the circumstances under which the 'three per cent budgetary deficit rule' may be overridden, and (2) the sanctions and fines imposed on euro Member States that are deemed to have violated that particular budgetary deficit rule.

The medium-term budgetary rule

In the context of the Council's power to define Broad Economic Policy Guidelines (BEPGs) for the Community and its Member States under 'Treaty' Article 99, the Ecofin Council stipulated (Council Regulation 1466/97/EC) that, beginning in mid 1998, all Member States (including Britain) should adhere to the medium term objective of budgetary positions that are close to balance or in surplus. Since the medium term is defined as the length of the business cycle, this rule would permit the Member State to benefit from the use of the automatic fiscal policy stabilisers during an economic downturn, provided that the Member State ran surpluses during 'good times'. In other words, discretionary budgetary policies should not be pro-cyclical. The Council, after a recommendation from the Commission, would examine the medium term budgetary positions, on the basis of the Stability Programmes and Convergence Programmes submitted once a year by each Member State participating in the single currency area and by each Member State outside the eurozone, respectively. The Council can only make recommendations to the Member State concerned and can only use peer pressure to force it to implement the recommendation. No sanctions can be imposed. Thus, secondary legislation adopted under 'Treaty' Article 99 is known in Community parlance as a 'soft law'. Yet, as has been observed in early 2002 when the Commission recommended to the Ecofin Council to send an 'early warning' letter to Germany and Portugal under the provisions of Article 6.2 of Council Regulation 1466/97/EC of the Stability and Growth Pact ('...significant divergence of the budgetary position from the medium-term budgetary objective, or the adjustment path towards it...'), even the threat of implementing a 'soft law' can have its desired effect (see Council 2002). Both the German and Portuguese governments made written commitments to the Council, in line with the concerns expressed by the Commission, to avoid the 'early warning' notice from the Council. These two governments promised in particular that they would not allow their planned government deficits for the year 2002 to 'slip' from their announced targets and that they would respect the 2004 target date to achieve a balanced budget, to prevent the 'medium-term budgetary position of close to balance or in surplus' from becoming a moving target.

The excessive deficit rule

In accordance with the Council's obligation to monitor excessive government deficits under the provisions of Article 104, the Member State's planned budgetary position of a current calendar year, submitted each year by the end of February at the latest, is examined to determine whether the Member State is in breach of the budgetary rule that prohibits a budgetary deficit of more than 3 per cent of GDP. If that should be the case, Ecofin makes a recommendation to the Member State to avoid such a situation. If, some nine months later, the Member State has not taken the appropriate measures, sanctions are imposed. This procedure, which is only outlined in the 'Treaty' Article 104, is clarified and described in detail in the Council Regulation 1467/97/EC as part of the Stability and Growth Pact adopted in 1997 and implemented at the beginning of Stage 3 of EMU. In particular, a strict time frame is placed on the process between the time a Member State submits a planned budget that is in breach of the deficit rule and the time that sanctions and fines are imposed. Thus, these provisions of the Stability and Growth Pact are known in Community language as a 'hard law'. The procedure also specifies the circumstances under which the '3 per cent deficit rule' may be overridden.

Exemptions to the excessive deficit procedure

The condition under which a Member State may have a planned government deficit over 3 per cent of GDP without being in breach of the Regulation is whenever the excess government deficit is the result of

- an exceptionally severe recession ('exceptionally severe economic downturn'), defined as an annual fall of real GDP of at least 2 per cent, which automatically exempts the Member State from the excessive deficit procedure, without the need for the Ecofin Council to adopt a decision to that effect, or
- a severe recession ('severe economic downturn'), defined as an annual fall of real GDP of at least 0.75 per cent but less than 2.0 per cent, coupled with a formal Ecofin decision for an exemption, adopted by a qualified majority and based on an assessment that takes into account the overall economic situation and any observations made by the Member State.

The Member States, in a Resolution adopted at the Amsterdam European Council meeting of June 1997, committed themselves not to invoke the exemption clause of the excessive deficit procedure for annual real GDP growth rates greater than −0.75 per cent. A study done by the Commission (Buti *et al.* 1997) shows that a 'severe recession' among the 15 Member States occurred 30 times over the period 1961–96, i.e. an average of two cases per country. The number of years of negative growth of between −0.75 per cent and −2.00 per cent is distributed unevenly among Member States. The Nordic countries as well as Belgium, Germany, Portugal and the United Kingdom registered a larger number of 'severe recessions' years compared with the average, while Spain, France, Luxembourg and the Netherlands recorded a small number of cases. There were seven cases – all small states, except for one (Italy) – where real GDP fell by 2 per cent or more in one year ('exceptionally severe recession').

The implementation of the excessive deficit procedure

Since the beginning of Stage 2 of EMU in 1994, Member States have to report their planned government deficits for year n twice a year to the Commission; the first time before 1 March of year n and the second time before 1 September of year n. Within three months of those reporting dates, the Ecofin Council has to decide whether an excessive government deficit for year n exists, and if so, the Council has to make a recommendation to the Member State concerned to take appropriate measures, within four months, to avoid an excessive deficit. If the Council decides that no effective action has been taken by the Member State, sanctions may be imposed within the next three months. Thus, within ten months of the reporting date by the Member State of its planned government deficit that is considered to be excessive, the sanctions are imposed.

When the Ecofin Council decides to apply sanctions to a eurozone Member State – the Member States outside the eurozone cannot have sanctions imposed on them – a non-interest bearing deposit is required. The amount of the first deposit is composed of a fixed component equal to 0.2 per cent of GDP and a variable component, equal to 0.1 per cent of GDP for each percentage point of excessive government deficit of year n above the reference value of 3 per cent. Moreover, any single deposit cannot exceed the upper limit of 0.5 per cent of GDP. If the excessive deficit persists more than one year, additional deposits are required following the same rule, but excluding the fixed component. Non-interest bearing deposits are converted into fines if, two years after the decision to require a deposit, the excessive deficit has not been corrected. The fines are, in turn, distributed to the eurozone Member States that do not run excessive deficits. To date (mid-2002), and since the start of the third stage of EMU in 1999, the excessive deficit procedure spelled out in Article 104 and in the provisions of Council Regulation 1467/97 (part of the Stability and Growth Pact) has not been applied to any Member State.

Lack of real progress on reduction of public deficits and debt

Sound public finances over the medium term are a necessary condition for sustained economic growth. Sound public finances contribute to maintaining a low interest rate, which is conducive to private investment – the engine of long-term growth and employment. Sound public finances require public budgetary surpluses for countries that already have high debt to GDP ratios (such as Italy, Belgium and Greece; see Table 4.1), to

Table 4.1 General government balance (as a percentage of GDP, 1998–2004)

Eurozone Member State	1998	1999	2000	2001	2002	2003	2004	Gross debt, % of GDP, 2002
Belgium	−0.8	−0.6	0.1	0.0	−0.2	0.2	0.6	104.3
Germany	−2.2	−1.6	−1.3	−2.7	−2.8	−2.1	−1.0	60.8
Greece				−0.4	0.3	0.5	1.2	97.9
Spain	−2.6	−1.1	−0.4	−0.2	−0.3	0.0	0.1	55.5
France	−2.7	−1.6	−1.3	−1.5	−2.0	−1.8	−0.5	57.4
Ireland	2.3	2.3	4.5	1.7	0.4	0.2	−0.6	33.6
Italy	−2.8	−1.8	−1.7	−1.4	−1.3	−1.3	0.0	107.8
Luxembourg	3.2	3.8	5.8	5.0	2.0	2.5	3.4	5.2
Netherlands	−0.8	0.4	1.5	0.2	0.0	−0.4	0.5	50.1
Austria	−2.4	−2.2	−1.9	0.1	−0.1	0.3	0.2	60.2
Portugal	−2.3	−2.2	−1.9	−2.7	−2.6	−2.5	0.0	56.2
Finland	1.3	1.9	7.0	4.9	3.3	2.7	2.6	43.1
Eurozone	−2.2	−1.3	−0.8	−1.3	−1.5	−1.2	−0.2	68.6
(Cyclically adjusted)	−2.1	−1.3	−1.3	−1.5	−1.2	−1.2		
USA	0.3	0.9	1.7	0.5	−0.7	−0.9		

Source:
European Commission (2002a). Figures for 2002 and 2003 are calculated by the Commission based on its Spring 2002 forecasts. Figures for 2004 are based on the obligatory Stability Programmes submitted by each eurozone Member State between October 2001 and January 2002. As of mid-2002, those figures have been amended by some Member States: Germany: 'close to balance', i.e. −0.5 per cent; France: figure is conditional on GDP growth rate of 3 per cent per year in 2003 and 2004; Italy: −0.3 per cent. Moreover, Italy was forced by the Commission to correct its accounting methods for the calendar 2001 deficit. Thus, with the restatement, the 2001 deficit is 2.2 per cent of GDP instead of the figure indicated in this table.

allow a reduction of the public debt and interest burden, creating room for reduction in taxes and/or increases in productive public spending. The Stability and Growth Pact seeks to promote sound public finances so as to provide the necessary room for the operation of the automatic stabilisers over the economic cycle. Thus, a Member State experiencing low or negative growth could allow an automatic budgetary deficit to appear to cushion the fluctuation of economic activity, provided that the Member State allowed a budgetary surplus to appear during periods of high growth. The need to allow the automatic budgetary stabilisers to function symmetrically over the cycle is all the more important for the Member States participating in the eurozone, since the monetary policy instrument can no longer be used by a particular Member State to cushion fluctuations in output.

Although the public deficit to GDP ratio in the eurozone Member States decreased from 2.2 per cent in 1998 to 0.8 per cent in 2000, and the public debt to GDP ratio decreased from 73.7 per cent to 70.2 per cent respectively, the goal of achieving a surplus budgetary position in an expansionary period, with a debt to GDP ratio declining to 60 per cent, is still far off (see Table 4.1). Compared with the US, the eurozone public finance ratios are clearly lagging the performance of the US in creating surpluses with a rapidly declining debt to GDP ratio. On the basis of the compulsory annual Stability Programmes submitted by the eurozone Member States between October 2001 and January 2002 in accordance with the requirements of the Stability and Growth Pact, the Commission calculated that, in 2004, the eurozone will still register a small deficit ratio of about 0.2 per cent of GDP (European Commission 2002a: 35).[4] Despite a real GDP growth rate of 3.4 per cent in 2000, the eurozone registered a public budgetary deficit to GDP ratio of 0.8 per cent, which does not include the government revenues from the one-off sale of UMTS (Universal Mobile Telecommunications System) licence sales. The improvement in the 'headline' public budgetary balances was primarily due to strong growth and lower debt service. In fact, the *cyclically adjusted primary* surpluses of the eurozone declined from 2.7 per cent of GDP in 2000 to 2.4 per cent of GDP in 2001. The debt/GDP ratio is projected to decline to 68.6 per cent by the end of 2002. As of 2002, there are still four eurozone Member States that are far from approaching a balanced budget, even if adjusted for the cyclical effect: Germany, France, Italy and Portugal. There is apprehension that the eurozone will not be able to generate surpluses before the next recession or before the slowdown in economic activity. Moreover, most Member States have not yet taken the necessary steps to meet the budgetary challenges of population ageing. On the other hand, the US has been running budgetary surpluses since 1998, with a budgetary surplus of 0.5 per cent to GDP in 2001 and a projected ratio of the publicly held federal government debt to GDP equal to 30 per cent by 2002. The US Treasury conducted highly visible buyback operations in

2000, repurchasing a total of $30 billion par value of its debt. Some recent projections in the US indicate that the publicly held federal debt may be entirely eliminated by the end of the decade (US Congress, 2000 and 2001).

'One-size-fits-all' monetary policy and national budgetary policies

Eurozone Member States that have been running persistent budgetary deficits need to achieve small budgetary surpluses and a lower debt to GDP ratio in the medium term to allow them, in the short-run, to benefit from the use of the automatic and discretionary mechanism of budgetary/fiscal policy to stabilise, if necessary, the national economy in the context of a single monetary policy. In a single currency area with a single monetary policy, the monetary policy decisions are always taken on the basis of the *average* variables in the single currency area, not the 'regional' (national) values of those variables.[5] This is true for an economy as large and as geographically diversified as the United States, Canada or the eurozone. However, unlike the case of a region in the US or Canada, a Member State in the eurozone cannot rely on labour mobility between Member States – since it is insignificant – or on the automatic countercyclical fiscal policy at the eurozone level to redistribute taxes and social benefits between Member States – since it does not exist – to absorb the effect of the single monetary policy that may be inappropriate for the Member State's current economic environment. At any given time, the economies of the eurozone may not be well synchronised in terms of either the cyclical growth rate of the GDP or the inflation rate. Since the single monetary policy is determined by an examination of the monetary, economic and financial variables based on the average variables in the eurozone, a Member State may need to rely on its national budgetary/fiscal policy to offset the effects of the single monetary policy that is inappropriate for its current economic environment. Given the constraints imposed by the Community Stability and Growth Pact, the Member State will only be able to use the automatic and discretionary fiscal stabilisers that result in a deficit if it has, in the past, respected the medium term rule of running, at a minimum, a balanced budget and has achieved a public debt to GDP ratio below 60 per cent.

Recent figures of real GDP growth rates between the individual Member States of the eurozone show that there are divergences both between the three major countries, namely Germany, France and Italy – which together represent 70 per cent of the eurozone GDP – and between those three countries and the periphery eurozone countries. The 1998–2001 figures shown in Table 4.2 indicate that France outperformed both Germany and Italy and that the periphery countries – namely Ireland, Finland, Spain and Portugal, which together account for 15 per

Table 4.2 GDP growth rates and HICP inflation rates, 1998–2002 for the eurozone and its Member States (EUR-11 prior to 2001 and EUR-12 from 2001 onwards)

Member States of eurozone; and USA	Annual percentage rate of growth of real GDP					Trend growth rate of real change of GDP, 1994–98, annual % rate**	Annual percentage rate of inflation as measured by the HICP				
	Years						Years				
	1998	1999	2000	2001	2002*		1998	1999	2000	2001	2002*
BE	2.2	3.0	4.0	1.0	1.1	2.2	0.9	1.1	2.7	2.4	1.7
DE	2.0	1.8	3.0	0.6	0.8	2.2	0.6	0.6	2.1	2.4	1.8
EL				4.1	3.7					3.7	3.6
ES	4.3	4.1	4.1	2.8	2.1	2.7	1.8	2.2	3.5	3.2	3.0
FR	3.4	2.9	3.1	2.0	1.6	2.0	0.7	0.6	1.8	1.8	1.7
IE	8.6	10.8	11.5	6.8	3.5	9.2	2.1	2.5	5.3	4.0	4.5
IT	1.8	1.6	2.9	1.8	1.4	1.3	2.0	1.7	2.6	2.3	2.2
LU	5.8	6.0	7.5	5.1	2.9	5.0	1.0	1.0	3.8	2.4	2.0
NL	4.3	3.7	3.5	1.1	1.5	3.1	1.8	2.0	2.3	5.1	3.5
AT	3.5	2.8	3.0	1.0	1.2	2.4	0.8	0.5	2.0	2.3	1.6
PT	4.5	3.4	3.4	1.8	1.5	2.9	2.2	2.2	2.8	4.4	3.1
FI	5.3	4.1	5.6	0.7	1.6	3.2	1.4	1.3	3.0	2.7	2.0
Eurozone	2.9	2.7	3.4	1.6	1.4	2.3	1.2	1.1	2.4	2.5	2.2
USA	4.3	4.1	4.2	1.2	2.7		1.6	2.2	3.4	2.8	1.4

Source: European Commission (2002a) and European Central Bank (see note below)

Notes:
*Figures for 2002 are based on forecasts calculated by the European Commission in April 2002 (European Commission 2002a); HICP = harmonised index of consumer prices.
**The trend growth rates of real GDP were calculated by the ECB (European Central Bank, *Monthly Report*, July 1999).
BE = Belgium, DE = Germany, EL = Greece, ES = Spain, FR = France, IE = Ireland, IT = Italy, LU = Luxembourg, NL = Netherlands, AT = Austria, PT = Portugal, FI = Finland.

cent of the eurozone GDP – had significantly higher growth rates than the three major core countries between 1998 and 2000.

The ECB examined (see European Central Bank, *Monthly Bulletin*, July 1999) the issue of divergences and similarities in economic developments across eurozone countries. In particular, it examined the recent patterns of real GDP growth rates between the individual Member States of the eurozone. The report shows that recent short-term cyclical differences between real GDP growth rates in the major eurozone countries are by no means exceptional from a historical perspective. The cyclical differences in the growth rates between the core countries may be partly explained by the asymmetric impact of external shocks on these countries, such as the 1998 Russian debt default affecting Germany more than France, or the Kosovo war affecting Italy more than Germany, or German reunification (an asymmetric shock on Germany) that created overinvestment in the German construction sector. The report shows a very similar trend in real GDP annual growth rates between France (2.0 per cent) and Germany (2.2 per cent) for the period 1994–98. The significant trend growth gap between Italy (1.3 per cent) and the two other major economies of the eurozone is in part explained by the extraordinary budgetary austerity imposed by the Italian government in order to satisfy, by the end of 1997, the Maastricht convergence criteria with respect to the public deficit target so as to qualify for membership in the first wave of eurozone countries. The report also shows that the Member States in the periphery of the eurozone had a higher trend growth rate than the core countries during that same time period: Ireland (9.2 per cent), Finland (3.2 per cent), Portugal (2.9 per cent) and Spain (2.7 per cent). These higher trend growth rates may reflect the fact that the periphery countries are in the process of 'catching up' the core countries.

Even if eurozone countries were perfectly synchronised in terms of output, a single monetary policy may still have a different impact on an individual Member State if the transmission mechanism of the single monetary policy is different in that country. Cecchetti (1999) presents the theoretical analysis for the model of monetary policy transmission based on financial structure, which can account for cross-country differences of the impact of a given monetary policy in the eurozone. This model, which is different from models that emphasise the interest rate and exchange rate channels of monetary policy on output and prices in the short run, is called the 'lending' or 'credit' transmission mechanism of monetary policy on prices and output. According to this model, the first impact of policy-induced changes in interest rates – which are both real and nominal changes because of the underlying assumption of sticky prices – depends on capital market imperfections, which have an effect on the ability of firms to obtain external financing. The second impact on output and prices is when the bank loan supply is affected by the central bank's policy-induced change in interest rate. This second impact, combined with a lack of alternative sources of investment funds for some firms, is the principal transmission channel of the 'credit' model. Capital market imperfections place a wedge between the cost of financing projects by using internal finance and by using external finance. These imperfections are related to information asymmetries, moral hazard problems and bankruptcy laws, all of which are, in turn, related to the country's legal structure (for an empirical assessment across eurozone countries, see Kieler and Saarenheimo 1998, Schmidt 1999, Suardi 2001). For instance, Suardi argues that a tightening of monetary policy in a single currency area would have a greater impact in a country with many small firms with a high degree of dependence on bank loans than in a country with large firms that have available alternative sources of financing other than banks. The ongoing efforts of the Commission to propose EU directives that would harmonise the legal framework (Financial Services Action Plan and the Risk Capital Action Plan) with a view of creating a single European financial market by 2005 should diminish the asymmetry in the transmission mechanism of the single monetary policy across the Member States.

Community oversight of structural unemployment policies of Member States: the Luxembourg process

Since the mid-1990s, the issue of employment has been central to the concerns of the European Union, yet the statistics on the whole do not indicate a significant improvement in the reduction of structural unemployment, apart from the cyclical decline in unemployment at the turn of the century, when the unemployment rate in the eurozone reached a ten-year low of 8.3 per cent in March 2001 and was forecast at 8.5 per cent for calendar year 2002 (European Commission 2002a). This fact can be highlighted by the stark contrast between EU and US unemployment rates. Since 1983, and in contrast to the post-war experience before that date, the EU unemployment rate has been consistently higher than the US rate. After falling to 7.5 per cent in 1990 (EEC-12) from a peak of just under 10 per cent in 1985 (EEC-10), the unemployment rate in the eurozone rose to a new peak of close to 12 per cent in 1997. By mid-2000, the eurozone unemployment rate only declined to 9 per cent. By contrast, in the US, unemployment declined to 4.9 per cent in 1997 from a high of 9.7 per cent in 1982, with the unemployment rate falling to 4.0 per cent by mid-2000 (see Blanchard 1998, Chapter 20, for a model based on wage setting/price setting behaviour, combined with structural labour market differences, that explains the higher structural level of unemployment in the EU).

The leaders of the European Union have raised the issue of combating unemployment at every opportunity since the publication of the Commission White Paper on *Growth, Competitiveness and Employment* (European Commission 1994) and its follow-up at the Essen European Council meeting of December 1994. The Presidency Conclusions (European

Council 1994) stipulated the five measures to be taken to improve the employment situation in the EU:

1. improving employment opportunities for the labour force by promoting investment in vocational training;
2. increasing the employment-intensiveness of growth, in particular by a more flexible organisation of work in a way that fulfils both the wishes of employees and the requirements of competition and by a wage policy that encourages job-creating investments and moderate wage agreements below increases in productivity;
3. reducing non-wage labour costs to ensure that there is a noticeable effect on decisions concerning the hiring of employees and, in particular, of unqualified employees;
4. improving the effectiveness of labour-market policy by avoiding practices that are detrimental to readiness to work;
5. improving measures to help groups – notably the young and the long-term unemployed – which are hard hit by unemployment.

(Presidency conclusions of the European Council meeting on 9 and 10 December 1994 in Essen)

The Essen European Council urged the Member States to transpose the recommendations in their individual policies into a multi-annual programme and urged the Commission and the Council (Ministers of Employment and Social Policy) to keep close track of employment trends, to monitor the relevant policies of the Member States and to report annually to the European Council. This process was similar to the one established by the European Union in setting the Broad Economic Policy Guidelines adopted by the Ecofin Council under Article 99 of the Maastricht Treaty, which came into force in late 1993. Such coordination of employment policies drew directly on the experience built up in the multilateral surveillance of economic policies under the Maastricht Treaty. In fact, the Essen employment policy process was incorporated as part of the Employment Title in the Amsterdam Treaty of 1997.

Despite these administrative efforts at the European level to prod Member States to implement national measures to reduce structural unemployment, the results so far have been meagre, not so much because of the lack of progress in reducing labour market rigidities, but rather because the labour rigidities have not been eliminated quickly enough in the face of a rapidly increasing competitive environment in the goods market. Progress has been made in implementing active measures to tackle youth and long-term unemployment. Most Member States focused on improving 'information and communication technology' equipment in schools. They also devoted increased attention to the promotion of lifelong learning. France has, since late 1997, implemented a youth job programme to improve the employability of the young unemployed. By the end of 2001, under that programme, 350,000 people aged between 18 and 25 were, or had been, given five-year contracts with state and para-statal organisations to acquire experience and training, and eventually to obtain a permanent job in the private sector. These people have been mainly hired to work as assistants or 'facilitators' in schools, in local government, and in the police. About 25 per cent have left the scheme to go to other jobs or training. Despite these efforts, youth unemployment (under 25 years old) in France only declined from 25 per cent in 1999 to 18 per cent in 2001, underlining the fact that the real problem lies with the unskilled who fall outside this scheme.

A number of Member States have taken steps to reduce the non-wage costs of labour, notably employers' social security contributions, especially at the lower end of the wage scale. The measures taken by France and Belgium in this area are characterised as having had a 'moderate' impact on the demand for labour, while the measures taken by Germany, Greece, the Netherlands, Austria and Finland have had either a 'small' or 'negligible' impact since 1998 (Economic Policy Committee 2001: Table 3.3). With the exception of France, Member States still have not tackled the combined incentive effects of taxes and unemployment benefits, which are more generous in Europe than in the US. France has adopted measures to reduce the disincentive for unemployed people to accept a low paid job by ensuring that they do not abruptly lose some of their social benefits when accepting the job. For example, the housing tax – from which the unemployed are exempted – the housing subsidy system, and the 'Revenu minimum d'insertion' (a welfare benefit for the unemployed) have been amended to avoid the entire loss of these benefits to persons finding jobs, so as to provide a tax and social welfare system that will effectively result in a higher net income to low paid workers than to unemployed people.

In the area of labour market regulation, few measures have been taken to reduce structural unemployment. Although some progress has been made in the modernisation of work organisation – such as the facilitation of part-time work in Germany, where a new law gives employees the right to change from full- to part-time work, and more flexible working arrangements in the Netherlands – nothing has been done to address strict employment protection legislation for permanent contracts in Spain, France, Italy and Portugal, which lead to large firing costs (severance pay) and make firms reluctant to hire permanent workers in the first place (see European Commission 2001a, Economic Policy Committee 2001). In fact, in the face of high profile plant and store closures (e.g. Danone, Marks and Spencer) in France, the French government adopted in mid-2001 legislation that makes it even more costly to shut down companies and lay-off permanent workers. Under the new law, redundancies will only be permitted in the case of a company experiencing financial difficulties caused by changes in technology or the need to reorganise activity. Even under those conditions, the employer must show that the redundant employees cannot be retrained and redeployed elsewhere in the company. Then, the company must pay for at least six months' free time for retraining and seeking new employment.

The Eurogroup

Although various articles of the Maastricht Treaty dealing with economic and monetary union issues stipulate that only the Finance Ministers representing EU Member States participating in the eurozone shall have voting rights in the Ecofin Council (see Article 122.5 of the 'Treaty' for the list), the 'Treaty' does not legally recognise the group of Finance Ministers from the eurozone Member States, called the Eurogroup. However, as of mid-1998, just before the launch of the single currency area, the European Council authorised the eurozone Finance Ministers to meet informally to discuss issues related to their particular responsibility:

> Under the terms of the Treaty, the Ecofin Council is the centre for the coordination of the Member States' economic policies and is empowered to act in the relevant areas. In particular, the Ecofin Council is the only body empowered to formulate and adopt the broad economic policy guidelines which constitute the main instrument of economic coordination.
>
> The defining position of the Ecofin Council at the centre of the economic coordination and decision-making process affirms the unity and cohesion of the Community.
>
> The Ministers of the States participating in the euro-area may meet informally among themselves to discuss issues connected with their shared specific responsibilities for the single currency. The Commission, and the European Central Bank (ECB) when appropriate, will be invited to take part in the meetings.
>
> Whenever matters of common interest are concerned they will be discussed by Ministers of all Member States.
>
> Decisions will in all cases be taken by the Ecofin Council in accordance with the procedures determined by the Treaty.
> (From Resolution I.6 of the Luxembourg European Council of 13 December 1997, in European Commission 1999b: 103)

This Resolution, formulated by the 15 EU Heads of State or Government, was adopted after it was argued that Member States composing a monetary union need more coordinated economic policies to guarantee the union's success in the long run, as stated in Resolution I.1 of the Luxembourg European Council of December 1997:

> [The third stage of] EMU will link the economies of the euro-area Member States more closely together. They will share a single monetary policy and a single exchange rate. Cyclical developments are likely

to converge further. Economic policies, and wage determination, however, remain a national responsibility, subject to the provisions of Article 104 of the Treaty and the Stability and Growth Pact. To the extent that national economic developments have an impact on inflation prospects in the euro area, they will influence monetary conditions in that area. It is for this basic reason that the move to a single currency will require closer Community surveillance and coordination of economic policies among euro-area Member States.

The Eurogroup, composed of the Finance Ministers from the eurozone Member States, the Commissioner responsible for economic and financial affairs and often a representative from the ECB, would provide the forum to discuss such coordination. The creation of this informal body is an example of a form of intergovernmental cooperation established on the margins of European Community Treaties, which over time could be integrated into the EC Treaty. For some eurozone Member States, such as France and Belgium, the creation of this informal body, the Eurogroup, was seen as the first political step towards the establishment of a visible EU 'economic government', a necessary counterweight to the single European Central Bank; for other Member States, such as Britain, the Eurogroup was simply to be considered as a sort of Ecofin Council 'committee', which may review and monitor the developments in the eurozone economy and prepare a common position on economic issues that appear on the Ecofin agenda, but which cannot have any decision-making power outside the established framework of the Ecofin Council, as laid out in the Treaty provisions.

Since mid-2000, a number of steps have been taken to strengthen the role of the Eurogroup. The Eurogroup Finance Ministers now meets the night before the regularly scheduled monthly meetings of Ecofin to prepare a common position on the issues to be discussed at the Ecofin meeting. In an effort to improve the coordination of economic policies between the eurozone Member States, the Commission prepares a quarterly report (European Commission 2002b) on the current economic trends, forecasts and risks in the eurozone, not in each Member State. This report provides the basis for a common assessment by the Eurogroup Finance Ministers of the overall economic situation in the eurozone. This is supplemented by the Commission's indicator-based forecast of the eurozone's quarterly GDP growth rate, released each month for the current quarter and the following quarter (Grasmann and Keereman 2001). The improved statistical information for the eurozone provides to the Eurogroup a more accurate evaluation of the stance of eurozone policy mix and, if need be, an evaluation of the coordinated approach between the eurozone Member States to change it.

ECB's participation in Community bodies

Although the eurozone monetary policy must be formulated and executed without any pressure from national governments or from Community institutions, there are formal and informal channels of communication between the ECB and the Community bodies responsible for setting the Broad Economic Policy Guidelines, the overarching instrument used for the coordination of economic policies between the Member States. In this regard, we examine below the ECB participation in the Eurogroup/Ecofin meetings, the Eurogroup/Ecofin Presidency participation in the ECB's Governing Council, and the ECB participation in the Economic and Financial Committee, the Economic Policy Committee, and the Macroeconomic Dialogue.

The ECB participation in Eurogroup/Ecofin meetings

The Luxembourg European Council Resolution of December 1997 states explicitly that the ECB is to be invited to participate at the meetings of the Eurogroup, where discussions of monetary, budgetary/fiscal, employment and structural policies of the eurozone take place in an informal forum. Since the first meeting of the Eurogroup in June 1998, an ECB representative, usually the President or Vice-President, has attended the monthly meetings of the Eurogroup. This resolution extends the formal 'Treaty' provision (see article 113.2) that requires the ECB President to be invited to Ecofin Council meetings when the Council is discussing matters relating to the objectives and tasks of the Eurosystem/ESCB, such as the exchange rate policy, or proposed legislation for the prudential supervision of banks. However, the current ECB President is reluctant to attend Ecofin Council, meetings for fear that the independence of the ECB would *appear* to be compromised. Duisenberg refuses to discuss, ex-ante, with the Ecofin Council, the policy mix between monetary and other economic policies. He fears that such a procedure would compromise the independence of the ECB. The informal nature of the Eurogroup meetings attenuates this fear for the participating ECB representative, who is usually an Executive Board member other than the President. Over the 18 Ecofin Council meetings covering the period May 2000 to March 2002, a member of the ECB Executive Board has attended nine such meetings. From the period January 1999 to April 2000, an ECB representative, the Vice-President, attended only two meetings of the Ecofin Council.

The Eurogroup/Ecofin Presidency participation in ECB's Governing Council

According to Article 113.1 of the 'Treaty', the Ecofin Council President has the right to sit in on the ECB Governing Council meetings, without a right to vote. The Ecofin Council President may even submit a motion to the Governing Council for deliberation. During the calendar years 1999–2000, the Ecofin President attended only three ECB meetings (two in 1999 and one in 2000) out of a total of some 50 meetings. During those first two years, the Ecofin President, who was also the Eurogroup President, could represent the views of the Eurogroup. In January 2001, when Sweden, a Member State not participating in the eurozone, took over the EU Presidency, the Ecofin and Eurogroup presidencies were held for the first time by two different individuals. In an effort to strengthen the cooperation between the Eurogroup and the ECB, it was agreed that the Eurogroup President would always replace the Ecofin President on the ECB Governing Council, whenever these two presidencies were not held by the same individual. Additionally, it was agreed that the Eurogroup President would henceforth attend the ECB Governing Council meetings once every two months.

The ECB participation in the Economic and Financial Committee

The Economic and Financial Committee (EFC), which in January 1999 replaced the Monetary Committee that had been established in 1958, meets about once a month, prepares the work of the Ecofin Council and, in many cases, provides recommendations and opinions to the Ecofin Council in areas such as the assessment of the annual Stability and Convergence Programmes submitted by the Member States, and the formulation of the annual Broad Economic Policy Guidelines. The EFC comprises two members from the ECB (the Vice-President and a member of the Executive Board), two members from each EU Member State (one senior official from the National Central Bank and another from the Finance Ministry) and two members from the Commission. The Committee provides an important forum where the dialogue between the Ecofin Council and the ECB is prepared and continued at the level of senior officials from the finance ministries, national central banks, the Commission and the ECB. The EFC, as the Committee that also prepares the economic dialogue between the Eurogroup and the ECB, each month drafts the assessment of the eurozone's current and future macroeconomic situation that is used as the framework for these discussions.

The ECB participation in the Economic Policy Committee

The Economic Policy Committee (EPC), originally established in 1974 when various Community economic committees were merged into one, comprises four representatives from each EU Member State and from the Commission. As of September 2000, the statute of the EPC was modified to include the ECB on an equal footing with the other members. Currently, the ECB is represented by three staff members. The work of the

EPC focuses primarily on issues dealing with structural reforms in the Member States in the context of the 'Luxembourg process' and 'Cardiff process', which were launched to coordinate reforms to bring about more flexibility in the labour markets and more integration in both the product and financial markets of the Member States. The EPC develops structural performance indicators and conducts annual reviews, submitted to the Ecofin Council, of each Member State's progress in the area of structural economic reforms. The ECB actively participates in this work, arguing that there is a link between structural reforms and monetary policy. Structural reforms could increase the long-run potential growth rate of the eurozone from the current range of 2–2.5 per cent to 3 per cent, which would allow a higher growth rate of money supply while maintaining the ECB's goal of price stability (see European Central Bank 2002).

The ECB participation in the Macroeconomic Dialogue

At the Cologne European Council meeting of June 1999, the Heads of State or Government and the President of the Commission endorsed a 'European Employment Pact', which added Macroeconomic Dialogue as a third pillar to the already existing 'Luxembourg process' and 'Cardiff process'. The Macroeconomic Dialogue, known also as the 'Cologne process', was adopted in the context of the ongoing effort, begun in 1997 with the 'Employment Title' entrenched in the Amsterdam Treaty, to establish a comprehensive Community policy framework to implement guidelines addressed to the Member States to reduce the structural level of unemployment and promote non-inflationary, employment-generating growth in the EU. The 'Cologne process' brings together representatives from the Ecofin Council and the Labour and Social Policy Council, the Commission, the European Central Bank, one non-eurozone EU national central bank, and the social partners (EU-level federations of employers and trade unions) to exchange views twice a year on the interaction between monetary policy, fiscal policy and wage developments. The exchange of information and opinions between the various economic policy actors and the private sector provides the employer and union federation representatives with a better appreciation and understanding of the current monetary and budgetary/fiscal measures taken by the ECB and the national Finance Ministers in light of the policy-makers' assessment of the macroeconomic environment. It also provides them with a better appreciation and understanding of the implications of wage developments for structural unemployment and for long-term employment-generating growth. These discussions take place without prejudice to the price stability goal and independence of the ECB and to the national budgetary deficit constraints placed on Member States by the Stability and Growth Pact. One of these twice-yearly meetings takes place before the drafting of the Broad Economic Policy Guidelines by the Ecofin Council; the other meeting takes place before the adoption, by the European Council, of the Employment Guidelines, which, following the decision taken at the Lisbon European Council meeting (March 2000), are adopted at the annual Spring European Council meeting. Since March 2001, these annual spring meetings are entirely devoted to economic and social (i.e. labour) issues, in accordance with the decision taken at the Stockholm European Council meeting.

External representation of the Eurosystem

Since the Second World War, central banks have played an increasingly more important role in international organisations, as multilateral economic and monetary cooperation became a more prominent feature of these international organisations. The central bank of a State that is a member of an international organisation or forum is usually indirectly represented by someone delegated to represent the State or directly represented by that state's central bank Governor. The representation of the Eurosystem outside the eurozone is complicated by the fact that a number of factors have to be taken into account under the 'Treaty' and the 'Statute'. First, under Article 111.4 of the 'Treaty', the exclusive competence of the Eurosystem with respect to the single monetary policy extends to the international level where only the Eurosystem, and not the eurozone Member States or the President of the Eurogroup Ministers of Finance, may represent the eurozone positions on this matter in international organisations or forums. Secondly, the exchange rate policy of the eurozone vis-à-vis non-Community currencies is a shared responsibility of the Eurogroup Finance Ministers and of the Eurosystem, while the banking prudential supervision policy of the EU15 remains the responsibility of the national authorities, albeit with cross-border cooperation/coordination and with the participation and contribution of the Eurosystem, as described below. Thirdly, article 6.1 of the 'Statute' deals with the question of which body of the Eurosystem – either the ECB or the National Central Banks, or both – retains that exclusive competence at the international level:

> In the field of international cooperation involving the tasks entrusted to the ESCB/[Eurosystem], the ECB shall decide how the ESCB/[Eurosystem] shall be represented.

The *International Relations Committee* of the ECB prepares a common position on all international matters that fall within the competence of the Eurosystem and the ESCB.

Below is a brief discussion of the representation of the Eurosystem and the ESCB in the major international organisations and forums in view of these binding constraints; an overview of the representation of the

166 *Economic policy coordination in the eurozone*

Eurosystem/ESCB in the external organisations and the EU forums is presented in Table 4.3.

The IMF and the OECD

The IMF Executive Board

Central to the International Monetary Fund's (IMF's) purposes and operations to maintain the stability of the international monetary system is the mandate, under its Articles of Agreement, to exercise surveillance over the economic, monetary and exchange rate policies of its member countries. To carry out this mandate, the IMF exercises both multilateral and bilateral surveillance. Multilateral surveillance consists of IMF Executive Board reviews of developments in the international monetary system, primarily based on the staff's *World Economic Outlook* reports, and on periodic discussions of developments, prospects, and key policy issues in international capital markets. Recently, multilateral surveillance has been extended to include regional surveillance of the developments in the major single currency areas, such as the eurozone. Bilateral surveillance takes the form of consultations with individual member countries, conducted annually for most members, under Article IV of the IMF's Articles of Agreement. IMF consultations with eurozone member states also involve discussions with the representatives of the relevant European Union institutions, such as the ECB and the Ecofin Council, when matters of monetary and exchange rate policies and 'policy mix' between monetary and fiscal policies are considered. The results of the consultations are presented to the IMF Executive Board, which comprises 24 Executive Directors, for discussion, with the relevant member of the IMF Executive Director representing the views of that member country to the Executive Board.[6] Of the 24 Executive Directors, eight represent solely their own country; each of the other 16 elected Executive Directors represents a 'constituency' comprising their own country plus a number of other countries. For the 15 EU Member States, the three Executive Directors from Germany, France and the United Kingdom represent solely their own country. The Executive Director from Italy – traditionally continuously re-elected because of its dominant economic size among the countries composing the constituency – represents a constituency that includes Greece and Portugal; the Executive Director from Belgium, who is continuously re-elected, represents a constituency that includes Austria and Luxembourg; the Executive Director from the Netherlands, who is continuously re-elected, represents a constituency that does not include any other EU state; Ireland is part of a constituency represented by the Executive Director from Canada, who is continuously re-elected. Finland is part of a constituency that includes a group of eight countries whose elected Executive Director rotates among Finland, Denmark, Sweden and Norway. Spain is

Table 4.3 Representation of the Eurosystem/ESCB in external and EU bodies

External organisation or forum	ECB	Eurozone NCBs	'Out' NCBs
IMF – Executive Board	Permanent representative (observer status)	–	–
– IMFC (formerly Interim Committee)	President (observer status)	Participation as alternate representative that parallels representation of all IMF members on the Executive Board	Participation as alternate representative that parallels representation of all IMF members on the Executive Board
OECD – relevant committees and working groups	Representative	Representative from each of the eurozone NCBs	Representative from each of the 'out' NCBs
G10 – Ministers and Governors under aegis of GAB	President (observer status)	Governors of the Deutsche Bundesbank, Banque de France, Banca d'Italia, De Nederlandsche Bank, and Banque nationale de Belgique	Governors of the Bank of England and Sveriges Riksbank
– Governors under aegis of BIS	President	Same as above	Same as above
G7 (Ministers' and Governors' Group)	President	Governors of the Deutsche Bundesbank, Banque de France and Banca d'Italia (only when certain issues are on the agenda)	Governor of the Bank of England
G20	President	Governors of the Deutsche Bundesbank, Banque de France and Banca d'Italia	Governor of the Bank of England
FSF (Financial Stability Forum)	Representative as an observer	Representatives from the Deutsche Bundesbank, Banque de France, Banca d'Italia and De Nederlandsche Bank	Representative from the Bank of England

continued

Table 4.3 Continued

EU bodies/forums	ECB	Eurozone NCBs	'Out' NCBs
Ecofin Council (EU15), meets monthly	President/Vice-President, or other members of the Executive Board (observer status) – the ECB may decline an invitation to attend if the purpose is to discuss ex-ante coordination of policy mix	–	–
Informal Ecofin Council (EU15), meets twice yearly	President	Governor from each of the eurozone NCBs	Governor from each of the 'out' NCBs
Eurogroup (Finance Ministers), meets one day prior to Ecofin Council meeting	President and Vice-President or other members of the Executive Board	–	–
Economic and Financial Committee (replaces Monetary Committee since 1 January 1999), meets once a month	Vice-President and a member of Executive Board	One representative from each of the eurozone NCBs	One representative from each of the 'out' NCBs
Economic Policy Committee, meets once a month	Three staff members, with voting rights	–	–
Economic and Monetary Affairs Committee of the European Parliament	President or Vice-President, monetary dialogue in the context of hearings, four times a year	–	–

Explanatory notes and definitions of initials and abbreviations:

ESCB	European System of Central Banks, which is composed of the Eurosystem and the 'out' EU national central banks.
ECB	European Central Bank.
NCB	National Central Bank; 'out' NCBs refer to the three EU national central banks of the Member States that have not adopted the single currency (United Kingdom, Sweden and Denmark).
IMF	International Monetary Fund, 183 member states.
OECD	Organisation for Economic Cooperation and Development (Paris), composed of 30 member states.
G7	Finance Ministers' and Governors' Group from the US, Japan, Germany, France, UK, Italy and Canada.
G10	In the context of the GAB, this is the Finance Ministers' and Governors' Group from the G7 and the Netherlands, Belgium, Sweden and Switzerland. In the context of the BIS, the G10 forum only includes the Governors of the central banks.
G20	Composed of representatives from the G7 countries plus Argentina, Australia, Brazil, China, India, Indonesia, Mexico, Russia, Saudi Arabia, South Africa, South Korea and Turkey, as well as representatives from the IMF-World Bank.
GAB	General Arrangements to Borrow established in the early 1960s by the G10 under the IMF framework.
BIS	Bank for International Settlements (Basel).
Ecofin Council	Composed of the Ministers of Economics and Finance of the 15 Member States of the European Union; the Commissioner responsible for economic and financial affairs usually attends the meetings; at the twice-yearly informal Ecofin Councils, no legally binding decisions are taken, but important resolutions may be taken.
Eurogroup	Composed of the Ministers of Economics/Finance from the eurozone Member States. This Group meets, under the Eurogroup Presidency, the day prior to each Ecofin Council meeting, but is not yet recognised as a formal body with the power to legislate in accordance with EC jurisprudence. If the Ecofin Presidency is not held by a eurozone Member State, then the Presidency of the Eurogroup is held by the member from the eurozone country next in line to take the Presidency of the Ecofin. This situation occurred for the first time during the first semester of 2001 when Sweden held the Presidency of the Ecofin Council. Belgium, being next in line to hold the Ecofin Presidency, took over the Presidency of the Eurogroup for the full year.
Economic and Financial Committee	Important forum where ECB has a role to play in the discussions of the annual Broad Economic Policy Guidelines (BEPG) and the surveillance of fiscal policies on the basis of annual Stability and Convergence Programmes. Participating in this forum are two members from the ECB Executive Board, one senior official from each NCB, one senior official from the Ministry of Finance of each Member State and two members from the Commission.
Economic Policy Committee	Forum where ECB fully participates in the drafting of policy recommendations to Council in the areas primarily related to the 'Cardiff process' (functioning of product, capital and services markets) and the 'Luxembourg process' (coordination among Member States of structural reforms in the labour market). The Member States and the Commission each appoint four members to the Committee, selected from among senior officials competent in the field of economic and structural policy.

part of a constituency composed of eight countries whose elected Executive Director rotates among Spain, Mexico and Venezuela.

Since the IMF's Articles of Agreement extend membership solely to countries, the Eurosystem – an independent institution that currently crosses over 12 countries – does not have an Executive Director on the IMF Executive Board to represent its views in the areas of its exclusive or shared competencies. Consequently, as there is no representative of the euro Member States who can speak on behalf of the European Central Bank, the ECB, in agreement with the IMF, appointed a permanent representative to sit on the IMF Executive Board, as an observer without the right to vote. It was agreed that the ECB permanent representative would participate in the discussions of the IMF Executive Board whenever the following topics were to be raised, some of which are within the exclusive competence of the Eurosystem and others are shared responsibilities with the Ecofin Council and the euro Member States:[7]

- IMF surveillance (Article IV) over the single monetary and exchange rate policies of the Euro area and over the policies of individual eurozone Member States, such as banking and prudential supervision;
- the role of the euro in the international monetary system;
- World Economic Outlook;
- International capital markets reports;
- World economic and market developments that specifically address the eurozone;
- other items recognised by the ECB and the IMF to be of mutual interest in the performance of their respective mandates.

To summarise, the ECB permanent representative who sits on the IMF Executive Board can represent the views of the Eurosystem on issues dealing with the single monetary policy; and the IMF Executive Director, whose constituency includes the euro Member State holding the Presidency of the Eurogroup, can represent the views of the eurozone on topics that are within the competence of the Eurogroup, such as exchange rate policy or budgetary policies in the context of the Stability and Growth Pact (Vienna European Council, Annex II of the Presidency Conclusions, 11–12 December 1998 in European Commission 1999b: 155).

Thus, whenever Germany, France or the Netherlands holds the Eurogroup Presidency, the IMF Executive Director from Germany, France or the Netherlands represents the views of the eurozone; whenever Italy, Portugal or Greece holds the Eurogroup Presidency, the IMF Executive Director from Italy represents the views of the eurozone; whenever Belgium, Austria or Luxembourg holds the Eurogroup Presidency, the IMF Executive Director from Belgium represents the views of the eurozone. Since Ireland holds a seat as Alternate Executive Director, with Canada as Executive Director, the IMF Alternate Executive Director from Ireland would represent the views of the eurozone in the event that Ireland holds the Eurogroup Presidency. Whenever Finland or Spain holds the Eurogroup Presidency and has not been elected as either an IMF Executive Director or Alternate Director, the IMF representative speaking on behalf of the Eurogroup would be from a non-eurozone country. This is possible since an IMF Executive Director from Denmark, Sweden or Norway could represent the constituency that includes Finland. Similarly, an IMF Executive Director from Mexico or Venezuela could represent the constituency that includes Spain, (see Lelart 2000 for details).

International Monetary and Financial Committee (IMFC)

As a permanent committee of the IMF since spring 2000, the International Monetary and Financial Committee's responsibilities are to advise and report to the Board of Governors (the highest decision making body of the IMF) on issues regarding the management and adaptation of the international monetary system, including sudden disturbances that may threaten the international monetary system, and on proposals to amend the IMF Articles of Agreement. To this end, the IMFC, whose predecessor was called the Interim Committee, meets twice a year at the level of Finance Ministers, with the participation of the Central Bank governors as Alternates, from the same 24 countries composing the IMF Executive Directors, who represent the 'constituencies' (country groups). Again, the President of the ECB attends those meetings as an observer, along with a representative from the European Commission. The relevant Minister of Finance sitting on the Committee representing the constituency that includes the country holding the Eurogroup Presidency, may speak on behalf of the Eurogroup. For instance, at the fourth meeting of the IMFC held in November 2001, the Belgian Minister of Finance, who held the rotating Presidency of the Eurogroup/Ecofin, could speak on behalf of his IMF constituency, which comprised Austria, Belarus, Belgium, the Czech Republic, Hungary, Kazakhstan, Luxembourg, the Slovak Republic, Slovenia and Turkey, as well as for the 12 EU Member States composing the eurozone.

Group of Ten (G-10)

The Group of Ten (G-10), comprising Belgium, Canada, France, Germany, Italy, Japan, the Netherlands, Sweden, Switzerland, the United Kingdom and the United States, is an informal international body established in the early 1960s to discuss issues related to IMF policy matters in the context of the General Arrangements to Borrow (GAB). Under the terms of the GAB, these countries are prepared to grant the IMF refinancing aid to supplement IMF resources. Whenever the G-10 countries meet, each country is represented by its Minister of Finance and its Central

Bank Governor. The President of the ECB also attends those meetings as an observer.

OECD

The Organisation for Economic Cooperation and Development (OECD), comprising 30 states that include all of the EU Member States, is a formal intergovernmental institution that deals with issues relating to cooperation in the field of microeconomic, macroeconomic and monetary policies. Thus, the OECD touches upon some of the basic tasks entrusted to the Eurosystem. There exists an agreement between the OECD and the ECB for allowing the ECB to participate as a separate member of the European Community delegation in the work of the relevant OECD committees and working groups, alongside the European Commission.

Group of Seven (G-7) ministers and governors and other such bodies

Since 1987, the G-7 Finance Ministers' and Governors' Group from the United States, Japan, Germany, France, the United Kingdom, Italy and Canada, has been an effective forum for informal and substantive discussions of important international economic issues, leading to greater coordination among policy makers in the field of monetary, financial and economic policies. The G-7 Finance Ministers' and Governors' Group meets four times a year. Two meetings are held in the host country, which rotates each calendar year; two other meetings are held in Washington in conjunction with the regular spring and fall meetings of the International Monetary Fund and the World Bank.

Since the creation of the eurozone in 1999, the G-7 Finance Ministers' and Governors' Group also includes the Minister of Finance representing the Eurogroup and the President of the ECB. The President of the ECB participates in the discussions that relate to the world economy, multilateral surveillance of the G-7 economies, and exchange rate policy. In order to limit the number of participants in the G-7 Group to a minimum, it was agreed – at the behest of the non-European members (the US, Canada and Japan) – that the Governors of the National Central Banks of France, Germany and Italy would not participate in the G-7 meetings devoted to those above-mentioned issues, but would attend – along with the President of the ECB – G-7 meetings devoted to all other issues concerning the international financial system, such as prudential supervision or ways to combat the financing of terrorism (Council [of the European Union] 1999).

The six-month rotating Presidency of the Eurogroup is held by the Finance Minister of the Member State holding the Presidency of the Ecofin Council. The President of the Eurogroup, who may at times be someone other than the Finance Minister from Germany, France or Italy, attends the G-7 meeting along with, on some occasions, the European Commission member responsible for economic and monetary affairs. When the Ecofin Presidency is held by the UK, Sweden or Denmark, the Eurogroup Presidency is held by the Minister of Finance from the euro Member State next in line to hold the Presidency of the Ecofin Council. In all instances, in the context of G-7 meetings, the six-month rotating Presidency of the Eurogroup is assisted on a rotating basis by the Finance Minister from one of the three eurozone permanent Member States of the G-7. For the period July–December 1999, when Finland held the EU presidency, the Finnish Finance Minister held the Presidency of the Ecofin Council as well as the Presidency of the Eurogroup. Therefore, at the meetings of the G-7, the eurozone ministerial representation was composed of the Finnish and German Finance Ministers. Similarly, for the period January–June 2000, when Portugal held the Presidency of the Eurogroup, it was composed of the Portuguese and French Finance Ministers. When the Belgian Finance Minister held the Presidency of the Eurogroup for the entire year of 2001 (since the Swedish Finance Minister held the Ecofin Presidency during the first semester of 2001, followed by the Belgian Presidency during the second semester), he was assisted by the Italian Finance Minister. The eurozone ministerial representation at the G-7 was therefore a Belgo-Italian tandem. For the first semester of 2002, the Presidency of the Eurogroup was held by the Spanish Finance Minister. Therefore, the eurozone ministerial representation at the G-7 meetings was composed of the Spanish and German Finance Ministers.

G-20

With the increasing globalisation of the international economy and financial system, the lack of emerging-market representation in the G-7 posed a problem to this informal forum for addressing certain questions dealing with the coordination and cooperation of policies in the area of the international economy and financial system. The establishment of the G-20 was designed to fulfil this need for representation from emerging markets. In September 1999, on the initiative of the G-7 Finance Ministers, the G-20 forum was established to study and review policy issues between the industrialised countries and emerging markets with a view to promote international financial stability. The G-20's task is to improve the dialogue between the industrialised countries and the emerging market economies in areas related to the international monetary and financial system and within the framework of the Bretton Woods institutional framework. The policy issues and recommendations raised by the G-20 are then considered by the decision-making bodies of the IMF and the World Bank, such as the IMFC and the Joint Development Committee of the IMF and the

World Bank. For instance, at the second G-20 meeting held in Montreal in October 2000, the Ministers and Governors discussed ways to reduce the frequency and severity of financial crises by choosing the appropriate exchange rate arrangement, by implementing prudent liability management in the private and public sectors, and by encouraging private sector involvement in crisis prevention and resolution – all issues that are under discussion at the IMF/World Bank. In the aftermath of the 11 September terrorist attacks in the US, the G-20 meeting of Ministers and Governors, held in Ottawa in November 2001, discussed an action plan to stop the financing of terrorism.

The G-20 countries represent two-thirds of the world population and 90 per cent of the global gross domestic product. The G-20 meets once a year at the level of the Finance Ministers and Central Bank Governors from the G-7 countries plus Argentina, Australia, Brazil, China, India, Indonesia, Mexico, Russia, Saudi Arabia, South Africa, South Korea, Turkey, and representatives from the Bretton Woods Institutions (IMF–World Bank). Both the President of the ECB and the Minister of Finance holding the EU presidency participate in this new forum. The Managing Director of the IMF and the President of the World Bank, as well as the Chairpersons of the International Monetary and Financial Committee and the Joint Development Committee of the IMF and the World Bank participate fully in the discussions.

Financial Stability Forum

In the wake of the Asian and Russian financial crises of 1997–98, and the risk to the banking sector posed in 1998 by the high losses of a large American hedge fund (LTCM) as a result of a large increase in interest rates on emerging-market bonds, the G-7 Finance Ministers and Central Bank Governors established in early 1999 – following the recommendation of the 'Tietmeyer Report', named after the then-President of the Deutsche Bundesbank – the Financial Stability Forum (FSF) to address specific issues directly related to matters of financial market stability. This forum is composed of the deputy Finance Ministers, deputy Central Bank Governors and country financial regulators and supervisors of the G-7 countries, as well as the representatives of the central banks of four non-G-7 countries that represent important financial centres (the Netherlands, Singapore, Australia and Hong Kong) and representatives of international organisations and bodies that deal with financial market stability, i.e. the Bank for International Settlements, the IMF, the World Bank, the Basel Committee on Banking Supervision, the Committee of the G-10 Central Banks on the Global Financial System, the International Organisation of Securities Commissions (IOSCO), the International Association of Insurance Supervisors (IAIS) and the OECD.

The FSF has been given a mandate to identify the gaps in the international financial system with respect to questions of financial stability and to improve the coordination and the exchange of information among the authorities responsible for financial stability in order to prevent systemic risk. To that end, the FSF has focused on three areas: proper financial supervision of offshore financial centres and highly leveraged institutions (HLIs), such as the American hedge fund LTCM; the possible risks associated with excessive short-term external debt in emerging market economies; and the promotion of internationally recognised standards and codes that each country should apply in its financial markets. In particular, the FSF evaluated the systemic risk emanating from offshore financial centres that are not well supervised and that do not cooperate with the EU. It also examined the destabilising influence of short-term capital flows in emerging market economies, which were seen as contributing to the Asian crisis of 1997. The FSF has identified 12 key standards and codes that each country should apply to place the private financial institutions and markets on a firm foundation so as to be more resistant to financial crises. The IMF is left with the task of monitoring compliance with these internationally recognised standards and codes. The ECB fully participates in the Financial Stability Forum that meets twice a year.

Central Banking Forums

The Bank for International Settlements (BIS) in Basel is an institution established to foster cooperation between central banks. The main forum of that international organisation consists of the meetings of the G-10 Governors, in which the President of the ECB and the Governors of five euro area NCBs (Belgium, France, Germany, Italy and the Netherlands), as well as the Governors of the national central banks of the United States, the United Kingdom, Japan, Canada, Sweden and Switzerland participate. This Group regularly monitors monetary and economic developments in international capital markets and provides guidance to the following committees set up under the BIS and on which sits an ECB representative: the Basel Committee on Banking Supervision, the Committee on the Global Financial System, the Committee on Payment and Settlement System, and the Committee on Gold and Foreign Exchange.

BANKING PRUDENTIAL SUPERVISION AND FINANCIAL STABILITY

When the single currency was launched at the beginning of 1999, the basic features of the prudential supervisory framework of credit institutions remained as they were prior to the creation of the single currency area, i.e. prudential supervision remained a competence of the national authorities, with either the national central bank or a non-central bank body or, in some cases, both together responsible for such supervision. In five Member States of the European Union, a *non*-central bank body has the primary responsibility for prudential supervision of credit institutions, the so-called 'separation principle' between monetary and prudential supervisory functions (the United Kingdom, Belgium, Luxembourg, Sweden and Denmark); in another six Member States, the National Central Bank has the primary responsibility for prudential supervision (Italy, Spain, the Netherlands, Greece, Portugal and Ireland); and in four Member States, the responsibility is shared between a non-central bank body and the National Central Bank (France, Germany, Austria and Finland). Moreover, the principles of 'home country' prudential supervision of EU cross-border credit institutions and of 'bilateral and multilateral' cooperation between prudential supervisors have remained in effect.

In France, the *Commission bancaire*, a six-member board, which includes the Head of the Treasury and which is chaired by the Governor of the Banque de France, is responsible for supervision of credit institutions established in metropolitan France, its Départements and Territoires d'Outre mer, and Monaco, as well as of branches of French credit institutions established in other EU countries. The *Commission bancaire* supervises compliance of credit institutions, including investment firms, with the prudential regulations. The inspections and on-site examinations are carried out by the Banque de France on behalf of the Commission bancaire. The Governor of the Banque de France also chairs the Comité des *Etablissements de Crédit et des Entreprises d'Investissement* (CECEI), which has the authority to grant and withdraw banking licences and to rule on bank mergers. Although the *Commission bancaire* is an autonomous public institution, it is clear that the Banque de France is directly involved in banking supervision.

With the growing role of financial conglomerates, resulting in the fusion of the banking, insurance and securities sectors, Germany established as of May 2002 a cross-sector supervisory authority, the Federal Agency for Financial Services Supervision (BAFin), which is responsible for supervising all credit institutions and financial services institutions. This new federal agency combines the former Federal Banking Supervisory Office (Bundesaufsichtsamt für das Kreditwesen), the Federal Supervisory Office for Insurance Enterprises, and the Federal Supervisory Office for Securities Trading into one integrated supervisory agency, which is, inter alia, responsible for banking supervision and which is authorised to issue licences and prudential banking regulations. This agency is accountable to the Ministry of Finance. The Federal Agency for Financial Services Supervision and the Bundesbank collaborate in supervising all credit institutions and financial services institutions. Although the Federal Agency is responsible for issuing prudential regulations and taking measures to implement them, the Bundesbank plays an important role in the supervision of all the financial institutions by evaluating their annual financial statements and assessing the adequacy of the institutions' capital, liquidity and risk management procedures. The observations of the Bundesbank are taken into consideration in the prudential surveillance of financial institutions by the Federal Agency (see Deutsche Bundesbank 2000, 2002: 163). Table 4.4 summarises the banking supervisory structure in the Member States of the European Union and in the United States.

The 'Treaty's' Article 105.2, which came into force with the creation of the eurozone, does not regard banking prudential supervision as a function of the ESCB but as a national responsibility, with the responsibility resting with the national central bank, with some other national body, or with a combination of both. However, given the close links between monetary policy, which is no longer within the jurisdiction of a eurozone national central bank, and the micro- and macro-prudential supervisory functions, Article 105.5 also ensures effective interaction between the Eurosystem and the national supervisory authorities:

> The ESCB [and thus, the Eurosystem] shall contribute to the smooth conduct of policies pursued by the competent authorities relating to the prudential supervision of credit institutions [micro] and the stability of the financial system [macro].

To that end, the ESCB set up a Banking Supervision Committee to provide the necessary cooperation between the Eurosystem/ESCB and national banking supervisors on matters related to prudential supervision and systemic stability. Moreover, Article 105.4 of the 'Treaty' gives the ECB a consultative role whenever national authorities legislate in the field of prudential supervision and the stability of the financial system. (This article applies to all EU countries with the exception of the UK.)

In the context of prudential supervision of credit institutions and the stability of the financial system, the issues of 'micro-prudential supervision' and of 'macro-prudential supervision' are usually raised. To deal with micro-prudential supervision, which focuses on the safety and soundness of individual credit institutions and which raises the 'solvency' issue, the EU Second Banking Coordination Directive (see below) provided significant harmonisation of national banking regulations and mandatory bilateral cooperation between the supervisory authorities of the Member States. Macro-prudential supervision deals with the response of the supervisory authorities to the unexpected 'failure' of a credit institution, as a result of either a solvency or liquidity problem, and its impact on the banking system as a whole – the so-called *systemic risk*. Macro-prudential supervision ultimately leads to the question of the role of the central bank as a 'lender of last resort', which is neither raised explicitly in the Community banking regulations nor assigned in the Maastricht Treaty or ESCB Statute as one of the functions of Eurosystem.

178 *Economic policy coordination in the eurozone*

Table 4.4 Bank supervisory structure in EU countries and the US

Country	Supervisory agency (agencies)
Belgium	Commission bancaire et financière (Banking and Finance Commission)[a]
Denmark	Finanstilsynet (Finance Inspectorate, Ministry of Industry)
Germany	Bundesaufsichtsamt für das Kreditwesen (Federal Banking Supervisory Office)/Deutsche Bundesbank (S[b]) As of 1 May 2002: Federal Agency for Financial Services Supervision/Deutsche Bundesbank (S[b])
Greece	Bank of Greece
Spain	Banco de España
France	Commission bancaire/Banque de France (C[c])
Ireland	Central Bank of Ireland
Italy	Banca d'Italia
Luxembourg	Commission de Surveillance du Secteur Financier
Netherlands	De Nederlandsche Bank[d]
Austria	Bundesfinanzministerium (Federal Ministry of Finance)/Oesterreichische Nationalbank
Portugal	Banco de Portugal[e]
Finland	Rahoitustarkastus (Financial Supervision Authority), chaired by a member of the Suomen Pankki
Sweden	Finansinspektionen (Financial Supervisory Authority)
United Kingdom	Financial Service Authority
United States[f]	
Bank holding companies	FR
(incl. Financial services holding companies)	
National Banks	OCC
State Banks	
Members	FR/state governments
Non-members	FDIC/state governments
Savings banks	OTS/FDIC/FR
Savings and loan associations	OTS
Edge Act and agreement corporations	FR
Foreign banks	
Branches & agencies	
State licensed	FR/FDIC
Federally licensed	OCC/FR/FDIC
Representative offices	FR

Sources: European Parliament (1998, adapted from Table 9, Annex III); Deutsche Bundesbank (2002: 163); European Central Bank (2001d).

Notes:
a In 2001, Belgium proposed integrating the Banking and Finance Commission (Ministry of Finance) into the National Bank of Belgium.
b S = Separated regime, with each body self financed. In Germany, as of 1 May 2002, the Federal Banking Supervisory Office is merged with the Federal Supervisory Office for Insurance Enterprises and the Federal Supervisory Office for Securities Trading to form a new cross-sector supervisory authority known as the Federal Agency for Financial Services Supervision.
c C = Combined regime, since the Governor of the Banque de France chairs the Commission bancaire and the Banque de France provides the staff and budget.

Harmonisation of EU banking supervisory regulations

The EU Second Banking Coordination Directive (89/646/EEC), which came into force on 1 January 1993, and the technical Community legislation dealing with the capital and solvency ratios of banks, described below, constituted one of the cornerstones in the development of common supervisory approaches towards credit institutions by various national banking supervisory offices.[8] The Directive introduced the concept of a single banking authorisation by which any credit institution duly authorised in its Member State of origin may establish a branch or provide services in any other Member State without having to seek additional authorisation.[9] This single banking licence, which implied mutual recognition between Member States of the authorisation granted to a credit institution, was based on the harmonisation of the conditions for such authorisation and of the requirements regarding prudential supervision. The level of harmonisation attained with this Community banking legislation allowed the principle of 'home country' prudential supervision to be applied. This means that the Member State that issues the single banking licence is primarily responsible for the prudential supervision of that credit institution throughout the Community.

The Second Banking Coordination Directive harmonised the following key provisions of the banking sector:

- the minimum capital required for obtaining the authorisation to establish a new institution (in general ECU [euro] 5 million);
- the 'own funds' of the bank (see below) must not fall below the amount of initial capital required in the case of new institutions, or below the highest level of 'own funds' reached after the date 22 December 1989 (date of notification of the Directive) in the case of existing institutions;

---

d A *Council of Financial Supervisors* was set up in July 1999 to provide enhanced cooperation between the agencies that supervise banks (De Nederlandsche Bank), securities firms and insurance companies.

e A *National Council of Financial Supervisors* was set up in September 2000 to provide enhanced cooperation between the sectoral supervisory authorities: the Banco de Portugal, the Securities Exchange Commission and the Portuguese Insurance Institute.

f FR = Board of Governors of the Federal Reserve System;
OCC = Office of the Comptroller of the Currency, a bureau established in 1863 within the US Treasury Department, supervises national banks (banks with a federal charter) and federally licensed branches and agencies of foreign banks in the US. State banks may choose to be either 'members' or 'non-members' of the Federal Reserve System. Edge Act corporations are chartered by the Federal Reserve, and agreement corporations are chartered by the states, to provide all segments of the US economy with a means of financing international trade;
FDIC = Federal Deposit Insurance Corporation, an autonomous agency which insures deposits up to $100,000;
OTS = Office of Thrift Supervision

180   *Economic policy coordination in the eurozone*

- the monitoring of the suitability of the principal shareholders;
- the limitation on holdings in the non-banking sector;
- the need for sound administrative and accounting procedures and adequate internal control mechanisms.

The harmonisation of the monitoring of the credit institutions' solvency was achieved by two additional Directives that were adopted at about the same time as the Second Banking Coordination Directive and that were largely based on the results of the work carried out by the Basel Committee on Banking Supervision.[10]

- The *Own Funds Directive* (89/299/EEC), effective as of 1 January 1993, sets minimum common basic rules for the own funds of all credit institutions authorised to do business in the Community. The Directive determines the items that may be taken into account in calculating the own funds of a credit institution, to be used as the base (numerator) for computing the solvency ratios (ratio of own funds to assets). The core capital (original own funds) consists of the highest quality items (equity capital and disclosed reserves); supplementary capital (additional own funds) consists of such items as revaluation reserves and securities of indeterminate duration, subordinated loan capital. The supplementary capital included in the original own funds may not exceed 100 per cent of core capital.
- The *Solvency Ratio Directive* (89/647/EEC), effective as of 1 January 1991, contributes to the harmonisation of prudential supervision so as to maintain banking stability and fixes at 8 per cent the ratio of a credit institution's own funds to its assets and off-balance-sheet items, weighted (from 0 to 100 per cent) according to the level of risk involved.
- The *Directive on the Monitoring and Control of Large Exposures of Credit Institutions* (92/121/EEC), effective as of the beginning of 1994, further harmonised essential banking supervisory rules in the EU. Credit institutions were obliged to report all large exposures to the competent supervisory authorities. A large exposure to a client or group of connected clients is defined as one whose value is equal to, or exceeds, 10 per cent of the lending institution's own funds. Moreover, a credit institution may not incur an exposure to a client or group of connected clients where the value of the exposure exceeds 25 per cent of own funds.

Since 1993, additional Community legislation (Council Directives) on the harmonisation of banking supervision has been adopted in light of the ongoing work in this area at the international level. The standards adopted by the Basel Committee on Banking Supervision, with the 1996 Market Risk Amendment introduced in the Capital Accord of 1988 to tackle new forms of prudential risk in banking, were incorporated into Community banking directives. Whereas common standards had been already established for the supervision and monitoring of credit risks in the Solvency Ratio Directive of 1989, it was necessary to develop common standards for market risks incurred by banks and to provide a complementary framework for the supervision of the risk incurred by banks with respect to counter-party/settlement risks and foreign-exchange risks. The EC *Capital Adequacy Directive* (93/6/EEC) was therefore adopted to translate at the European level the new and evolving international standards to be applied for measuring the capital adequacy of banks. In 1998, an amendment to the EC Capital Adequacy Directive allowed credit institutions to use internal risk management models to determine the prudential capital requirements for market risk, in accordance with guidelines set by the Basel Committee.

The European Commission, in collaboration with EU national banking regulators/supervisors and the ECB, is reviewing the present EU rules on bank capital requirements, in parallel with the work done in the Basel Committee on Banking Supervision (BCBS), known as Basel 2. This review is expected to result in an overhaul of the European Union's bank capital framework, which will provide a refined treatment of credit risk and will introduce new risk categories, such as operational risk from system failures and fraud and reputational risks. Unlike the rules set by the BCBS, the EU banking regulatory framework is legally binding on all EU credit institutions. The Commission plans to have a proposal for an EU Directive on capital requirements as an integral part of the banking supervision framework by the end of 2003. The Commission's legislative proposals will then have to be approved by the Ecofin Council and the European Parliament, with the Directive translated into national laws for implementation in each Member State by the end of 2006.

Bilateral and multilateral cooperation of supervisory authorities

While the supervisory authorities of the Member State that issues the banking licence (country of origin) are primarily responsible for the overall supervision of a credit institution, including its cross-border operations, the *Second Banking Coordination Directive* strengthens and extends the First Banking Coordinating Directive of 1977 with respect to the principle of bilateral cooperation between the supervisory authorities in the country of origin and those in the host country:

> The competent authorities of the Member States concerned shall collaborate closely in order to supervise the activities of credit institutions operating, in particular by having established branches there, in one or more Member States other than that in which their head offices are sit-

182 *Economic policy coordination in the eurozone*

uated. They shall supply one another with all information concerning the management and ownership of such credit institutions that is likely to facilitate their supervision and the examination of the conditions for their authorisation, and all information likely to facilitate the monitoring of such institutions, in particular with regard to liquidity, solvency, deposit guarantees, the limiting of large exposures, administrative and accounting procedures and internal control mechanisms.

(Article 14.1 of the Second Banking Coordination Directive 89/646/EEC)

To implement this principle, the Member States began to negotiate bilateral 'Memoranda of Understanding' to supervise credit institutions that have cross-border activities. By the end of 1997, 78 bilateral Memoranda of Understanding had been signed between the banking supervisory authorities of the European Economic Area (EEA), which includes the 15 EU Member States plus Liechtenstein, Norway and Iceland. These Memoranda of Understanding regulate in detail the nature of the bilateral cooperation between the banking supervisory authorities, with particular reference to the reciprocal information and consultation obligations.

At a multilateral level, the *Banking Supervision Committee* of the ESCB, which is composed of representatives of all EU national central banks and national supervisory authorities as well as representatives of the ECB, is the key instrument established to promote multilateral cooperation at the EU level with respect to prudential supervision and financial stability. The Eurosystem may provide supervisory authorities with confidential information on individual credit institutions obtained from its activities in the fields of monetary policy, foreign exchange policy and payment systems. Conversely, the national supervisory authorities may provide the Eurosystem with supervisory information on individual institutions, such as compliance with minimum reserves. The so-called 'Post-BCCI Directive' (95/26/EC), adopted in 1995 after the collapse of multinational bank BCCI in the early 1990s, enlarged the list of institutions with which the supervisory authorities could share confidential information of credit institutions, and required external auditors of credit institutions to inform the supervisory authorities of any and all irregularities observed in the performance of their tasks. Additionally, according to that Directive, a credit institution may no longer have its registered office and head office in two different Member States, as was the case with BCCI. That situation left a gap in the prudential supervision of BCCI since the authorities could not agree on the 'home country' of that bank.

Macro financial stability and crisis management

The stability of the banking system can be compromised by an unexpected 'liquidity' or 'solvency' crisis of a major credit institution, which can spread to other participants in the banking sector. An isolated crisis can quickly evolve into a 'systemic' crisis for the entire eurozone. The current situation in the eurozone does not explicitly allow the ECB to provide liquidity support to individual banks. Within the Eurosystem, the principle regarding the provision of emergency liquidity to individual financial institutions is that the competent national central bank would be responsible for providing such assistance to those institutions operating within its jurisdiction. However, the ECB would have to assess these operations in the context of its monetary policy with a view to maintaining price stability.

In the eurozone, there is no explicit central provider or coordinator of emergency liquidity in the event of a serious problem with a credit institution and the Eurosystem cannot officially play the role of 'lender of last resort' as is de facto the case of most central banks, such as the Federal Reserve System. However, the ECB Governing Council may decide to provide such liquidity, which it could legally do by way of collateralised credit, under the terms of the 'structural' open market operations, in the event of a liquidity problem resulting from a gridlock in the payment system or from a bank failure with systemic consequences in the eurozone. In case the eligible collateral from the bank proves insufficient, the Eurosystem could agree to accept 'ineligible paper' as collateral.

The lack of clarity of the response of the monetary authority in the event of a financial stability crisis creates what the architects of the Eurosystem call 'constructive ambiguity' for the private financial sector. The underlying principle of the EU framework for crisis management with systemic implications in the banking sector is that every crisis has unique features and has to be managed in the light of the particular circumstances (see Economic and Financial Committee 2001). These institutional principles are similar to the ones existing in Germany, whereby the Bundesbank does not have either the explicit responsibility for the stability of the German banking system, or the power to act as a lender of last resort. This reflects the German view with respect to 'moral hazard', whereby the very existence of a safety net may encourage imprudent behaviour on the part of credit institutions and their clients. Although the Maastricht Treaty does not grant the Eurosystem the explicit power to be the 'lender of last resort', it allows the prudential supervision function to be transferred from the national authorities to the Eurosystem, provided that the Commission, the Ecofin Council, the ECB, and the European Parliament are all in agreement (Article 105.6). In fact, the ECB is seeking a larger role for its Banking Supervisory Committee in the prudential supervision of banks in the EU. However, the German and British governments do not want to see the ECB directly involved in banking supervision and would rather see the creation of a 'European Stability Forum' to increase the coordination between national regulators, finance ministries, and the Eurosystem.

Banking consolidation in the EU

The consolidation of the banking sector taking place in each EU Member State, together with the prospects of more cross-border mergers, has raised for the supervisory authorities the question of the impact of bank mergers on the stability of the financial system. While cross-border consolidation can reduce the probability of failure, it can increase the risk of a bank failure spreading across Member States, should such a failure occur. Cross-border reorganisation of financial institutions raises another issue for the supervisory authorities. As financial institutions reorganise themselves on a cross-border basis, their nationality may become less clear, raising the question of which supervisory authorities should assume responsibility in the event of a solvency crisis.

Despite the adoption of Community legislation in the late 1980s/early 1990s to create a single market in the banking sector, the combined market share of cross-border branches and subsidiaries established by credit institutions domiciled in the 15 EU Member States plus Liechtenstein, Norway and Iceland – known as the European Economic Area (EEA) – was, at the end of 1997, below 10 per cent in terms of banking assets in all eurozone countries, with the exception of Belgium, Ireland and Luxembourg (see Table 4.5). Since 1990, there have been two tendencies in the EEA banking sector: first, a gradual increase of the number of cross-border institutions, and second, a strong domestic consolidation (mergers or acquisitions) *within* each national banking sector.

The first tendency reflects an increase in the establishment of branches of banks domiciled in other EEA countries. It is partly the result of the implementation of the single market measures that simplified the procedures for opening up cross-border branches with the single 'passport'

Table 4.5 Market share of branches and subsidiaries of foreign credit institutions as a percentage of the total assets of domestic credit institutions, end-1997

Eurozone Member State	From EEA countries	
	Branches	Subsidiaries
Belgium	9.0	19.2
Germany	0.9	1.4
Spain	4.8	3.4
France	2.5	–
Ireland	17.7	27.8
Italy	3.6	1.7
Luxembourg	19.4	71.1
the Netherlands	2.3	3.0
Austria	0.7	1.6
Portugal	2.5	6.8
Finland	7.1	0

Source: European Central Bank, *Monthly Bulletin*, April 1999: 48.

introduced in the Second Banking Coordination Directive. The second tendency is the result of both a defensive and an offensive strategy on the part of banks in response, on the one hand, to the anticipated increase in competition coming from the creation of the European single financial market with a single currency, and, on the other hand, to the anticipated acquisition threats coming from the large banks in the US, such as Citigroup and J. P. Morgan Chase & Co, and in Japan, such as MTFG (Mitsubishi Tokyo Financial Group), Mizuho Holdings (formed from an alliance of Dai-Ichi Kangyo Bank, Fuji Bank and Industrial Bank of Japan), UFJ and SMBC. The net result of these two tendencies in the banking sector is that the concentration at the national level has either remained the same or increased since the early 1990s (see Table 4.6). This table also shows that the national concentration levels in the banking sector differ significantly over the eurozone Member States. The five largest banks represent over 75 per cent of total bank assets in Finland, the Netherlands and Portugal; between 40 per cent and 60 per cent in Austria, Belgium, France, Ireland and Spain; and below 25 per cent in Germany and Italy.

While most bank mergers/acquisitions in Europe have involved small banks, an increasing proportion of the most recent domestic bank mergers has involved two larger institutions (see Box 4.1). Cost savings in the back office and functional diversification between private banking, fund management and bancassurance are the main factors explaining these mergers between large banks. Although some high-profile EU cross-border bank mergers or acquisitions have recently made the headlines, these relatively few large cross-border mergers and acquisitions in the banking sector have primarily involved Belgian–Dutch and Scandinavian institutions seeking to expand out of their mature and relatively small

Table 4.6 Concentration at the national level: assets of the five largest credit institutions as a percentage of the total assets of domestic credit institutions

Member State	1985	1990	1995	1997
Belgium	48.0	48.0	54.0	57.0
Germany	–	13.9	16.7	16.7
Spain	38.1	34.9	45.6	43.6
France	46.0	42.5	41.2	40.3
Ireland	47.5	44.2	44.4	40.7
Italy	20.9	19.1	26.1	24.6
Luxembourg	–	–	21.2	22.4
Netherlands	69.3	73.4	76.1	79.4
Austria	35.9	34.6	39.2	48.3
Portugal	61.0	58.0	74.0	76.0
Finland	51.7	53.5	68.6	77.8

Source: European Central Bank, *Monthly Bulletin*, April 1999: 46.

domestic markets. Cultural as well as legal and regulatory hurdles can explain the limited number of important cross-border mergers/ acquisitions. Included in the first set of hurdles are the national governments' opposition to foreign takeovers, so as to create or maintain 'national champions' (see the example of Portugal in Box 4.1), and the identification of national customers with their national banks, making it difficult for a foreign bank to enter the national market. Included in the second set of hurdles are the national labour laws that may preclude layoffs in the reorganisation of the financial institution, and the new accounting and reporting requirements, all limiting the cost savings in cross-border mergers.

Box 4.1 Examples of recent domestic and cross-border mergers or acquisitions (or proposals) in the eurozone banking sector

In Italy

Banca Ambroveneto merged with Cariplo (1998), the Milan savings bank, which together with Banca Commerciale Italiana and Banco Ambrosiano Veneto (1999), now form *Banca IntesaBci*, Italy's largest banking group (total assets: €266 billion).

San Paolo, the Turin commercial bank, combined with IMI, the Rome financial group, to form *San Paolo-IMI*, which plans to buy a controlling share of Banco de Napoli from INA, the insurer acquired by Assicurazioni Generali, Italy's largest insurer that was unsuccessful in acquiring French insurer AGF (total assets of San Paolo-IMI: €140 billion).

Credito Italiano acquired control of the Bologna-based Rolo bank and subsequently merged with three of the largest north Italian savings banks (Unicredito) to form the *UniCredito Italiano* (1998) banking group (total assets: €150 billion).

UniCredito Italiano, after forming an alliance with Banca Nazionale del Lavoro, in which Banco Bilbao Viscaya Argentaria, Spain's second largest bank, has a 10 per cent stake, failed in its attempt to get BBVA to transfer its 10 per cent holding in BNL in exchange for a stake in the Milan bank of between 3.5 and 4 per cent. UniCredito Italiano tried to acquire control of BNL. UniCredito Italiano acquired Pioneer, the Boston-based mutual funds group.

In late 2001, Banca Monte dei Paschi di Siena, Italy's fifth largest bank tries to merge with Banca Nazionale del Lavoro, the sixth largest bank.

In Spain
Banco Santander, the largest bank, absorbed Banco Central Hispanoamericano, the third largest bank to become *Banco Santander Central Hispano (BSCH)* (1999) (total assets: €236 billion).

Banco Bilbao Vizcaya (BBV), Spain's second largest bank, merged with Argentaria, Spain's third largest bank, to become *BBVA* (2000), which is Spain's second largest bank (total assets: €202 billion).

BBVA and Telefonica, Spain's largest telecommunications group, have bought First-e, a Dublin-based bank, to develop a European online bank.

In Portugal
Banco Comercial Português acquired the Mello banking and insurance group, and Banco Português do Atlantico (1995).

Banco Comercial Português, Portugal's second largest bank, launched a hostile takeover (1999) for the Champalimaud financial group (composed of four banks and an insurer), after the Portuguese government blocked the friendly bid by Banco Santander Central Hispano, Spain's largest bank, for Champalimaud; the European Commission launched legal procedures against Portugal's violation of European single market regulations, after which Portugal lifted its veto on the BSHC bid for Champalimaud. As Banco Comercial Português dropped its hostile bid for Champalimaud, but maintained its offer for Banco Pinto e Sotto Mayor, the biggest bank in the Champalimaud group, Champalimaud is divided between BSCH and state-owned Caixa Geral de Depôsitos, Portugal's biggest bank, resulting in BSCH having 11 per cent of the Portuguese banking market. With BCP's acquisition of BPSM, BCP became Portugal's largest financial group.

Banco Espirito Santo and Banco Português de Investimento merged to create a group known as BES.BPI with a market share of 25 per cent of Portugal's retail banking.

In France
The Caisse des Dépôts et Consignations (CDC), a state institution, and the Groupe Caisse d'Epargne, a mutual savings bank, launched in 2001 a partnership by pooling some of their assets, to the amount of €8.3 billion, to create a joint subsidiary, Eulia.

HSBC Holdings of the UK, the world's second largest bank behind Citigroup of the US, acquired (in 2000), in a friendly bid, the

Crédit Commercial de France, France's fourth largest bank. The deal is the most significant cross-border acquisition of a European bank and comes after ING's failed bid to buy CCF.

The Banque Nationale de Paris bid (1999) for Paribas and Société Générale, but failed to acquire the latter, which originally wanted to merge with Paribas (total assets of BNP and Paribas €574 billion).

Crédit Agricole, France's largest bank, planned in late 2001 to take over Crédit Lyonnais, France's third-biggest bank.

Investment bank Banque Indosuez sold (1996) to Crédit Agricole, which renamed it Crédit Agricole Indosuez.

Société Générale purchased Crédit du Nord, owned by Paribas, in 1998.

In Germany
Vereinsbank and Hypo-Bank merge to create Bayerische HypoVereinsbank, Germany's second largest bank, which changed its name to HVB in 2001; in 2000, HypoVereinsbank acquired Bank of Austria; Munich Re, the world's largest reinsurer, acquired 26 per cent of HVB in 2001, exerting a strong influence on the bank, in line with the European trend to create bancassurance in the banking sector.

Deutsche Bank, Germany's largest bank, which acquired Bankers' Trust (1999) (US) initially proposed to merge its retail banking with the retail business of Dresdner Bank, Germany's third largest bank (the four largest German banks control only 25 per cent of the retail market, since much of the retail banking is in the hands of 13 lander banks and 578 savings banks); the Banque Nationale de Paris' interest in Dresdner Bank suspended temporarily the Deutsche–Dresdner merger proposal; then Dresdner Bank and Bayerische HypoVereinsbank announced a possible merger, but in early March 2000 Deutsche Bank and Dresdner Bank agreed to merge to form one of the world's largest banks; however, in April 2000 a dispute over the future of Dresdner Kleinwort Benson, the London-based investment banking arm of Germany's Dresdner Bank led to a collapse of that merger agreement; in October 2000, Deutsche Bank announced that it will purchase the retail, private banking, corporate banking and asset management arms of Banque Worms (France) from Axa, the French financial services group.

In July 2000, Commerzbank, Germany's fourth largest bank,

engaged in merger talks with Dresdner Bank; as these talks foundered, Commerzbank announced in August 2000 that, instead of seeking a cross-border merger partner, it will seek cross-shareholdings with its cooperation partners: Crédit Lyonnais (France); BSCH (Spain); Banca Intesea, Mediobanca and insurer Generali (Italy), and Erste Bank (Austria); in 2001, Dresdner is finally acquired in a €24 billion takeover by Munich-based insurer Allianz, creating a bancassurance.

In February 2001, GZ Bank and DG Bank announced a merger worth €6 billion.

In October 2001, Bayerische Landesbank, Germany's second largest public sector bank, signed a partnership agreement with Caisse des Dépôts et Consignations (CDC) and Groupe Caisse d'Épargne of France.

In the Netherlands
NMB Postbank and the insurer Nationale-Nederlanden merged to create ING.

ING bought Banque Bruxelles Lambert (1998), Belgium's third largest bank.

ING acquired BHF-Bank of Germany (1999) (total assets: €440 billion).

ING set up internet banking branches in France and Spain; ING took a 49 per cent participation in Allgemeine Deutsche Direktbank with a view to taking full control in the future.

ABN-Amro acquired (1999) Banca di Roma (Italian) over rival Italian bidder San Paolo-IMI whose bid was deemed hostile, and therefore blocked by Italy's central bank.

In Belgium
Fortis, a Belgo-Dutch financial group formed in 1990, acquired (1999) Générale de Banque, over rival bidder ABN Amro (Dutch). This cleared the way for Fortis to integrate Générale's operations with those of ASLK-CGER, a Belgian bank that Générale de Banque had previously acquired.

Bacob Bank acquired Paribas Banque Belgium, renaming itself Artesia.

Kredietbank, a retail and corporate bank, merged with CERA Bank, a rural coop bank, and with ABB, the insurance group, to create a new bancassurance giant called KBC.

Crédit Local de Belgique merged (1996) with Crédit Communal

de Belgique to create *Dexia* (total assets : €204 billion), which purchased Artesia in 2001 for €3.2 billion.

In Nordic countries

Merita (Finland) merged in 1998 ($10.7 billion) with Nordbanken (Sweden) to form MeritaNordbanken.

MeritaNordbanken acquired, for $4.5 billion Unidanmark, Denmark's second largest banking group; it also acquired, for $2.9 billion Christiania Bank, Norways' second largest bank, giving MeritaNordbanken 40 per cent of the Finnish banking market, 25 per cent in Denmark and 20 per cent in Sweden. The new group is named Nordea and becomes the largest Nordic bank.

In Greece

Alpha Bank and National Bank of Greece, Greece's two leading banking groups decided in late 2001 to merge, but in a dispute over senior management appointments, this €10 billion merger is scuttled in early 2002.

CONCLUDING REMARKS

During the late 1980s and the early 1990s when the Member States of the European Community and the Community institutions were preoccupied with negotiating the framework for the creation of a single currency area with a single central bank, it was clear that the future European Central Bank would have to 'look like' and 'act like' the Bundesbank. Under those conditions, the German people were willing to give up their beloved Deutsche mark and Bundesbank as the price to pay to continue the long and sometimes difficult post-war process towards further European economic and political integration that would forever anchor Germany in a Europe at peace with itself, composed of nation states that could eventually become the United States of Europe. Post-war Germany was committed to form 'an ever closer union' with its European neighbours so as to create a 'destiny henceforward shared', which would substitute for age-old rivalries and bloody conflicts between the nations of Europe.

The framework for the European Central Bank outlined in the Maastricht Treaty and its Protocol convinced the Germans, and more importantly the Bundesbank, that the future European Central Bank would indeed look like the Bundesbank in all its essential elements: a primary statutory objective of price stability and independence from all national governments and Community bodies in the execution of its monetary policy to achieve and maintain its primary objective. The ECB, like the

Bundesbank, would be accountable, and only within the narrow terms of its mandate, directly to the people of Europe and to no one else. Its Executive Board would be comparable to the Bundesbank's Directorate; the National Central Bank Governors, who would sit on the ECB's Governing Council and who would have to be entirely independent from their national governments and parliaments, would be comparable to the Presidents of the Land Central Banks sitting on the pre-euro Bundesbank's Central Bank Council. The icing on the cake would be the request from the German government to have the ECB headquartered in Frankfurt to guarantee a 'Bundesbank culture', and in return, as a gesture to Europe, the German government would decline to propose its candidate for the position of the first ECB President, although the first ECB chief economist, an important and influential position on the Governing Council, would come from the Bundesbank.

Some in Europe, such as the French government and the then-President of the European Commission, Jacques Delors, would have preferred a European Central Bank designed more along the lines of the Fed: a limited statutory independence, no single primary objective, and accountable to the European Parliament, which would involve more than just periodically reporting to it. The European Parliament, and even perhaps national parliaments, along with the European Commission and the Ecofin Council, should be ultimately able to change or influence the ECB, if required. More importantly, a eurozone 'economic government' would be set up to act as a counterweight to the ECB. All of that was not to be. The German people and the Bundesbank would never accept such a framework for the new European Central Bank. That was clearly demonstrated by the German reaction to the remarks of President Mitterrand of France in 1992, when in a last-ditch effort to convince French voters to vote in favour of the Maastricht Treaty, interpreted certain provisions of the Treaty by claiming that the 'politicians' would ultimately have the last word on the policies of the European Central Bank.

The long transition period between the entry into force of the Maastricht Treaty in late 1993 and the establishment of the European Central Bank in mid-1998 would be an opportunity for the Bundesbank to prepare, in cooperation with all the other EU national central banks, the groundwork for a final decision on the monetary policy strategy to be followed by the ECB. It is here that the ECB seems to deviate slightly from the Bundesbank model. The ECB monetary policy strategy based on two pillars – one of which uses a reference value, not on a target value, of a broad monetary aggregate, while the other uses a wide range of economic and financial indicators to assess future price developments – looks like a monetary policy strategy that is close to the Fed's, notwithstanding the fact that the Fed has two policy objectives of maintaining a low rate of inflation and stabilising aggregate demand growth around the potential growth rate of output. Although it refuses to release the votes of the Governing

192 *Economic policy coordination in the eurozone*

Council meetings, the ECB is a very communicative institution compared with the pre-euro Bundesbank. For the most part, the communication attempts to place its monetary policy decisions in the context of its two-pillar based monetary policy strategy, which the public perceives as complicated. The numerous appearances of Executive Board members before a European Parliamentary committee and the monthly publication of its 'Editorial' explaining in detail the basis for the monetary policy decision are just two examples that set it apart from the pre-euro Bundesbank.

The ECB does not have a good press. Yet its performance judged over its first three years – a short period of time to pass judgement on a central bank – is as good as, if not better than, the much praised Fed. The average annual inflation rates over the years 1999–2001 were 1.97 per cent and 2.8 per cent for the eurozone and the US, respectively (see Table 3.5). And the Fed, for all its claimed flexibility to 'fine tune' the economy owing to its dual objective of maintaining price stability and a sustainable growth of output, was unable to prevent the US recession that began in March 2001 and ended in December 2001. It probably reduced the recession's amplitude and duration by aggressively reducing the target federal funds rate by 4.75 percentage points over a 12-month period. The ECB critics do not so much find fault with the ECB's performance in terms of its stated objectives, but rather criticise its monetary policy strategy, which the market has difficulties understanding and so therefore the market has difficulty predicting the next move of the ECB. In order to overcome this shortcoming, the ECB either will have to define, as part of its monetary policy strategy, a target zone for a reliable eurozone monetary aggregate and thus behave more like the pre-euro Bundesbank, or will have to guide the markets more carefully before changing its key interest rates and thus behave more like the Fed. Finally, the 'question-and-answer' period with the press (the 'Frankfurt follies') that immediately follows the Governing Council's monthly monetary policy meeting could be discontinued without any loss, and possibly a gain, to the reputation of the ECB. There are more productive ways for a central bank to communicate information. In that regard, the ECB should learn from both the pre-euro Bundesbank and the Fed.

Appendix

Table of equivalencies between the previous numbering and the new numbering in the 'Treaty establishing the European Community', following the coming into force on 1 May 1999 of the Treaty of Amsterdam (1997).

Previous numbering	*New numbering**
Article 2	Article 2
Article 3a	Article 4
Title VI	Title VII
Chapter 1	Chapter 1
Article 102a	Article 98
Article 103	Article 99
Article 103a	Article 100
Article 104	Article 101
Article 104a	Article 102
Article 104b	Article 103
Article 104c	Article 104
Chapter 2	Chapter 2
Article 105	Article 105
Article 105a	Article 106
Article 106	Article 107
Article 107	Article 108
Article 108	Article 109
Article 108a	Article 110
Article 109	Article 111
Chapter 3	Chapter 3
Article 109a	Article 112
Article 109b	Article 113
Article 109c	Article 114
Article 109d	Article 115
Chapter 4	Chapter 4
Article 109e	Article 116
Article 109f	Article 117
Article 109g	Article 118
Article 109h	Article 119
Article 109i	Article 120
Article 109j	Article 121

continued

Appendix

Previous numbering	New numbering*
Article 109k	Article 122
Article 109l	Article 123
Article 109m	Article 124
Title VIa	Title VIII
Article 109n	Article 125
Article 109o	Article 126
Article 109p	Article 127
Article 109q	Article 128
Article 109r	Article 129
Article 109s	Article 130
Protocol (TEU) no. 3	Protocol no. 18
Protocol (TEU) no. 5	Protocol no. 20
Protocol (TEU) no. 6	Protocol no. 21
Protocol (TEU) no. 11	Protocol no. 25

*All citations in this text use the 'new numbering'.

Notes

1 Historical background and basic institutional features

1 Resolution of the Council and of the Representatives of the Governments of the Member States of 22 March 1971:

> ...express their political will to establish an economic and monetary union, during the coming decade, in accordance with a plan by stages beginning on 1 January 1971. The steps to be taken must be such that, at the conclusion of this process, the Community will:
> ...
> Form a single currency area within the international system, characterized by the total and irreversible convertibility of currencies, the elimination of margins of fluctuation of exchange rates, the irrevocable locking of parities – all of which are essential preconditions for the creation of a single currency – and including a Community organisation of the Central Banks;...
>
> (Monetary Committee 1974)

Resolution of the Heads of State or Government on 19–21 October 1972:

> ...The Heads of State and Government reaffirm the resolve of the Member States of the enlarged Community [the original six Member States plus the United Kingdom, Ireland and Denmark] to move irrevocably the Economic and Monetary Union, by confirming all the details of the Acts passed by the Council and by the Member States representatives on 22 March 1971 and 21 March 1972 [authorizing the central banks of the Member States to reduce the margins of fluctuation between any two currencies of the Member States]. The required decisions will have to be taken during 1973 to allow transition to the second stage of the Economic and Monetary Union on 1 January 1974 and in view of its complete realization by 31 December 1980 at the latest.
>
> (Monetary Committee 1974)

2 With the coming into force of the Treaty of Amsterdam (1997) on 1 May 1999, the articles of the Treaty on European Union (1992) and of the Treaty establishing the European Community (1957) have been re-numbered. The correspondence between the original numbers and the new numbers, which are cited in this text, is given in the Appendix.

3 For the initial appointments of the Executive Board members, the requirement of consulting the 'Governing Council' is replaced by the requirement of

consulting the members of the 'European Monetary Institute', which was the precursor of the European Central Bank during the period 1994–98 leading up to the launch of the single currency.

4 In practice, the President of the ECB has indicated that, at the meetings of the Governing Council, the monetary policy decision is taken by achieving a broad consensus in a 'collegial' manner. Thus, a formal vote is not necessary. However, a consensus, according to Duisenberg, 'does not indicate in all cases that, if there had been a vote, it would have been unanimous' (Duisenberg 1999b, c; *Financial Times*, June 8, 1999: 3; Barber 1999). Nayeri (2002) reports that Duisenberg usually defines a broad consensus as requiring at least 14 members (from a total of 18) to agree to a monetary policy decision.

5 In Denmark, the government decided to hold a referendum on 28 September 2000 on whether it should abrogate its 1992 decision to retain its national currency. In this latest referendum, the people of Denmark rejected joining the eurozone by a 53 per cent majority. This result does not exclude the possibility of another referendum at some future date. In fact, with the successful changeover to the euro banknotes and coins in the eurozone at the beginning of 2002, combined with the election of a new centre-right Danish government in late 2001, the new government has indicated that another referendum on the euro may take place in early 2003. With a majority voting in favour of the euro, Denmark could join the eurozone soon thereafter, since the Danish krone has participated in ERM II since 1999 and its national central bank already satisfies the independence requirements of the 'Treaty'.

In March 2000, the Swedish ruling party of Social-Democrats took a 'yes, but later' stance on joining the eurozone, with a then-expected national referendum on the question slated for Autumn 2002, followed by a decision of the Swedish Parliament, which would have put the expected entry date of Sweden into the eurozone in early 2004. The Danish 'no' vote in 2000 delayed that timetable. A referendum is now expected in March 2003, after the general election in September 2002. According to that new timetable, Sweden could thus participate in ERM II as of June 2003 and join the eurozone in January 2005 (see Leonard 2002: 12).

The British Labour government decided in 1997 that the question of British entry into the single currency area would not be considered before the next elections, which were held on 7 June 2001. In the meantime, the government policy is to 'plan and prepare' in order that the UK may have a genuine option to join the eurozone, if that is what the government, Parliament and the people in due course decide. In February 1999, HM Treasury published its first *Outline of the National Changeover Plan*. The *Second Outline of the National Changeover Plan* was published in March 2000. Provided that 'five economic tests' are met, the government will decide to launch the process to join the single currency area, a process that would include a non-binding referendum on the question within four months of the decision that the UK had met the economic tests. In total, the length of the period between a positive referendum and the introduction of euro notes and coins in the UK is estimated to be 24–30 months, but the changeover plan does not specify the length of the period between a positive referendum result and entry into the third stage of EMU, when sterling would be irrevocably fixed against the euro. Before the UK could join, as is the case for all Member State applications for eurozone membership, the European Commission and the ECB would need to report to the Ecofin Council on whether the UK economy had achieved a high degree of sustainable convergence with the euro area, including a stable exchange rate against the euro within the exchange rate regime known as ERM II for a two-year period prior to the evaluation period. It is expected, as promised by the

Labour government, that the Chancellor of the Exchequer will have completed his analysis of the five economic tests by Autumn 2002, at the earliest, or by June 2003 at the latest. Most observers believe that this scenario suggests that Britain's entry into the eurozone would not be before late 2005 or early 2006. The Treasury's five economic questions, as defined by the ruling Labour government, that need a positive answer in order to launch a referendum for joining the eurozone are (see HM Treasury 2001):

1 Are business cycles and economic structures compatible so that the UK and the eurozone could live comfortably with euro interest rates on a permanent basis?
2 If problems emerge is there sufficient flexibility to deal with them?
3 Would joining the single currency create better conditions for firms making long-term decisions to invest in Britain?
4 What impact would entry into the single currency have on the competitive position of the UK's financial industry, particularly the City's wholesale market?
5 Would joining the single currency promote higher growth, stability and a lasting increase in jobs?

6 The ECB has subsequently requested (in November 1998), and received authorisation from the Ecofin Council (Regulation 2000/1009/EC of 8 May 2000), to increase, if necessary, the capital base of the ECB up to €10 billion.
7 In accordance with the transitional provisions of the EMU in the 'Treaty', the three 'out' NCBs (Bank of England, Danmarks Nationalbank, and Sveriges Riksbank) also made a minimal contribution to the ECB's capital by the amount of 5 per cent of their subscribed capital share. The net return generated on this capital represents their contribution to the operational costs that have arisen from their participation in some activities of the ECB. However, the 'out' NCBs are not entitled to receive any share of the distributable profits of the ECB.
8 However, during the interim period of 1999–2001, the pooled seigniorage income derived from the aggregate deposit liabilities of the euro NCBs to credit institutions was calculated by using the so-called indirect method, i.e. by multiplying a defined liability base by a specified reference interest rate. The liability base was defined as all deposit liabilities of euro NCBs to credit institutions, which included current accounts, the deposit facility, fixed-term deposits, deposits related to margin calls, liquidity absorbing repurchase agreements and liabilities of euro NCBs arising from the issuance of debt certificates by the ECB. The reference interest rate used was the latest available two-week repo rate and was applied on a daily basis to the liability base. This indirect method was used during the first three years of operation of the Eurosystem because, in the judgement of the ECB Governing Council, the balance sheet structures of the eurozone National Central Banks were too heterogeneous to calculate directly meaningful seigniorage income figures.
9 On 1 January 1999, the total value of the banknotes in circulation from the then 11 eurozone NCBs amounted to €342 billion (European Central Bank, *Annual Report 1999*); the total value of the Deutsche mark denominated banknotes in circulation amounted to €131 billion (Deustche Bundesbank, *Annual Report 1999*); the total value of the French franc denominated banknotes in circulation amounted to €42 billion (Banque de France, *Rapport annuel – Exercice 1999*).
10 On 1 January 1999, the opening date of the financial statement of the Eurosystem composed of the original 11 participating NCBs and the ECB, the reserve

assets amounted to €329.4 billion, composed of gold (€99.6 billion), Special Drawing Rights (€5.1 billion), reserve position in the IMF (€23.4 billion) and foreign exchange (€199.8 billion). The foreign exchange figure refers to non-euro area currencies, since euro-area currency-denominated foreign exchange positions held on 31 December 1998 were transformed automatically into domestic positions through the transition to Stage Three. For example, Deutsche mark denominated assets held by the Banque de France were automatically transferred as 'domestic' assets in the accounts of the Eurosystem. According to the harmonised accounting rules of the Eurosystem, the initial gold and foreign exchange holdings were valued at market rates and prices prevailing on 31 December 1998. Foreign currency reserves and gold are revalued at the end of each quarter, using the market exchange rates and prices prevailing at the end of the quarter (for current data, see any issue of the European Central Bank, *Monthly Bulletin*, Table 8.7.2).

11 With the integration of the Deutsche Bundesbank in the European System of Central Banks in June 1998, this requirement had to be changed to 'not less than five years' to be in line with the provisions of the Maastricht Treaty.
12 It is sometimes said that, in Europe, the reverse is true: the European Central Bank is a central bank without a sovereign nation. This statement is not entirely correct. Although the eurozone is composed of 12 sovereign nations, the sovereignty of each nation is partly transferred to the eurozone level since most EU laws, which supersede national laws, are adopted by a qualified majority in the EU Council of Ministers and, depending on the legislative area, by a majority of the members of the European Parliament.
13 The Comptroller of the Currency was, and still is today, at the time of writing, a member of the Executive branch of government responsible for the supervision of private banks with a national charter.
14 Thus, the Federal Reserve Banks of Richmond, Atlanta, St Louis, Minneapolis, Kansas City, Dallas and San Francisco were excluded from this Committee.
15 If the appointment of a member is to complete the unfinished 14-year term of another member who died or resigned before the end of his/her term, the member may be reappointed for only one full 14-year term. For example, the current Chairman, Alan Greenspan, was appointed in August 1987 to complete an unfinished term expiring at the end of January 1992 of a previous Governor, and was reappointed in 1992 for a full 14 year term expiring at the end of January 2006. His mandate as the Chairman expires in June 2004.
16 The allocation formula among the Federal Reserve Banks of US Government and Federal Agency Securities held in the SOMA account stemming from the open market operations executed exclusively by the Federal Reserve Bank of New York is subject to a number of exceptions (see Federal Reserve Bank of New York 1999: 50–53). We simply note here that the allocation formula does not use the criterion of the relative size of each Reserve Bank, as measured by the total paid-in capital contributed to each Reserve Bank by its member banks.

2 Objectives, independence, transparency and accountability

1 Article 3 of the Bundesbank Act of 26 July 1957, with its amendments up to and including the Fifth Act of 8 July 1994, states:

> The Deutsche Bundesbank shall regulate the amount of money in circulation and of credit supplied to the economy, using monetary powers conferred on it by this Act, with the *aim of safeguarding the currency* and shall arrange for the execution of domestic and international payments.

(From Deutsche Bundesbank 1995 [emphasis added])

2 Usually, 'price stability' is operationally defined as a low rate of inflation (less than 2 or 3 per cent per year) as measured by the Consumer Price Index, which allows for the possible upward bias in the measurement of the rate of inflation. Under this definition of 'price stability', the central bank usually allows a 'base drift', which means that any short-run deviation from its definition of 'price stability' is not offset by a lower (or higher) rate of inflation in subsequent periods. In other words, the central bank will not attempt to offset any short-term deviation from 'price stability' caused by one-time, random shocks.

3 The Maastricht Treaty stipulates that the primary objective of the ECB and all EU national central banks (with the exception of the Bank of England by virtue of Protocol no. 25 of the 'Treaty') is to maintain price stability:

> The primary objective of the ESCB shall be to maintain price stability...
> (Article 105.1 of the 'Treaty' and Article 2 of the 'Statute')

Article 105.2 stipulates that 'The basic tasks to be carried out through the ESCB [Eurosystem] shall be to *define* [emphasis added by author] and implement the monetary policy of the Community [eurozone]...'

4 For more details, see Hetzel (1985) and Fisher (1934).

5 The Employment Act of February 20, 1946 states in Section 2: 'The Congress hereby declares that it is the continuing policy and responsibility of the Federal Government to use all practicable means ... to promote maximum employment, production, and purchasing power.'

6 There have been recent Congressional attempts to legislate price stability as the primary objective of the Federal Reserve System. In 1989, 1991 and 1993 Representative Steven Neal, a Democrat from North Carolina, introduced legislation directing the Federal Reserve to adopt and pursue monetary policies leading to, and then maintaining, zero inflation. Zero inflation was defined to be identical to Greenspan's definition of price stability. In 1995, 1997 and 1999, Senator Connie Mack, a Republican from Florida, and Representative James Saxton, a Republican from New Jersey, introduced legislation (the Mack–Saxton Bill) to adopt price stability as the primary objective of the Fed and to direct the Fed to define price stability numerically. All of these Congressional initiatives remained in committee.

7 There was one minor exception to this rule. Article 13.2 of the Bundesbank Act of 1957 gave the German government the right to defer a decision of the Bundesbank's Central Bank Council for up to two weeks, a privilege that had never been used by the German government.

8 Under the Full Employment and Balanced Growth Act (Humphrey–Hawkins Act) of 1978, the Federal Open Market Committee was required, until mid-2000, to set yearly target growth rates of monetary aggregates and to explain to Congress any deviations of the monetary aggregates from the announced targets. Title 12, Section 225a, of the US Code pursuant to the Full Employment and Balanced Growth Act of 1978 stipulates:

- The Board of Governors of the Federal Reserve System and the Federal Open Market Committee shall maintain long run growth of the monetary and credit aggregates commensurate with the economy's long run potential to increase production, so as to promote effectively the goals of maximum employment, stable prices, and moderate long-term interest rates.
- In furtherance of the purposes of the Full Employment and Balanced

> Growth Act of 1978, the Board of Governors of the Federal Reserve System shall transmit to the Congress, not later than February 20 and July 20 of each year,... the objectives and plans of the Board of Governors and the Federal Open Market Committee with respect to the ranges of growth or diminution of the monetary and credit aggregates for the calendar year during which the report is transmitted ... [and] the Board of Governors shall include an explanation of the reasons for any revisions to or deviations from [the announced target rates of the previous year].

With the coming into force of the Federal Reports Elimination and Sunset Act (1995) in mid-2000, and the resulting amendments to the Federal Reserve Act of 27 December 2000, the content of the twice-yearly 'Monetary Policy Report to Congress' has been modified. The Federal Open Market Committee is no longer required to set – and no longer sets – monetary target ranges. In fact, as explained below, since the late 1980s little attention had been put on these target ranges either as a guide to monetary policy or in the context of Congressional oversight of the Federal Reserve System.

9 Although the discussion takes place in the Ecofin Council, the voting rights of the Ministers from Member States outside the eurozone are suspended.
10 Article 6.1 of the Bundesbank Act of 1957, which provided for the Central Bank Council's competence to determine the monetary policy of the Bank, states:

> The Central Bank Council determines the monetary policy of the Bank...

11 Article 15, Bundesbank Act of 1957: 'In order to influence the amount of money in circulation and of credit granted, the Deutsche Bundesbank sets the interest and discount rates to be used in its transactions and defines the principles governing its lending and open market operations.'

Article 16, Bundesbank Act of 1957: '(1) In order to influence the amount of money in circulation and of credit granted, the Deutsche Bundesbank may require credit institutions to hold certain percentages of the liabilities in respect of sight deposits, time deposits and savings deposits, and of their liabilities in respect of short and medium-term borrowed funds...'
12 The initial terms of office of the members of the ECB Executive Board have various durations to introduce continuity of the Board when the posts change hands (see Article 50 of the 'Statute').
13 A casual empirical observation of the comparative rates of inflation between Germany, with its independent pre-euro Bundesbank, which had a single primary objective of price stability, and the US, with its less independent Federal Reserve System, which has no single primary objective, would seem to confirm this relationship over the period 1975 to 1998: Germany with an average annual inflation rate of 3.12 per cent and the US with an average annual inflation rate of 4.78 per cent (see Table 3.7). Of course, the German inflation outcome was not necessarily 'caused' by the independent pre-euro Bundesbank – it may just be the result of a different inflation culture in the two countries, stemming from different historical experiences with the consequences of inflation (see Hayo 1998).
14 Federal Reserve Act, Section 10, par. 10, as added by the Banking Act of 23 August 1935
15 However, whenever the Board of Governors decided to approve the request of a district Federal Reserve Bank to change its discount rate, the Board released an immediate statement. This policy still applies today.

Notes 201

16 At regularly scheduled meetings, the press release is issued at 2:15 pm, Eastern time.
17 Article 113.3 of the 'Treaty' stipulates: 'The ECB shall address an annual report on the activities of the ESCB and on the monetary policy of both the previous and current year to the European Parliament, the Council and the Commission, and also to the European Council. The President of the ECB shall present this report to the Council and to the European Parliament, which may hold a general debate on that basis. The President of the ECB and the other members of the Executive Board may, at the request of the European Parliament or on their own initiative, be heard by the competent Committees of the European Parliament.'
18 Article 15.1 of the 'Statute' stipulates: 'The ECB shall draw up and publish reports on the activities of the ESCB at least quarterly.'

3 Monetary policy: strategy, instruments and actions

1 The annual rate measures the rate of the price index change between the current month and the same month of the previous year. This measure is less responsive to recent changes in the price levels than the month-on-month rate of change. However, the year-on-year measure can be influenced by one-off effects in either end month.
2 This time period is the ECB's unofficial definition of the 'medium term', the period of time that may be required for the inflation rate to return to the ECB's definition of price stability following a one-off price shock (see Duisenberg 2001a: 3).
3 The ECB argues that the unemployment rate for the eurozone, published by Eurostat and calculated according to International Labour Office (ILO) definitions is not a reliable measure of slackness in the labour market and that a high rate of unemployment does not, by itself, indicate downward pressure on wages since the bulk of the unemployment in the eurozone is of a structural nature, which is related to specific labour market regulations and institutional features governing individual labour markets. Thus, the ECB prefers to examine the changes in unemployment rate rather than the underlying level of the unemployment rate (European Central Bank, *Monthly Bulletin*, April 1999: 35; European Central Bank, *Monthly Bulletin*, May 2000: 57–74).
4 Since June 1997, the Bank of England targets a rate of inflation (RPIX = retail price index excluding mortgage interest payments) of 2.5 per cent; the Sveriges Riksbank targets a rate of inflation (UNDIX = CPI excluding interest expenditure and direct effects of altered indirect taxes and subsidies) of 2 per cent with a tolerance of ±1 percentage point; the Bank of Canada's monetary policy aims at keeping the year-over-year rate of inflation at the 2 per cent midpoint of a range defined with a floor of 1 per cent and a ceiling of 3 per cent. The core rate of inflation is used as an operational guide. The core rate of inflation includes 84 per cent of the CPI basket. It excludes fruits, vegetables, gasoline, fuel oil, natural gas, intercity transportation, tobacco, mortgage interest and indirect taxes (see Bank of Canada 2001).
5 In addition to the regular standard tender on 27 April 2001, the ECB conducted an additional standard refinancing operation with a *one-week* maturity. This additional operation was purely technical because of the low volume financing demanded by the credit institutions during the previous two main refinancing operations. The credit institutions were unwilling to bid for funds in the expectation that the minimum bid rate would be reduced by the ECB at the following weekly tender (see European Central Bank 2001a).
6 By virtue of Council Regulation 98/2531/EC of 23 November 1998, based on

Article 19.2 of the 'Statute', the Governing Council of the ECB has the right to set the minimum required reserve ratio, which may not exceed 10 per cent of any relevant liabilities of the financial institutions, but may be 0 per cent.
7 However, as a transitional measure, between 4 and 21 January 1999 the interest rate for the marginal lending facility was set at 3.25 per cent and the interest rate for the deposit facility at 2.75 per cent. This last measure of a technical nature, as explained above, was taken to guide the overnight market interest rate in a narrow corridor of 50 basis points, so as to help the credit institutions in the 11 eurozone Member States to adapt to the new environment (see Fig. 3.3).
8 The basic formula is sometimes called Fisher's money exchange equation, whereby the exogenous money supply times the income velocity of money is equal to the product of the equilibrium level of real income and of the general price level, or

$$M \times V = P \times Y$$

where M is the exogenous money supply, V is the income velocity of that money, P is the general price level, and Y is real income. By taking the time derivative of the log expression of the above equation, we obtain the result that the money supply growth rate times the rate of change of the income velocity of money is equal to the product of the growth rate of real income and of the rate of change of the general price level. Consequently, for a constant rate of change over time of income velocity of money and a constant rate of change over time of real income (usually equal to the potential growth rate of the economy), Fisher's equation implies a well-defined relation between the growth rate of money supply and the inflation rate, namely that, in long-run equilibrium, the inflation rate is equal to the sum of the growth rate of the money supply and the income velocity of that money, less the potential growth rate of output.
9 This section draws heavily on the Meulendyke (1998).
10 The various definitions of money stock are as follows: M1 is currency plus demand deposits; M2 is M1 plus time and savings deposits at commercial banks other than large certificates of deposit (CDs); and M3 is M2 plus deposits at non-bank thrift institutions.
11 The Federal Reserve Reform Act, Section 2A, 16 November 1977 requires that the Board of Governors and the Federal Open Market Committee 'maintain long-run monetary and credit aggregates commensurate with the economy's long-run potential to increase production so as to promote effectively the goals of maximum employment, stable prices, and moderate long-term interest rates'. The Full Employment and Balanced Growth Act of 1978 requires the President, the Congress, and the Federal Reserve to work together to achieve those goals and, in particular, requires the Fed to set annual target ranges for growth in monetary and credit aggregates, to report these targets to Congress twice each year, and to explain deviations from the announced targets.
12 Edge Act and agreement corporations are special purpose banks limited to internationally oriented business.
13 Required reserves must be held in the form of deposits with Federal Reserve Banks or vault cash. Non-member institutions may maintain reserve balances with a Federal Reserve Bank indirectly, on a pass-through basis, with certain approved institutions. According to the Monetary Control Act of 1980, the Board of Governors has the right to impose reserve requirements on transaction deposits and on non-personal time deposits. However, the reserve requirements on non-personal time deposits with a maturity of 1.5 years or more and

with a maturity of less than 1.5 years were eliminated by the Board of Governors in 1983 and 1991, respectively. Moreover, the first $4.9 million (1999 figure) of transaction deposits are not subject to any required reserves; the balance of reservable liabilities up to $46.5 million (1999 figure) is subject to a required reserve ratio of 3 per cent; reservable liabilities over that amount are subject to a required reserve ratio of 10 per cent. To allow depository institutions flexibility in meeting their reserve requirements, the Federal Reserve requires these institutions to hold an average amount of reserves over a two-week maintenance period rather than a specific amount on each day. Since 1982, the Federal Reserve has required depository institutions to maintain their reserves against transaction deposits on a virtually contemporaneous basis.

4 Economic policy coordination in the eurozone

1 Council Decision of 17 July 1969 (69/227/EEC), Council Decisions of 22 March 1971 (71/141/EEC) and (71/142/EEC), Council Decision of 18 February 1974 (74/120/EEC) and Council Decision of 12 March 1990 (90/141/EEC). All Council Decisions are available in the *Official Journal of the European Communities* (Luxembourg).
2 Article 2 of the 'Treaty' provides that:

> The Community shall have as its task, by establishing a common market and an economic and monetary union and by implementing common policies or activities referred to in [Article 4], to promote throughout the Community a harmonious, balanced and sustainable development of economic activities, a high level of employment and of social protection, equality between men and women, sustainable and non-inflationary growth, a high degree of competitiveness and convergence of economic performance, a high level of protection and improvement of the quality of the environment, the raising of the standard of living and quality of life, and economic and social cohesion and solidarity among Member States.

Article 4, paragraph 1 stipulates:

> For purposes set out in Article 2, the activities of the Member States and the Community shall include, as provided in this Treaty and in accordance with the timetable set out therein, the adoption of an economic policy which is based on the close coordination of Member States' economic policies, on the internal market and on the definition of common objectives, and conducted in accordance with the principle of an open market economy with free competition.

Article 4, paragraph 3 adds:

> The activities of the Member States and the Community shall entail compliance with the following guiding principles: stable prices, sound public finances and monetary conditions and a sustainable balance of payments.

3 According to the 'Community method' of legislation, a 'recommendation' from the Commission to the Ecofin Council is weaker than a 'proposal' since the Ecofin Council can amend a Commission 'recommendation' by a qualified majority whereas a Commission 'proposal' can only be amended by unanimity.
4 This figure is based on the German government's 2004 target deficit of 1 per

cent of GDP, but at the February Ecofin Council meeting of 2002, the German government committed itself to a budget close to balance by 2004. On the other hand, this figure is based on the French government's 2004 target deficit of 0.5 per cent of GDP, but at the June Ecofin Council meeting of 2002, the new centre-right French government declared that this target was conditional on France achieving a growth rate of at least 3 per cent per year over the period 2003–04. Moreover, this figure is based on a balanced budget target for Italy in 2004. In mid-2002, the Italian government was targeting a revised deficit of 0.3 per cent of GDP for 2004.

5 The President of the ECB rejected demands by the European Parliament to provide, in its monthly reports, economic developments in each of the eurozone countries, to avoid the type of economic and financial assessment that may lead to the 'regionalisation' of monetary policy in the eurozone (*Financial Times*, 27 October 1999: 1; Duisenberg 2001b).

6 There are 24 Executive Directors, with 182 IMF member states. Consequently, an Executive Director may represent more than one member of the IMF. Only the Executive Directors from the United States, Germany, Japan, France, the United Kingdom, Saudi Arabia, Russia and China represent exclusively their member state. All the other Executive Directors represent a 'constituency' composed of their own member state and other IMF member states. For instance, the Executive Director from Canada represents (and votes for) not only Canada but also the following IMF members: Antigua and Barbuda, the Bahamas, Barbados, Belize, Dominica, Grenada, *Ireland*, Jamaica, St Kitts and Nevis, St Lucia, and St Vincent and the Grenadines.

7 For the shared responsibilities between the Eurosystem and the eurozone Member States, such as prudential supervision of banks and exchange rate policies, the views of the eurozone Member States would also be presented at the IMF Executive Board by the IMF Executive Director representing the EU Member State holding the Eurogroup Presidency.

8 Although, prior to that time, other Community legislation was adopted to harmonise the supervision of credit institutions, this Directive was the most comprehensive. The First Banking Coordination Directive (77/780/EEC), adopted on 12 December 1977 and implemented on 15 December 1979, was the first attempt to get minimum Community standards set for regulating banks and other credit institutions that take deposits and lend money.

9 Setting up a subsidiary in another Member State requires the authorisation from the host Member State, but such authorisation should be granted under the same terms as that of a domestic request to carry on the business of a credit institution in a Member State's national jurisdiction.

10 The Basel Committee on Banking Supervision is an informal group composed of the banking supervisors – including central bank representatives – of the Group of Ten countries (G-7, Benelux countries, Sweden, Switzerland and Spain since 2001). The Committee was created in 1975 following the failure of the German Bankhaus Herstatt, and is based in Basel at the Bank for International Settlements (BIS). The Committee became better known through the agreement on minimum capital adequacy rules for internationally active banks (the Basel Capital Convergence Accord of 1988). The Basel Committee has no legislative authority, but is an internationally recognised standard setter.

References

Alesina, A. (1989) 'Politics and business cycles in industrial democracies', *Economic Policy*, 8, pp. 55–98.

Alesina, A. and Summers, L. (1993) 'Central bank independence and macroeconomic performance: some comparative evidence', *Journal of Money, Credit and Banking*, 25(2), pp. 151–62.

Bakhshi, H., Haldane, A. G. and Hatch, N. (1998) 'Some costs and benefits of price stability in the United Kingdom', Bank of England Working Paper No. 78, London.

Bank of Canada (2001) 'Renewal of the inflation-control target', *Background Information*, Ottawa, May.

Banque de France [year *n*] *Rapport annuel (Exercice n-1)* (Paris).

Barber, A. (1999) 'Interview of Duisenberg', *Financial Times* (London), 26 November.

Beattie, A. and Fidler, S. (2000) 'Careful planning behind bank's euro surprise', *Financial Times* (London), 25 September.

Bernanke, B. and Mihov, I. (1997) 'What does the Bundesbank target?' *European Economic Review*, 41, pp. 1025–53.

Bindseil, U. (1997) 'Reserve requirements and economic stabilization', *Monatsbericht*, Nr 1/97 (Deutsche Bundesbank, Frankfurt am Main).

Blanchard, O. (1998) *Macroeconomics* (Upper Saddle River, NJ: Prentice-Hall).

Blanchard, O. and Fischer, S. (1989) *Lectures on Macroeconomics* (Cambridge, MA: The MIT Press).

Brainard, W. C. (1967) 'Uncertainty and the effectiveness of policy', *American Economic Review*, 57, pp. 411–25.

Browne, F. X., Fagan, G. and Henry, J. (1997) 'Money demand in EU countries: a survey', *Staff Paper*, no. 7, March (Frankfurt am Main: European Monetary Institute).

Bryant, R. C., Henderson, D. W., Holtham, G., Hooper, P. and Symanski, S. (eds) (1988) *Empirical Macroeconomics for Interdependent Economies* (Washington, DC: Brookings Institution).

Bundesministerium der Finanzen (2001) 'Allfinanzaufsicht und Bundesbankstrukterreform starken Finanzplatz Deutschland', *Pressemitteilungen*, F.18 (d.8), 25. Januar, Berlin.

Buti, M., Franco, D. and Ongena, H. (1997) 'Budgetary policies during recessions – retrospective application of the "stability and growth pact" to the post-war period', *Economic Papers*, No. 121 (Brussels: European Commission, Directorate General for Economic and Financial Affairs).

References

Cecchetti, S. G. (1999) 'Legal structure, financial structure, and monetary policy transmission mechanism', *Economic Policy Review*, Federal Reserve Bank of New York, 5(2), pp. 9–28.

Central Banking (1997) 'Dispute over ESCB profits', *Central Banking*, 6(4).

Coenen, G. and Vega, J. L. (1999) 'The demand for M3 in the euro area', *European Central Bank Working Paper Series*, no. 6, September, Frankfurt am Main.

Committee of Governors of the Central Banks of the European Communities (1990) 'Draft statute of the European system of central banks and of the European central bank', in *Europe Documents*, 1669/70, 8 December, Brussels.

Council [of the European Union] (1999) *Minutes of the '2196th Council Meeting'*, Ecofin, 12 July, Brussels. Available on website http://ue.eu.int/Newsroom.

Council [of the European Union] (2001) *Minutes of the '2329th Council Meeting'*, Ecofin, 12 February, Brussels.

Council [of the European Union] (2002) *Minutes of the '2407th Council Meeting'*, Ecofin, 12 February, Brussels.

Cukierman, A. (1992) *Central Bank Strategy: Credibility and Independence* (Cambridge, MA: The MIT Press).

Delors Committee [Committee for the Study of Economic and Monetary Union] (1989) *Report on Economic and Monetary Union in the European Community* [Delors Report] (Luxembourg: Office for Publications of the European Communities).

Destler, I. M. and Henning, C. R. (1989) *Dollar Politics: Exchange Rate Policymaking in the United States* (Washington DC: Institute for International Economics).

Deutsche Bundesbank (1985) 'Recent developments with respect to the Bundesbank's securities repurchase agreement's, *Monthly Report*, October, pp. 18–24, Frankfurt am Main.

Deutsche Bundesbank (1990) 'Statement on the establishment of an economic and monetary union in Europe', *Monthly Report*, October, Frankfurt am Main.

Deutsche Bundesbank (1995) *The Monetary Policy of the Bundesbank*, Frankfurt am Main, October.

Deutsche Bundesbank (1996) *Annual Report 1995*, Frankfurt am Main.

Deutsche Bundesbank (1999) 'Reflections and proposals concerning the future organisational structure of the Deutsche Bundesbank', *Monthly Report*, July, pp. 5–16, Frankfurt am Main.

Deutsche Bundesbank (2000) 'The Deutsche Bundesbank's involvement in banking supervision', *Monthly Report*, September, pp. 31–43, Frankfurt am Main.

Deutsche Bundesbank (2002) *Annual Report 2001*, Frankfurt am Main.

Deutschland (1991) 'Projet de traité sur l'UEM présenté par l'Allemagne, Bruxelles, 26 février 1991', in Ministère de l'Économie, des Finances et du Budget, Direction du Trésor, Bureau G3, *Travaux sur la conférence intergouvernementale sur l'union économique et monétaire européenne* (Paris). [This is the French translation of the German text. The English translation is not very good. The original German text was reprinted in Krägenau, H. and Wetter, W. (1993) *Europäische Wirtschafts-und Währungsunion: Vom Werner-Plan zum Vertrag von Maastricht–Analysen und Dokumente*, Baden-Baden: Nomos Verlagsgesellschaft].

Duisenberg, W. (1998) 'ECB press conference of 22 December', Frankfurt am Main, available on website www.ecb.int.

Duisenberg, W. (1999a) 'ECB press conference', 8 April, Frankfurt am Main.
Duisenberg, W. (1999b) 'ECB press conference', 6 May, Frankfurt am Main.
Duisenberg, W. (1999c) 'ECB press conference', 7 October, Frankfurt am Main.
Duisenberg, W. (1999d) 'Presentation of the ECB's Annual Report 1998 to the European Parliament', *Introductory statement* delivered by Duisenberg, 26 October, European Parliament, Strasbourg. Available on website www.ecb.int.
Duisenberg, W. (2000a) 'ECB press conference', 8 June, Frankfurt am Main.
Duisenberg, W. (2000b) 'Introductory statement', Hearings before the Committee on Economic and Monetary Affairs of the European Parliament, 23 November, Brussels.
Duisenberg, W. (2001a) 'ECB press conference', *Transcript of the questions and answers*, 10 May, Frankfurt am Main.
Duisenberg, W. (2001b) 'ECB press conference', *Introductory Statement*, 21 June, Dublin.
Economic and Financial Committee [former Monetary Committee] (2001) *Report on Financial Crisis Management* ('Brouwer Report'), 17 April, Brussels.
Economic Policy Committee (2001) 'Annual Report on Structural Reforms 2001' Report addressed to the Council and the Commission, Brussels, 6 March.
Economic Report of the [US] President (2001) together with the *Annual Report of the Council of Economic Advisers*, January (Washington, DC: United States Government Printing Office).
Eijffinger, S., Schaling, E. and Hoeberichts, M. (1998) 'Central bank independence: a sensitivity analysis', *European Journal of Political Economy*, 14, pp. 73–88.
Emerson, M., Gros, D., Italianer, A., Pisani-Ferry, J. and Reichenbach, H. (1992) *One Market, One Money* (Oxford: Oxford University Press).
European Central Bank [year], *Monthly Bulletin*, [month], Frankfurt am Main.
European Central Bank [year *n*], *Annual Report [year n-1]*, April, Frankfurt am Main.
European Central Bank (1998a) *The Single Monetary Policy in Stage Three: General Documentation on ESCB Monetary Policy, Instruments and Procedures*, September, Frankfurt am Main.
European Central Bank (1998b) 'ECB press conference of 3 November', Frankfurt am Main, available on website www.ecb.int.
European Central Bank (1998c) 'Interest rates in the European Monetary Union', *ECB Press Release*, 3 December, Frankfurt am Main, available on website www.ecb.int.
European Central Bank (1999a) *Compendium: Collection of Legal Instruments*, Frankfurt am Main.
European Central Bank (1999b) 'Possible effects of EMU on the EU banking systems in the medium to long term', *Monthly Bulletin*, February.
European Central Bank (2000) 'Potential output growth and output gaps: concept, uses and estimates', *Monthly Bulletin*, October, pp. 37–48, Frankfurt am Main.
European Central Bank (2001a) 'Additional refinancing operation with one week maturity on 27 April 2001', *ECB Press Release*, 23 April, Frankfurt am Main.
European Central Bank (2001b) 'Decisions on the issue of euro banknotes and on the allocation of monetary income', *ECB Press Release*, 6 December, Frankfurt am Main.
European Central Bank (2001c) 'Review of the quantitative reference value for monetary growth', *ECB Press Release*, 6 December 2001, Frankfurt am Main.

208 References

European Central Bank (2001d) 'The role of central banks in prudential supervision', March, Frankfurt.

European Central Bank (2002) 'Labour market mismatches in euro area countries', *Monetary Policy Committee of the European System of Central Banks*, March, Frankfurt.

European Commission [Commission of the European Communities] (1991) 'Draft treaty amending the treaty establishing the European Economic Community with a view to achieving economic and monetary union', *Bulletin of the European Communities*, Supplement 2 (Luxembourg: Office for Official Publications of the European Communities).

European Commission (1994) 'Growth, competitiveness and employment: the challenges and ways forward into the 21st century', White Paper (Brussels: Secretariat-General of the Commission).

European Commission (1999a) 'Spring 1999 forecasts for 1999–2000', in *European Economy*, Supplement A, No. 4, April (Luxembourg: Office for Official Publications of the European Communities).

European Commission (1999b) *Economic and Monetary Union – Compilation of Community Legislation*, June (Luxembourg: Office for Official Publications of the European Communities).

European Commission (2000a) 'Spring 2000 forecasts for 2000–2001', in *European Economy*, Supplement A, Economic Trends, No. 1/2, April (Luxembourg: Office for Official Publications of the European Communities).

European Commission (2000b) 'Autumn 2000 forecasts for 2000–2002', in *European Economy*, Supplement A, Economic Trends, No. 10/11, October/November (Luxembourg: Office for Official Publications of the European Communities).

European Commission (2000c) 'Action plan on EMU statistical requirements', Directorate General for Economic and Financial Affairs in close collaboration with the European Central Bank, Brussels, 25 September.

European Commission (2001a) 'Report on the implementation of the 2000 broad economic policy guidelines', *European Economy*, Report and Studies no. 2, Directorate General for Economic and Financial Affairs, Brussels.

European Commission (2001b) 'Spring 2001 Forecasts for 2001–2002', in *European Economy*, Supplement A, Economic Trends, no. 3/4, March/April, Directorate-General for Economic and Financial Affairs (Luxembourg: Office for Official Publications of the European Communities).

European Commission (2001c) 'The EU economy: 2001 Review', *European Economy*, no. 73, Directorate-General for Economic and Financial Affairs, Brussels.

European Commission (2002a) 'Economic Forecasts, Spring 2002', in *European Economy*, no. 2, Directorate-General for Economic and Financial Affairs (Luxembourg: Office for Official Publications of the European Communities).

European Commission (2002b) 'Quarterly report on the euro area', no. 2002/I, Directorate-General for Economic and Financial Affairs, Brussels.

European Commission (2002c) *Report from the Commission*: 'on the implementation of the 2001 Broad Economic Policy Guidelines', 21 February, COM (2002) 93 final, Brussels.

European Council [various years] 'Presidency conclusions' available at website http://europa.eu.int [European Council meetings are designated by venue and date, e.g. Essen 1994].

European Parliament (1998) 'Prudential supervision in the context of EMU', Working Paper, Directorate-General for Research, Economic Affairs Series, February.

Eurostat (2000) Eurozone data can be obtained from this official EU statistical agency headquartered in Luxembourg by consulting its website at http://europa.eu.int/comm/eurostat.

Eurostat (2002) 'Euro-indicators', *News Release*, No. 34/2002, 18 March, Luxembourg.

Fagan, G., Henry, J. and Mestre, R. (2001) 'An area-wide model (AWM) for the euro area', ECB Working Paper Series, Working Paper no. 42, January, Frankfurt am Main.

Favero, C. A., Freixas, X., Persson, T. and Wyplosz, C. (2000) *One Money, Many Countries*, Monitoring the ECB Series, February (London: Center for Economic Policy Research).

Federal Reserve Bank of New York (1991) 'Monetary policy and open market operations during 1990', *Quarterly Review*, 16(1), pp. 52–78.

Federal Reserve Bank of New York (1999) *Eighty-Fifth Annual Report*, for the year ended 31 December, 1999 (New York: Second Federal Reserve District).

Federal Reserve System (1978) *Sixty-Fifth Annual Report of the Board of Governors of the Federal Reserve System, 1978* (Washington, DC).

Federal Reserve System (1993) *Eightieth Annual Report of the Board of Governors of the Federal Reserve System, 1993* (Washington, DC).

Federal Reserve System (1994) *Purpose and Functions*, 8th edn, Board of Governors of the Federal Reserve System, Washington, DC.

Federal Reserve System (1998) *Eighty-Fifth Annual Report of the Board of Governors of the Federal Reserve System, 1998* (Washington, DC).

Federal Reserve System (2000a) 'Modifications to the FOMC's disclosure procedures', *Press Release*, 19 January (Washington, DC).

Federal Reserve System (2000b) *Eighty-Seventh Annual Report of the Board of Governors of the Federal Reserve System, 2000* (Washington, DC).

Fender, I. and Galati, G. (2001) 'The impact of transatlantic M&A activity on the dollar/euro exchange rate', *BIS Quarterly Review*, December, pp. 58–68 (Basel: Bank for International Settlements).

Fisher, I. (1934) *Stable Money: a History of the Movement*, Chapters V and VI (New York: Adelphi).

Forder, J. (1998) 'The case for an independent European central bank: a reassessment of evidence and sources', *European Journal of Political Economy*, 14, pp. 53–71.

France (1991) *Travaux sur la conférence intergouvernementale sur l'union éeconomique et monétaire européenne*, Ministère de l'Économie, des Finances et du Budget, Direction du Trésor, Bureau G3, février, Paris.

Gilbert, R. A. (1994) 'A case study in monetary control: 1980–82', *Review*, 76(5), September, pp. 35–55 (Federal Reserve Bank of St-Louis).

Grasmann, P. and Keereman, F. (2001) 'An indicator-based short-term forecast for quarterly GDP in the euro area', *Economic Papers*, no. 154, June, Directorate-General for Economic and Financial Affairs, European Commission, Brussels.

Greenspan, A. (1989) 'Statements to Congress', *Federal Reserve Bulletin*, 75, pp.: 272–77 (Washington, DC).

References

Grilli, V., Masciandaro, D. and Tabellini, G. (1991) 'Political and monetary institutions and public financial policies in the industrial countries', *Economic Policy*, 13, pp. 341–92.

Gros, D., Mayer, T., Davanne, O., Tabellini, G., Emerson, M. and Thygesen, N. (2000) *Quo Vadis Euro? The Cost of Muddling Through*, Second Report of the CEPS Macroeconomic Policy Group (Brussels: Centre for European Policy Studies).

Hansen, J. and Roeger, W. (2000) 'Estimation of real equilibrium exchange rates', *Economic Papers*, no. 144, September (Brussels: European Commission, Directorate General for Economic and Financial Affairs).

Hayo, B. (1998) 'Inflation culture, central bank independence and price stability', *European Journal of Political Economy*, 14, pp. 241–63.

Hetzel, R. L. (1985) 'The rules versus discretion debate over monetary policy in the 1920s', Federal Reserve Bank of Richmond, *Economic Review*, 71(6), November–December, pp. 3–14.

HM Treasury (1991) *Economic and Monetary Union – Beyond Stage I: Possible Treaty Provisions and Statute for a European Monetary Fund*, January (London: HM Treasury).

HM Treasury (2001) *Preliminary and Technical Work to Prepare for the Assessment of the Five Tests for UK Membership of the Single Currency*, November (London: HM Treasury).

Hoffmann, J. (1998) 'Problems of inflation measurement in Germany', *Monatsbericht*, Nr 1/98, Deutsche Bundesbank, Frankfurt am Main.

Hoffman, R. and Schröder, U. (1997) 'The euro – a challenge to the dollar?', Deutsche Bank Research, *EMU Watch*, No. 33, 25 June.

IFO Institute for Economic Research (2001) 'The IFO business climate index', Munich, available at website www.ifo.de.

Illmanen, A. (1997) 'EMU trades: insights from post-1999 forward rates', Salomon Brothers Economic and Market Analysis, *Euro Strategist*, 21 May.

International Monetary Fund (1998) *Annual Report 1998* (Washington, DC: International Monetary Fund).

International Monetary Fund (2001) *World Economic Outlook*, May (Washington, DC: International Monetary Fund).

Issing, O. (1999) 'The monetary policy of the ECB: stability, transparency, accountability', speech at the Royal Institute of International Affairs, London, 25 October. Available at the *European Central Bank* website www.ecb.int.

Issing, O., Gaspar, V., Angeloni, I. and Tristani, O. (2001) *Monetary Policy in the Euro Area: Strategy and Decision Making at the European Central Bank* (Cambridge, UK: Cambridge University Press).

Jones, T. (2000a) 'Champions of ECB openness notched up significant victory', *European Voice*, 17–23 February, 6(7), pp. 12–13.

Jones, T. (2000b) 'First salvo in battle for eurozone control', *European Voice*, 27 July–2 August, 6(30), p. 8.

Kenny, G. and McGettigan, D. (1997) 'Low inflation or price stability? A look at the issues', *The Irish Banking Review*, Winter, pp. 2–16.

Kieler, M. and Saarenheimo, T. (1998) 'Differences in monetary policy transmission? A case not closed', *Economic Papers*, no. 132, November, European Commission, Directorate-General for Economic and Financial Affairs, Brussels.

Kremers, J. M. and Lane T. D. (1990) 'Economic and monetary integration and the aggregate demand for money in the EMS', *IMF Staff Papers*, 37(4), pp. 777–805.

Lelart, M. (2000) 'Le Fonds Monétaire international et la Monnaie unique', *Document de Recherche*, no. 2000–14 (Orléans: Laboratoire d'Économie d'Orléans).

Leonard, D. (2002) 'Sweden back on the road to the euro', *European Voice* (Brussels), 8(11), 21–27 March.

Luce, E. (1998) 'Fund managers predict euro will soon rival strength of dollar', *Financial Times* (London), November 10, p. 16.

Mangano, G. (1998) 'Measuring central bank independence: a tale of subjectivity and of its consequences', *Oxford Economic Papers*, 50(3), pp. 468–92.

Mankiw, G. (1985) 'Small menu costs and large business cycles: a macroeconomic model of monopoly', *Quarterly Journal of Economics*, 100(2), May.

McMorrow, K. (1998) 'Is there a stable money demand equation at the Community level?–Evidence, using a cointegration analysis approach for the eurozone countries and for the Community as a whole', *Economic Papers*, no. 131, November (Brussels: European Commission, Directorate-General for Economic and Financial Affairs).

McMorrow, K. and Roeger, W. (2001) 'Potential output: measurement methods, 'new' economy influences and scenarios for 2001–2010 – a comparison of the EU15 and the US', *Economic Papers*, no. 150, April (Brussels: European Commission, Directorate-General for Economic and Financial Affairs).

Meulendyke, A-M. (1998) *US Monetary Policy and Financial Markets*, New York: Quarterly Review, Federal Reserve Bank of New York.

Mishkin, F. S. and Posen, A. S. (1997) 'Inflation targeting: lessons from four countries', *Economic Policy Review*, Federal Reserve Bank of New York, 3(3), August, pp. 9–110.

Monetary Committee of the European Communities (1974) *Compendium of Community Monetary Texts* (Luxembourg: Office for the Official Publications of the European Communities).

Monetary Committee of the European Communities (1990) 'Economic and monetary union beyond stage I', in *Europe Documents*, 1609, 3 April (Brussels).

Nayeri, F. (2002) 'European Central Bank's many chefs cause confusion', Bloomberg.com/Top Financial News, London, 25 January.

O'Reilly, B. (1998) 'The benefits of low inflation: taking stock', *Bank of Canada Technical Report*, no. 83 (Ottawa).

Owens, A. (1996) 'Dollar's role under threat', (London: Julius Bear Investments) 2 July.

Parkin, M. and Bade, R. (1980) 'Central bank laws and monetary policies'. Unpublished manuscript, University of Western Ontario, London (Canada).

Prati, A. and Schinasi, G. J. (1998) 'Ensuring financial stability in the euro area', *Finance and Development*, 35(4), December, pp. 12–15.

Prati, A. and Schinasi, G. J. (1997) 'European Monetary Union and international capital markets: structural implications and risks', *IMF Working Paper*, 97/62 (Washington, DC: International Monetary Fund).

Pringle, R. (ed.) (1992) 'The currency crisis: a seven part feature', *Central Banking*, 3(2), Autumn.

Roeger, W. (2001) 'The contribution of information and communication technologies to growth in Europe and the US: a macroeconomic analysis', *Economic*

Papers, no. 147, January (Brussels: European Commission, Directorate-General for Economic and Financial Affairs).

Rogoff, K. (1985) 'The optimal degree of commitment to an intermediate monetary target', *Quarterly Journal of Economics*, 100, pp. 1169–90.

Schmidt, R. H. (1999) 'Differences between financial systems in European countries: consequences for EMU', paper 26 March, forthcoming in the proceedings volume, H. Remsberger (ed.) (London: Macmillan).

Schröder, G. (2001) 'Responsibility for Europe' *SPD* [ruling Social Democratic Party] *Position Paper*, 30 April, Berlin.

Suardi, M. (2001) 'EMU and asymmetries in the monetary policy transmission', *Economic Papers*, no. 157, July, Directorate General for Economic and Financial Affairs, European Commission, Brussels.

Taylor, J. (1993) 'Discretion versus policy rules in practice', *Carnegie-Rochester Conference Series on Public Policy*, 39, pp. 195–214.

US Congress (2000) *The Long-Term Budget Outlook*, October (Washington, DC: Congressional Budget Office).

US Congress (2001) *The Budget and Economic Outlook: Fiscal Years 2002–2011*. A Report to the Senate and House Committees on the Budget, January (Washington, DC: Congressional Budget Office).

US House of Representatives (1894), *House Miscellaneous Documents*, 53rd Congress, 2nd Session, 1893–94, II, pp. 576–91 (Washington, DC).

Verhofstadt, G. (2000) Speech, *Office of Prime Minister*, Brussels, 26 October.

Werner Committee (1970) 'Report to the Council and the Commission on the realisation by stages of economic and monetary union in the community, definitive text [Werner Report], *Bulletin of the European Communities*, Supplement 11 (Luxembourg: Office for Official Publications of the European Communities).

Wynne, M. A. (1999) 'Core inflation: a review of some conceptual issues', *Working Paper Series*, no. 5, May (Frankfurt am Main: European Central Bank).

Index

ABN-Amro 189
accountability 62–3
acquisitions and mergers 100, 105–6, 184–90
Aetna 105
AGF 186
Alcatel 105, 106
Aldrich plan 20
Alesina, A. 56
Allianz 105
Alpha Bank 190
American Cyanamid 105
American-style auctions 84, 86
Amsterdam Treaty 145, 147, 164
Asian crisis 136
ASM Lithography 105

Bacob Bank 189
Bade, R. 56
Bakhshi, H. 29
Banca Ambroveneto 186
Banca IntesaBci 186
Banca Monte dei Paschi di Siena 186
Banco Bilbao Vizcaya 187
Banco Comercial Português 187
Banco Santander 187
BancWest 106
Bank for International Settlements (BIS) 175
Bankers' Trust 188
Banking Act: (1933) 22; (1935) 22–3
banking sector: consolidation 184–90; cooperation of supervisory authorities 181–2; crisis management 182–3; financial stability 182–3; in France 176; in Germany 176–7; prudential supervision policy 165, 175–8; supervisory regulations 179–81

Banking Supervision Committee 177, 182
Banque de France 12, 63, 176; accountability 63; *seigniorage* income 12
Basel Accord 44
Basel Committee on Banking Supervision 180, 181
BASF 105
Bayerische HypoVereinsbank 188
BBVA 187
Beattie, A. 45
Beige Book 61–2
BEPGs (Broad Economic Policy Guidelines) 145–8, 149, 162
Bernanke, B. 25, 128
Bestfoods 105
Biddle, Nicholas 19
Bies, Susan 25, 26
Blanchard, O. 55
BNP Paribas 106
Board of Governors (Federal Reserve) 21, 22–3, 26, 54–5
bond issues 102
bond yields 79
borrowed reserve targets 134–5
Brainard, W.C. 109
Bretton Woods monetary system 2, 50
Broad Economic Policy Guidelines (BEPGs) 145–8, 149, 162
Browne, F.X. 69
Bryant, R.C. 56
budgetary policies 146–7, 148–57; excessive deficit rule 149–51; medium-term budgetary rule 149; public deficits to GDP ratio 153–4; in recessions 150–1
Bundesbank 14–17; accountability 62;

Index

Bundesbank *continued*
  banking prudential supervision policy 176–7; Central Bank Council 17, 18, 54; Directorate 14; historical background 14; institutional features 14–17; institutional independence 34–8, 39; as lender of last resort 50, 183; Lombard/discount rate 109, 128–9; objectives 28–30, 34–8, 39; operational independence 49–50; personal independence 54; reserve requirements 87–8; *seigniorage* income 12; voting system 8; *see also* monetary policy, Bundesbank
Bundesrat 16
Business and Consumer Surveys 73, 98
Buti, M. 150

capacity utilisation 75
Capital Adequacy Directive 181
capital base of the ECB 9–10, 11
capital outflows 100, 105–6
Cardiff process 148
Cariplo 186
Caruana, J. 7
Cecchetti, S.G. 156
Central Bank Council (Bundesbank) 17, 18, 54
Central Banking Forums 175
Chrysler Corporation 105
Coenen, G. 70
Cologne process 164–5
Commerzbank 188–9
Commission bancaire 176
Constâncio, V. 7
consumer confidence surveys 73
consumer price indexes 66–8, 74
Crédit Agricole 188
credit institutions *see* banking sector
credit model 157
Credito Italiano 186
crisis management 102–3, 143, 182–3
Cukierman, A. 57

Daimler-Benz 105
decentralisation principle 5, 8
Delors, Jacques 2, 3, 191
demand/output conditions 75, 96; money demand function 68–9; negative output gap 29
deposit interest rates 87
Destler, I.M. 52
Deutsche Bank 105, 188
Deutsche Telekom 105

Dexia 190
Directorate (Bundesbank)) 14
disclosure policy: of the ECB 57–9; of the FOMC 59–62, 110–15
discount rates 22, 109, 128–9, 130, 141–2
dollar exchange rate 45–8
Domingo-Solans, E. 6
Dresdner Bank 188
Duisenberg, W. 6, 46, 59, 71, 104, 106, 118–19, 162
Dura Pharmaceuticals 105
Dutch-style auctions 84, 86, 130

ECB *see* European Central Bank (ECB)
Ecofin Council 2, 42, 145–6, 149, 161; ECB participation in meetings 162, 168; participation in ECB Governing Council 162–3; Presidency 173
economic data/indicators 78, 101
Economic and Financial Committee (EFC) 163
economic government 144–5, 161
economic growth, sustainability of 51
Economic and Monetary Union (EMU) 1–3
economic policies in the eurozone 143–94; Broad Economic Policy Guidelines (BEPGs) 145–8, 149, 162; budgetary policies 146–7, 148–57; coordination Decisions, Regulations and Directives 144–5; employment policies 147–8, 157–60; hard laws 150; microeconomic structural reforms 147, 148; sanctions on Member States 151; soft laws 149
Economic Policy Committee (EPC) 163–4
Edge Act 140
EEC (European Economic Community) 2
EFC (Economic and Financial Committee) 163
effective exchange rate index 76, 79
Eijffinger, S. 55, 56
Elan 105
Emerson, M. 57
Employment Act (1946) 31–2
employment policies 147–8, 157–60; redundancies 159–60; unemployment rate 79, 96, 98
employment protection legislation 159
EMS (European Monetary System) 50
EMU (Economic and Monetary Union) 1–3

Index 215

Eniro 106
enlargement of the EU 9
E.ON 105
EPC (Economic Policy Committee) 163–4
ESCB *see* European System of Central Banks (ESCB)
Essen European Council 158
euro exchange rate 45–8, 96, 99–103, 119
Eurogroup 145, 160–1; ECB participation in meetings 162; participation in ECB Governing Council 162–3; Presidency 172–3
European Central Bank (ECB) 190–2; accountability 62–3; capital base 9–10, 11; crisis management 102–3, 143; decentralisation principle 5, 8; and enlargement of the EU 9; Executive Board 4, 5, 6, 53; external representation 165–75; foreign exchange intervention 12–13, 45–8; foreign reserve assets 12–13; General Council 8; Governing Council 4–7, 9, 53, 58, 162–3; historical background 1–4; income of 8–12; institutional features 4–8; institutional independence 33–9; *International Relations Committee* 165; as lender of last resort 42, 143; *Monthly Bulletin* 58, 59, 63; objectives 30, 34–8, 57, 66–8; operational independence 41–9; participation in community bodies 162–5; personal independence 53–4; President of 4; publication of forecasts 58–9; shareholders 8–9; statements from officials/key events 118–24; transparency 57–9; voting system 4–5, 8, 9; *see also* monetary policy, ECB
European Economic Community (EEC) 2
European Monetary System (EMS) 50
European System of Central Banks (ESCB) 3, 4; Banking Supervision Committee 177, 182
Eurosystem 4, 5; external representation 165–75
excessive deficit rule 149–51
Exchange Rate Mechanism 50
Exchange Rate Mechanism II 43–9
exchange rates: dollar exchange rate 45–8; effective exchange rate index 76, 79; euro exchange rate 45–8, 96, 99–103, 119; foreign reserve assets 12–13; independence in policy 42–3, 49–50, 52; intervention by the ECB 12–13, 45–8; Irish punt 90; and positive supply shocks 99
Executive Board (ECB) 4, 5, 6, 53

Favero, C.A. 80
Fazio, A. 7
Federal Deposit Insurance Corporation (FDIC) 22
federal funds rate 110–15, 133, 139–42
Federal Open Market Committee (FOMC) 23, 24–7, 51, 133–42; disclosure policy 59–62, 110–15; minutes of meetings 61–2; public speeches/press interviews 62
Federal Reports Elimination and Sunset Act (1995) 40, 136
Federal Reserve 17–27; Board of Governors 21, 22–3, 26, 54–5; discount rate changes 22; federal funds rate 110–15, 133, 139–42; historical background 17–21; institutional features 24–7; institutional independence 34–8, 40–1; objectives 31–2, 34–8; Open Market Investment Committee (OMIC) 22; open market operations 23–4; Open Market Policy Conference (OMPC) 22, 23; operational independence 51–2; organisational structure 21–4; personal independence 54–5; policy bias 110–15; reserve requirements 88; target federal funds rate 110–15; transparency 59–62; voting system 8, 25, 26–7; *see also* monetary policy, Federal Reserve
Federal Reserve Act (1913) 20, 21, 40
Federal Reserve Banks 20–1, 25–7; appointment of chief executive officers 23; excess earnings 24; reserve requirements 23; *seigniorage* income 23–4
Federal Reserve Reform Act (1977) 32
Fender, I. 100
Ferguson, Roger W. 25, 26
Fidler, S. 45
financial stability 182–3
Financial Stability Forum (FSF) 167, 174–5
fine-tuning operations 86, 104, 106, 108–9

Index

First Bank of the United States 17, 19
First Banking Coordination Directive 181–2
fiscal policies *see* budgetary policies
Fischer, S. 55
Fisher equation 70
fixed rate tenders 81, 84
FOMC *see* Federal Open Market Committee (FOMC)
Forder, J. 56
forecasts (projections) 58–9, 73, 76–7
Foreign Direct Investment (FDI) outflows 105–6
foreign exchange policy *see* exchange rates
foreign reserve assets 12–13
Fortis 189
France: banking sector 176, 187–8; Banque de France 12, 63, 176; Commission bancaire 176; social benefit systems 159
France Telecom 105
Full Employment and Balanced Growth Act (1978) 32, 40, 136

G-7 167, 172–3
G-10 167, 171–2
G-20 167, 173–4
Galati, G. 100
Garganus, N. 7
GDP growth rates 91, 93, 95–8, 100–1, 116; across eurozone countries 156–7; and inflation 155; public deficits to GDP ratio 153–4
General Council (ECB) 8
Gilbert, R.A. 135
gold standard 31
Governing Council (ECB) 4–7, 9, 53, 162–3; minutes of meetings 58
government budget deficits *see* budgetary policies
Gramlich, Edward M. 25, 26
Grasmann, P. 161
Greenspan, Alan 25, 26, 51
Grilli, V. 56, 57
Gros, D. 80, 100

The Hague Summit 1
Hämäläinen, S. 6
Hamilton, Alexander 19
Hansen, J. 99
hard laws 150
harmonisation of banking supervisory regulations 179–81

Harmonised Index of Consumer Prices (HICP) 66–8, 74
Henning, C.R. 52
Hoffmann, J. 66
Houghton Mifflin 106
HSBC 187–8
Humphrey-Hawkins Act 32, 40, 136
Hurley, J. 7
HypoVereinsbank 188

IMF (International Monetary Fund) 166–71, 173–4
IMFC (International Monetary and Financial Committee) 167, 171
IMI 186
income of the ECB 8–12
independence: and inflation 55–7; institutional 33–41; operational 41–52; personal 52–5
Independent Treasury System 20
industrial confidence surveys 73, 98
industrial production 93–4
inflation: and bond yields 79; consumer price indexes 66–8, 74; core rate of inflation 67–8; in the Eurozone 95, 116–17; forecasts (projections) 58–9, 73, 76–7; and GDP growth 155; and the gold standard 31; and independence of central banks 55–7; and interest rates 29–30; and monetary reference values 68–73; target rates 28, 30, 66–8, 126–7; *see also* price stability
inflation targeting policies 64
ING 105, 189
institutional independence: Bundesbank 34–8, 39; ECB 33–9; Federal Reserve 34–8, 40–1
interest rates: on deposit facilities 87; discount rates 22, 109, 128–9, 130, 141–2; federal funds rate 110–15, 133, 139–42; and inflation 29–30; and launch of single currency area 90–1, 92, 104; Lombard rate 109, 128–9; and public finances 151; setting by ECB 8; size of rate changes 108–9; *see also* main refinancing operations
International Monetary and Financial Committee (IMFC) 167, 171
International Monetary Fund (IMF) 166–71, 173–4
International Relations Committee 165
investment flows 100, 105–6

Ireland: budgetary plans 146; Irish punt 90
Issing, O. 6, 28, 54, 118

Jackson, Andrew 19
Jefferson, Thomas 17, 19
Jones, T. 59
Jordan, Jerry L. 25

Keereman, F. 161
Kenny, G. 28
Kieler, M. 157
Kohl, Helmut 2
Kohn, Donald 25
Korean War 32
Kremers, J.M. 69

labour costs 79, 159
labour mobility 154
Lafontaine, Oskar 118
Land Central Banks 8, 14, 16, 17, 18
Lane, T.D. 69
legal structures 157
lender of last resort 42, 50, 143, 183
Liebscher, K. 7
Liquidity Consortium Bank 50
liquidity providing operations 81–6
Lombard rate 109, 128–9
longer-term refinancing operations 85–6
Lucent Technologies 106
Luxembourg process 147, 157–60
Lycos 105

M3 monetary aggregate 69–73, 93, 95–6, 103–4, 116
Maastricht Treaty 1, 2, 3–4, 144–6, 148–9, 160
McDonough, William J. 25
McGettigan, D. 28
McMorrow, K. 69, 99
Macroeconomic Dialogue 164–5
McTeer, Robert D. 25
Madison, James 19
main refinancing operations 81–5, 93–109; in 1999 93–6; in 2000 96–8; in 2001 103–4; size of rate changes 108–9
Major, John 3
Mangano, G. 57
Mankiw, G. 30
Mannesmann 100
marginal lending facility 87
Market Risk Amendment (1996) 180–1
matched sale-purchase transactions 139–41

medium-term budgetary rule 149
menu costs 30
mergers and acquisitions 100, 105–6, 184–90
Merita 190
Mersch, Y. 7
Meulendyke, A.-M. 21, 202
microeconomic structural reforms 147, 148
Mihov, I. 128
minutes of meetings 58, 61–2
Mishkin, F.S. 80
Mitterrand, François 2
Monetary Control Act (1980) 51, 140, 142
monetary policy, Bundesbank 15, 64, 117–32; inflation objectives 126–7; Lombard/discount rate 109, 128, 130; monetary targeting 64, 117, 124–8; operational instruments 49, 82–3, 128–32; reference values 124
monetary policy, ECB 65–117, 154, 191–2; evaluation of 109, 116–17, 192; inflation forecasts 73, 76–7; M3 monetary aggregate 69–73, 93, 95–6, 103–4, 116; National Central Bank actions 90–1; operational instruments 81–90; policy actions in 1999 91–6; policy actions in 2000 96–8; policy actions in 2001 103–4, 116–17; reference values 68–73; statements from officials/key events 118–24; two pillars strategy 64, 65–6, 80; *see also* open market operations, Eurosystem; price stability
monetary policy, Federal Reserve 64–5, 133–42; borrowed reserve targets 134–5; monetary targets 133, 134–5; non-borrowed reserve targets 134–5; operational instruments 82–3, 139–42; policy during 197–78 133; policy during 197–89 134–5; policy during 1990–present 135–9; target federal funds rate 110–15, 133, 139–42; Taylor rule 138–9
monetary reference values 68–73, 124
monetary stability *see* price stability
monetary targeting 64, 117, 124–8
money demand function 68–9
Monitoring and Control of Large Exposures of Credit Institutions Directive 180
Monthly Bulletin 58, 59, 63

moral hazard 183
Morgan, J. Pierpont 20
MP3.com 106
National Bank of Greece 190
National Banking Act 19
National Central Banks 8, 12–13, 90–1; *seigniorage* income 10–12, 24
National Discount Brokers 105
Nayeri, F. 117
negative output gap 29
New York Fed Trading Desk 60–1, 135, 138, 139, 140
Newbridge Networks 105
Nice Treaty 9
Nicholas Applegate 105
NMB Postbank 189
non-borrowed reserve targets 134–5
Nordea 190
Noyer, C. 6

objectives: of the Bundesbank 28–30, 34–8, 39; of the ECB 30, 34–8, 57, 66–8; of the Federal Reserve 31–2, 34–8
OECD (Organisation for Economic Cooperation and Development) 167, 172
Olson, Mark W. 25, 26
One2One 105
Open Market Investment Committee (OMIC) 22
open market operations, Eurosystem 8, 10, 81–6; counterparties 81; fine-tuning operations 86, 104, 106, 108–9; longer-term refinancing operations 85–6; main refinancing operations 81–5, 93–109; main refinancing operations in 1999 93–6; main refinancing operations in 2000 96–8; main refinancing operations in 2001 103–4; size of rate changes 108–9
open market operations, Federal Reserve 23–4; *see also* Federal Open Market Committee (FOMC)
Open Market Policy Conference (OMPC) 22, 23
operational independence: Bundesbank 49–50; ECB 41–9; Federal Reserve 51–2
operational instruments: Bundesbank 49, 82–3, 128–32; Eurosystem 81–90; Federal Reserve 82–3, 139–42
Orange 105

O'Reilly, B. 29
Organisation for Economic Cooperation and Development (OECD) 167, 172
output *see* demand/output conditions
outright purchases and sales 141
Own Funds Directive 180

Padoa-Schioppa, T. 6
Parkin, M. 56
part-time working 159
personal independence: Bundesbank 54; ECB 53–4; Federal Reserve 54–5
Pimco 105
Pioneer Group 105
political union 2
portfolio investment flows 100, 105–6
Posen, A.S. 80
positive supply shocks 99
PowerGen 105
price stability 28–30, 30, 34–8, 57, 66–8; and the Federal Reserve System 31–2, 51; macroeconomic benefits 29–30; operational meaning 41; *see also* inflation
Pringle, R. 50
production costs 79
prudential supervision policy 165, 175–8
public finances *see* budgetary policies

Quaden, G. 7

recessions 150–1
redundancies 159–60
reference values 68–73, 124
refinancing operations *see* main refinancing operations
ReliaStar Financial Corporation 105
repurchase agreements 139–41
reserve requirements: Eurosystem 87–90; Federal Reserve 88; Federal Reserve Banks 23
Reuters-NTC Research surveys 73
reverse transactions 81, 82–3
Roeger, W. 99
Rogoff, K. 55
Rome Treaty 2, 144
Russian debt default 94, 136
RWE 106

Saarenheimo, T. 157
safeguarding the currency objective 28, 39
San Paolo 186

sanctions on Member States 151
Santomero, Anthony M. 25
Schmidt, R.H. 157
Schröder, G. 103
Seagram 105
Seat Pagine Gialle 106
Second Bank of the United States 19
Second Banking Coordination Directive 177, 179–80
seigniorage income 10–12, 23–4
separation principle 176
shareholders of the ECB 8–9
shoe-leather costs 30
Silicon Valley Group 105
Single European Act (1986) 2
snake 44
social benefit systems 159
Société Générale 105, 188
soft laws 149
Solvency Ratio Directive 180, 181
Stability and Growth Pact 118, 147, 150, 153
standing facilities 87
Stern, Gary H. 25
Strausskahn, Dominique 118
Strong, Benjamin 22
structural reforms 147, 148
Suardi, M. 157
Summers, L. 45, 56
sustainability of economic growth 51
System Open Market Account (SOMA) 139, 140

takeovers *see* mergers and acquisitions
target federal funds rate 110–15, 133, 139–42

Taylor rule 138–9
TCW Group 105
Telefonica 187
tenders 81, 84–5, 130
Terra Networks 105
Thames Water 106
transparency 57–62
Trichet, J.-C. 7

unemployment rate 79, 96, 98; *see also* employment policies
UniCredito Italiano 105, 186
Unilever 105
unit labour costs 79

Vanhala, M. 7
variable rate tenders 84–5, 130
Vega, J.L. 70
velocity of circulation of money 124
Verhofstadt, G. 103
Vivendi 105, 106
Vodafone 100
VoiceStream Wireless 105
voting systems: Bundesbank 8; ECB 4–5, 8, 9; Federal Reserve 8, 25, 26–7

wage negotiations 97
Wellink, N. 7
Welteke, E. 7, 16
Werner Report 1–2
World Bank 173–4
World Economic Outlook 166
Wynne, M.A. 68